STUDIES OF THE AMERICAS

edited by

Maxine Molyneux
Institute of the Americas
University College London

Titles in this series include cross-disciplinary and comparative research on the United States, Latin America, the Caribbean, and Canada, particularly in the areas of politics, economics, history, anthropology, sociology, development, gender, social policy, and the environment. The series publishes edited collections, which allow exploration of a topic from several different disciplinary angles by eminent scholars, and book-length studies, which provide a deeper focus on a single topic.

Titles in this series published by Palgrave Macmillan:

Cuba's Military 1990-2005: Revolutionary Soldiers during Counter-Revolutionary Times
By Hal Klepak

The Judicialization of Politics in Latin America
Edited by Rachel Sieder, Line Schjolden, and Alan Angell

Latin America: A New Interpretation
By Laurence Whitehead

Appropriation as Practice: Art and Identity in Argentina
By Arnd Schneider

America and Enlightenment Constitutionalism
Edited by Gary L. McDowell and Johnathan O'Neill

Vargas and Brazil: New Perspectives
Edited by Jens R. Hentschke

D1446510

When Was Latin America Modern?
Edited by Nicola Miller and Stephen Hart

Debating Cuban Exceptionalism
Edited by Bert Hoffman and Laurence Whitehead

Caribbean Land and Development Revisited
Edited by Jean Besson and Janet Momsen

Cultures of the Lusophone Black Atlantic
Edited by Nancy Priscilla Naro, Roger Sansi-Roca, and David H. Treece

Democratization, Development, and Legality: Chile, 1831-1973
By Julio Faundez

The Hispanic World and American Intellectual Life, 1820-1880
By Iván Jaksić

The Role of Mexico's Plural in Latin American Literary and Political Culture: From Tlatelolco to the "Philanthropic Ogre"
By John King

Faith and Impiety in Revolutionary Mexico
Edited by Matthew Butler

Reinventing Modernity in Latin America: Intellectuals Imagine the Future, 1900-1930
By Nicola Miller

The Republican Party and Immigration Politics: From Proposition 187 to George W. Bush
By Andrew Wroe

The Political Economy of Hemispheric Integration: Responding to Globalization in the Americas
Edited by Diego Sánchez-Ancochea and Kenneth C. Shadlen

Ronald Reagan and the 1980s: Perceptions, Policies, Legacies
Edited by Cheryl Hudson and Gareth Davies

Wellbeing and Development in Peru: Local and Universal Views Confronted
Edited by James Copestake

The Federal Nation: Perspectives on American Federalism
Edited by Iwan W. Morgan and Philip J. Davies

Base Colonies in the Western Hemisphere, 1940-1967
By Steven High

Beyond Neoliberalism in Latin America? Societies and Politics at the Crossroads
Edited by John Burdick, Philip Oxhorn, and Kenneth M. Roberts

Visual Synergies in Fiction and Documentary Film from Latin America
Edited by Miriam Haddu and Joanna Page

Cuban Medical Internationalism: Origins, Evolution, and Goals
By John M. Kirk and H. Michael Erisman

Governance after Neoliberalism in Latin America
Edited by Jean Grugel and Pía Riggirozzi

Modern Poetics and Hemispheric American Cultural Studies
By Justin Read

Youth Violence in Latin America: Gangs and Juvenile Justice in Perspective
Edited by Gareth A. Jones and Dennis Rodgers

The Origins of Mercosur
By Gian Luca Gardini

Belize's Independence & Decolonization in Latin America: Guatemala, Britain, and the UN
By Assad Shoman

Post-Colonial Trinidad: An Ethnographic Journal
By Colin Clarke and Gillian Clarke

The Nitrate King: A Biography of "Colonel" John Thomas North
By William Edmundson

Negotiating the Free Trade Area of the Americas
By Zuleika Arashiro

History and Language in the Andes
Edited by Paul Heggarty and Adrian J. Pearce

Cross-Border Migration among Latin Americans: European Perspectives and Beyond
Edited by Cathy McIlwaine

Native American Adoption, Captivity, and Slavery in Changing Contexts
Edited by Max Carocci and Stephanie Pratt

A New Chapter in US-Cuba Relations

Social, Political, and Economic Implications

Edited by

Eric Hershberg and
William M. LeoGrande

Editors
Eric Hershberg
Center for Latin American and Latino Studies
American University
Washington, DC, USA

William M. LeoGrande
School of Public Affairs
American University
Washington, DC, USA

Studies of the Americas

ISBN 978-3-319-31151-7   ISBN 978-3-319-29595-4 (eBook)
DOI 10.1007/978-3-319-29595-4

Library of Congress Control Number: 2016013236

© The Editor(s) (if applicable) and The Author(s) 2016
This work is subject to copyright. All rights are solely and exclusively licensed by the Publisher, whether the whole or part of the material is concerned, specifically the rights of translation, reprinting, reuse of illustrations, recitation, broadcasting, reproduction on microfilms or in any other physical way, and transmission or information storage and retrieval, electronic adaptation, computer software, or by similar or dissimilar methodology now known or hereafter developed.
The use of general descriptive names, registered names, trademarks, service marks, etc. in this publication does not imply, even in the absence of a specific statement, that such names are exempt from the relevant protective laws and regulations and therefore free for general use.
The publisher, the authors and the editors are safe to assume that the advice and information in this book are believed to be true and accurate at the date of publication. Neither the publisher nor the authors or the editors give a warranty, express or implied, with respect to the material contained herein or for any errors or omissions that may have been made.

Cover illustration © dpa picture alliance / Alamy Stock Photo

Printed on acid-free paper

This Palgrave Macmillan imprint is published by Springer Nature
The registered company is Nature America Inc. New York

Contents

Figures and Tables

Figures

Tables

Acknowledgments

This book originated in a web forum assembled in early 2015 with the sponsorship of American University's Center for Latin American and Latino Studies (CLALS) and the Cuba program at the Social Science Research Council (SSRC). The forum afforded us an opportunity to provide well-informed yet inevitably preliminary reflections on the potential implications of the surprising announcement of December 17, 2014, that the United States and Cuba would seek to restore diplomatic ties and set out on a new course in bilateral relations. As the objectives outlined by Presidents Castro and Obama in their simultaneous speeches of that dramatic morning advanced, culminating in the opening of embassies in Washington and Havana during the summer of 2015, we concluded that it would be opportune to delve more deeply into the dynamics unleashed by the quest toward normalization. Our inclination to prepare this expanded collection of essays, along with some new contributions, was reinforced by the favorable response that the forum elicited from readers in the United States, Cuba, and beyond. This brief volume first appeared in print just slightly more than a year after the presidents announced plans for a rapprochement.

Producing such an ambitious collection in such a short time would not have been possible without able coordination and editorial assistance from CLALS Program Coordinator Jacquelyn Dolezal, as well as the support and encouragement of Sara Doskow and her colleagues at Palgrave Macmillan. Marcie Neil delivered high-quality translations of Chapters 10 and 11. Their support was funded through grants provided to the CLALS Cuba Initiative by the Christopher Reynolds Foundation, and to the SSRC Cuba Program by the Ford Foundation. Their generosity is greatly appreciated; without this foundation support, we would not have been able to sustain our Cuba-related work over the past several years.

Contributors

Holly Ackerman is the Librarian for Latin American, Iberian, and Latino Studies at Duke University. She is the author of *The Cuban Balseros: Voyage of Uncertainty*, which established the foundational demography and history of the 1994 Cuban raft crisis, and is an editor of the recently published collection of essays *Cuba: People, Culture, History* (Charles Scribner's Sons, 2011).

Philip Brenner is Professor of International Relations and Affiliate Professor of History at American University. He is co-editor (with Marguerite Rose Jiménez, John M. Kirk, and William M. LeoGrande) of *A Contemporary Cuba Reader: The Revolution Under Raúl Castro* (Rowman and Littlefield, 2014), and co-author (with Peter Eisner) of *Cuba's Quest for Sovereignty: A 500-Year History* (Rowman and Littlefield, forthcoming).

Ted A. Henken is Associate Professor of Sociology and Latin American Studies at Baruch College, City University of New York. He is the co-author with Archibald R. M. Ritter of *Entrepreneurial Cuba: The Changing Policy Landscape* (FirstForumPress, 2015) and the President ex-officio of the Association for the Study of the Cuban Economy.

Eric Hershberg is Professor of Government at American University and Director of its Center for Latin American and Latino Studies. He is co-editor with Maxwell A. Cameron and Kenneth Sharpe of the recent book *New Institutions for Participatory Democracy in Latin America: Voice and Consequence* (Palgrave Macmillan, 2012), and with Maxwell Cameron of the book *Latin America's Left Turns: Politics, Policies, and Trajectories of Change* (Lynne Rienner, 2010).

Bert Hoffmann is Senior Research Fellow at the GIGA German Institute of Global and Area Studies in Hamburg and Professor of

Political Science at Freie Universität Berlin. His publications include: Debating Cuban Exceptionalism (with L. Whitehead; published by Palgrave, 2007), and Charismatic Authority and Leadership Change: Lessons from Cuba's Post-Fidel Succession published in *International Political Science Review* (2009; 30: 229–248).

William M. LeoGrande is Professor of Government in the School of Public Affairs at American University in Washington, DC, and co-author with Peter Kornbluh of the recent book, *Back Channel to Cuba: The Hidden History of Negotiations between Washington and Havana* (University of North Carolina Press, 2014).

Arturo Lopez-Levy is a doctoral candidate at the Joseph Korbel School of International Studies of the University of Denver. He is co-author of the book *Raul Castro and the New Cuba: A Close-Up View of Change* (McFarland, 2011).

Emily Morris is an Honorary Research Associate in Development Economics at University College London's Institute of the Americas.

Marifeli Pérez-Stable is Professor of Political Sociology at Florida International University. Her most recent books are *The Cuban Revolution: Origins, Course and Legacy* (2012, third edition) and *The United States and Cuba: Intimate Enemies* (2011). In 2001–2003, she chaired the Task Force on Memory, Truth and Justice, which issued the report *Cuban National Reconciliation.*

Omar Everleny Pérez Villanueva is Professor of Economics at the University of Havana, and former director of the Centro de Estudios de la Economia Cubana. He has served as a visiting professor at universities in the United States, Japan, and France, and has published more than 70 research articles in a variety of areas related to the Cuban and global economies.

Andrés Serbin is the President of the "Coordinadora Regional de Investigaciones Económicas y Sociales–CRIES," Councilor of the Argentine Council of International Relations (CARI), and former Director of Caribbean Affairs at the Latin American Economic System (SELA). He is Professor Emeritus from the Central University of Venezuela and Emeritus Researcher from the Venezuelan National Council of Science and Technology (CONYCET).

Ana Serra is Associate Professor of Spanish and Latin American Studies at American University in Washington, DC, and author of the book *The "New Man" in Cuba: Culture and Identity in the Revolution* (2007), as well as other publications on Cuban culture and its diaspora.

Ricardo Torres is Professor of Cuban Economy at the Centro de Estudios de la Economía Cubana, Universidad de La Habana. He is co-editor with Omar Everleny Pérez Villanueva of the book *Miradas a la Economía Cubana* (Editorial Caminos, 2015).

Gabriel Vignoli is a lecturer in International Relations at the Julien J. Studley Graduate Program in International Affairs (Milano School of International Affairs, Management, and Urban Policy, The New School), and defended his dissertation "Schizonomics: Remapping La Habana's Black Market" at the New School's Department of Anthropology in 2014.

Chapter 1

Introduction: US-Cuba Diplomatic Rapprochement and Washington's Relations with Latin America

Eric Hershberg

Introduction

For long-time observers of Cuban-US relations, and for anyone concerned with Cuban affairs, "17D" has become universally recognized as shorthand for the December morning in 2014 when Presidents Barack Obama and Raúl Castro appeared on television simultaneously to announce their intentions to restore diplomatic ties and endeavor to normalize relations between their two countries. Catalyzed by 1.5 years of secret negotiations directed by senior confidants of the two presidents, bypassing normal diplomatic channels, the unexpected announcements provoked elation in some quarters and consternation in others. After 55 years of estrangement and hostility, the two presidents acknowledged that an alternative path for relations between the two governments, based on mutual respect and reciprocity, was both possible and desirable.

To advance in that direction, their statements outlined a series of measures that had been taken that very day, including an exchange of long-imprisoned spies and the release of USAID contractor Alan Gross from prison in Cuba. President Castro agreed to free a number of jailed political dissidents, and President Obama committed his administration to take a series of executive actions that would loosen the infamous embargo, even though the embargo itself would remain in effect because, by law, only Congress could fully abolish what the Cubans have long referred to as the blockade. It was widely recognized that this was improbable given that Republicans controlled both legislative chambers, and that the Republican majority in Congress was unlikely to confirm an ambassadorial nominee. But this did not preclude the July 20 opening of embassies in both countries, with Secretary of State John Kerry traveling to Havana to hoist the American flag the following month. Along the way, the Obama administration had removed Cuba from the list of state sponsors of terrorism, relaxed restrictions on both financial transactions and banking and investments in communication technology, and substantially broadened the categories of US citizens who are free to travel to Cuba without seeking a special license. Additional regulatory changes were introduced in September, further encouraging engagement of US businesses and citizens with Cuba. Even as Republican Party politicians castigated the President for what they labeled unilateral concessions to a totalitarian dictatorship, US citizens began flooding hotels in Havana as well as private homes in arrangements facilitated by the American firm Airbnb, one of countless US companies scrambling to launch business deals that appeared on the horizon in the wake of the diplomatic opening.

Meanwhile, throughout 2015, senior diplomats from the two countries met regularly in an effort to negotiate agreements on a wide range of issues that go beyond the restoration of diplomatic relations. Not surprisingly, these conversations did not produce instant results, and both sides repeatedly introduced demands that they knew would be problematic for their counterparts. But this was to be expected, and by all accounts the exchanges have been as cordial and constructive as they have been candid. Of course, the path toward full "normalization" of US-Cuban relations is replete with obstacles. As Philip Brenner points out in his contribution to this book, it may well be that, as Marifeli Pérez-Stable (2011) wrote years ago, there has never existed a "normal" relationship between the United States and Cuba (see also Perez 2008). Despite widespread relief and optimism among many advocates of normalization, a long road lies ahead before the two countries will achieve the "civilized relationship" that Raúl Castro has defined as entailing mutual interaction amid respect for one another's sovereignty and independence.

Countless op-ed pieces have been written since 17D, and many of them have been very insightful; however, as befits the genre, they have largely provided soundbites or reflections on particular aspects of the negotiations rather than deep analysis of the far-reaching implications of efforts by both regimes to transform the bilateral relationship. The chapters presented in this volume are mostly expanded and updated versions of essays that appeared in a web forum sponsored by the Center for Latin American and Latino Studies at American University and the Cuba Program at the Social Science Research Council posted in April 2015 (CLALS 2015). Contributors aim to delve deeply into the ramifications of changes in US-Cuba relations by drawing on their own scholarship and the substantial body of academic research that can inform our understanding of the present conjuncture and potential trajectories in the future. We are especially pleased to include contributions from leading experts from Europe and Latin America, as well as from the United States and Cuba.

The analyses encompass a variety of themes, ranging from US-Cuba relations to the hemispheric implications, and to the consequences for ongoing political, economic, and cultural change in Cuba. What does it mean to contemplate "normalization" between two countries with such a fraught history of interaction? How might experiences of "normalization" between the United States and other countries with which it maintained longstanding hostilities provide lessons for those who seek to understand the likely course of events involving the United States and Cuba? Will rapprochement between the United States and Cuba have consequences for domestic political dynamics inside Cuba? What impact will the changed bilateral relations and a relaxation of US sanctions have on ongoing efforts to "update" and perhaps transform Cuba's economic model? To what degree do 17D and its aftermath alter the landscape of international relations in the western hemisphere? How might Cuban cultural production and everyday life engage differently with US audiences and with members of the Cuban diaspora? These are among the myriad questions examined directly and indirectly in the essays that follow this introductory chapter.

The remainder of this chapter consists of two separate sections. The first situates the 17D watershed moment in the context of US-Latin American relations during the Obama years. While primarily focused on the implications for Cuba and for bilateral relations, the book affords an opportunity for pondering the broader significance of rapprochement for hemispheric relations, and particularly US ties to the western hemisphere more broadly. The analysis in this chapter thus explores the degree to which the US policy shift responded to an assessment of broader hemispheric dynamics and, in turn, the consequence of the Obama administration's shift in its stance toward Cuba for US-Latin America diplomatic relations. The analysis addresses issues such as the Americans' standing in the OAS and prospects for more constructive dialogue between Washington and major countries in the region about bilateral issues and common concerns not directly related to Cuba. The section concludes with a consideration of how the evolution of the Obama administration's Cuba policies during 2016 and contemporaneous debates about Cuba during the American presidential campaign may shape regional perceptions of the United States as a diplomatic interlocutor and regional partner during the remainder of the Obama presidency and beyond.

The final section provides a roadmap through the book, signaling key themes addressed by each of the authors and drawing connections across the contributions. There is no doubt that dimensions of the contemporary US-Cuba relationship and its effects have escaped our gaze, all the more so because the book was completed a mere 9 months since the announcements of December 17. Unanticipated dimensions deserving of dispassionate analysis will inevitably arise as the two sides navigate the diplomatic waters that, like the Florida Strait, have separated the two polities despite geographic proximity and deeply rooted demographic, cultural, and historical ties. Future scholars will thus face no shortage of topics to address as they seek to illuminate the nature and trajectory of Cuban-US affairs. Our aspiration in publishing this book is to contribute a perspective that will inform observers at this critical juncture in the two countries' intertwined histories and provide valuable points of reference for researchers grappling with the peaks and valleys of the relationship as it unfolds.

17D and US-Latin American Relations

Barack Obama was elected to the presidency in 2008, on the heels of a campaign that hinged on optimistic promises to effect wholesale "change we can believe in." The country's first African American president pledged to end US involvement in unpopular wars in the Middle East, talk with America's foes, close the US military prison in Guantánamo Bay, and enact comprehensive immigration reform that would address the status of nearly ten million undocumented individuals of Latin American origin. Coming on the heels of a campaign in which he characterized the half-century-old policy toward Cuba as anachronistic and ineffective, many observers in Latin America and in the United States anticipated more than a cosmetic opening to Cuba (Brenner and Hershberg 2014). This, and the fact that Obama was replacing a predecessor who was singularly unpopular in the region, was one of several factors fueling anticipation across the region of a new era in US-Latin American relations. Nowhere was this more evident than in the April 2009 OAS Presidential Summit in Port of Spain, where Obama was met with thunderous applause when he acknowledged that the United States had not always acted as an equal partner in the Americas and pledged a new era of mutual respect and reciprocity.

The passage of time, however, dampened regional enthusiasm toward the new administration. There was no discernible movement on Cuba—modest steps to liberalize travel and permit remittances by Cuban Americans had little echo in Latin America, where observers mostly took note of the continuation of US programs to effect "regime change" in Cuba—and the administration continued its predecessor's intransigence with regard to drug policy and devoted little attention to building relationships in the region. Guantánamo remained open, immigration reform was noteworthy for its absence, and from Argentina to Venezuela, US diplomats retained the unwelcome habit of conveying US government opinion regarding how countries should govern themselves. The President himself, occupied with extricating the United States from two wars, avoiding a Great Depression, and securing passage of his landmark healthcare reform, was perceived as completely disengaged from the region, and the advisors he had appointed for the region were considered weak and often imperious in their dealings with Latin American counterparts.

The extent of region-wide dismay was exhibited forcefully at the April 2012 Summit of the Americas in Cartagena, as noted by Serbin in Chapter 13 of this volume. Only three years had elapsed since the meeting in Port of Spain, but the atmosphere could not have been more different. Testy exchanges between Obama and Latin American presidents focused especially on Cuba, whose President had not been invited because of US insistence that the Inter-American Democratic Charter preclude its presence, although this was but the most glaring of a litany of complaints regarding the administration's dismissive attitude toward the region. Speaking to the press, Obama lamented that in obsessing about Cuba, his counterparts were acting as if mired in the Cold War, seemingly unaware that the point of his critics was that the United States was perpetuating policies toward Cuba and the region as a whole that were themselves a lamentable example of Cold War-era behaviors. The Summit was widely declared a failure, and several Latin American presidents, including some of those typically most sympathetic to Washington, made clear that they would not attend the next Summit, which was scheduled to take place in Panama in April 2015, if the Cuban President were not invited (Armstrong and Hershberg 2014; Hakim 2012).

In hindsight, the Cartagena debacle was a critical turning point because it demonstrated to President Obama that his own credibility in the region was being undermined by the continued intransigence regarding Cuba. Perhaps the President's memoirs will shed further light on the relative weight of Latin American opinion and his own desire to resolve the Cuba matter simply as part of his legacy as a competent leader unwilling to prolong what he had termed a "stupid policy." It is apparent, however, that after Cartagena, Obama came to realize that his Latin American legacy would be determined by whether he took meaningful steps to put aside the failed approach of isolation that had driven US policy toward Cuba for more than half a century. Approximately one year later, nearly two years before the Panama Summit, his emissaries would begin secret talks with representatives of Raúl Castro, and the path had been opened toward the announcements of 17D.

The consequence of the shift in paradigm was on display at the Summit of the Americas in Panama, which took on an all but celebratory tone in the afterglow of the 17D announcements and signs of continued progress in the bilateral relationship between Washington and Havana. Without this dominant narrative of mutual respect and reconciliation, American hostility toward the Venezuelan government would have taken on greater prominence at the Summit. Amid all of the praise directed toward President Obama from leaders of Brazil, Chile, Colombia, Mexico, and other countries, claims by ALBA countries regarding putative aggressions from Washington carried a great deal less weight.

And those claims almost certainly will continue to fade in relevance, and not just because of the decay of several governments that espoused them most vociferously. Indeed, symbolizing as it does the administration's commitment to forging a new tone for relations with the region and rekindling the spirit of Obama's 2009 remarks in Port of Spain, the opening to Cuba lends credibility to a broader shift in policy toward the region that progressive advocates in the United States have long desired and that is equally welcome throughout Latin

America. With the Cuba embarrassment out of the way, greater space has opened up for cooperation between Washington and counterparts in the hemisphere around shared objectives in a wide array of areas. Indeed, one can hope that, as progress in the bilateral relationship continues to advance, opportunities will grow for collaboration in new domains, ranging from energy to the environment, and even contentious issues such as trade and the drug war. During the year since the 17D announcements, progress is evident in each of these domains and, to a much greater degree than at any time in memory, Latin American interlocutors are willing to give Washington the benefit of the doubt.

This underscores the importance for US-Latin American relations staying the course with regard to Cuba. At this juncture, the costs of a reversal of American policy should not be underestimated. There is a consensus throughout the region regarding the desirability of multilateralism in international affairs, and the need for unequivocal respect for national self-determination and the inviolability of domestic political affairs. The United States backtracking on these principles with regard to Cuba would reverberate powerfully throughout the region, undermining prospects of cooperative relationships far beyond diplomatic questions involving the island itself.

However, the commitment to multilateralism is not shared across the political spectrum in the United States, as evidenced by the strident rhetoric of Republican leaders in Congress condemning the nuclear nonproliferation agreement negotiated between Iran and a coalition of major powers. In the case of Iran, regarding the question of relations with Cuba, rather than go along with the consensus of the international community, GOP leaders—and presidential candidates— are united in calling for a unilateral prolonging of sanctions, regardless of global opinion. That there seems little concern about the potential response of third parties to an abandonment of the negotiating stance regarding Cuba is evident in rhetoric along the campaign trail. Even though this may in large part involve playing to an internal party constituency, the fact that strong majorities of Americans surveyed express support for reaching out to Cuba needs not preclude meaningful steps backward in the event of a Republican presidency beginning in 2017. Given that the likely Republican nominee will almost surely continue the drumbeat of rhetoric against the restoration of diplomatic relations, there can be little doubt that an incoming GOP administration would begin its Latin American diplomacy with a major point of contention with virtually every government in the region.

As for whether that situation will come to pass, it comes down to the result of the 2016 presidential election. Although, to date, Cuba policy is the only foreign policy issue that has been understood to motivate Latino voters—primarily among virulent anti-Castro groups in Florida—it would be ironic if disillusion with US administration among Latin American governments were to further widen the GOP's existing deficit in support among Latino residents, who are a growing portion of the American electorate and who trace their origins to countries elsewhere in the region.

Outline of the Book

In Chapter 2, Philip Brenner offers a reflection on the degree to which imbalance has been the defining characteristic of US-Cuban relations since the latter part of the nineteenth century. Understood from this perspective, the confrontational dynamic of the relationship since Fidel Castro's triumphant entry into Havana in 1959 is but the latest chapter in a much more deeply rooted estrangement that, as noted, suggests that an eventual "normalization" will hardly represent a return to normality. To achieve that objective, Brenner concludes that the two sides will need to develop empathy, a quality that has eluded both sides until now and that, as many historians have noted, is particularly absent in the record of US interaction with its far less powerful neighbor (Perez 2008; Schoultz 2009). Indeed, that record suggests that beneath the undoubtedly sharp ideological differences that set them apart, the resistance and antipathy toward US hegemony that has characterized the Castro regime from its inception can be traced to nationalist impulses that have shaped currents of Cuban ideas and practices since at least the days of Martí (Kapcia 2008).

Whereas Brenner puts forth a social–psychological perspective on the bilateral relationship, drawing on constructivist currents in international relations scholarship, in Chapter 3 Arturo Lopez-Levy emphasizes a power politics dimension. Seen through the analytic lens of realist scholars, extreme asymmetries of power and resources such as those between the United States and Cuba can motivate the strong state to attempt to deny the sovereignty of the weaker one, and the weak state to reject the stronger one's claims to authority in the international system. Revolutionary Cuba's resistance to US imperialism extended far beyond the island, encompassing a rejection of American leadership more broadly. A solution to such confrontational situations, Lopez-Levy notes, is "recognition," whereby the weaker state's sovereignty is acknowledged and the stronger state's interests in the international order are deemed acceptable (Womack 2009). Full-fledged normalization of US-Cuban relations will be possible (as this line of thinking would suggest) if the two countries can sustain the spirit of mutual recognition that has characterized their interactions since 17D.

In Chapter 4, Bert Hoffmann identifies instructive comparisons between the controversial *Ostpolitik* pursued by West German Chancellor Willy Brandt at the height of the Cold War and the *Südpolitik* undertaken by President Obama in a very different geopolitical environment. By extending an olive branch across the Berlin Wall, Brandt opened the path toward undermining the East German state's claim to symbolize antifascist resistance. While Obama's gesture of reconciliation may exhibit noteworthy parallels to that earlier Cold War experience, Hoffman emphasizes several key differences above and beyond separation in world historical time. In particular, in contrast to the circumstances in Germany in the 1970s, the ties between Cuban and American society have been growing stronger for some time. 17D marked an instance of states catching up to their respective societies. Hoffmann's comparison of 17D to *Ostpolitik* is partly about the bilateral relationship between the governments, but it especially calls attention to the potential impact of détente inside Cuba. Greater ties with the United States in recent years have fueled class and racial inequalities in Cuba that call into question key legitimating tenets of the state. Accelerated opening may exacerbate those inequalities, with consequences for social cohesion on the island that may prove challenging.

Whether that implies a likelihood of fundamental political change in Cuba is uncertain. What is clear, however, is that the intensity of Cuban resistance to US imperial aspirations has both fueled and provided a rationale for many of the most controversial policies pursued by the Cuban state both at home and abroad since the Revolution. William M. LeoGrande considers in Chapter 5 whether the attenuation of hostilities with the United States may disrupt a longstanding foundation for cohesion in revolutionary Cuba. An extensive social science literature posits that political systems resort to extraordinary measures in response to existential threats, and from the Cuban perspective the animus of Washington (and Miami) surely qualified. Indeed, the blockade and US aggression was seen in Havana as embodying not only justified policies that took a toll on the Cuban population but also provided the country's rulers with a ready explanation for the system's shortcomings. For many years, some observers have speculated that the embargo and diplomatic confrontation with the United States were actually a source of Cuba's stability during the same time that they caused hardship. The coming years may test whether that was, in fact, the case.

The embargo and the ostracism that it was designed to sustain ironically provided a template through which Cuba became perceived as alluring in many circles abroad, including in the United States. In Chapter 6, Ana Serra analyzes how this constrained but also augmented the profile of Cuban art, literature, and film, making them "forbidden fruit" from an exotic and, for Americans, legally inaccessible place. Cuban artistic production thrived in this environment, and artists attained privileged positions as a result of the international popularity of their work. Serra reflects on how normalization might impact the distinctiveness of Cuban arts, the ways in which they are received by US audiences, and the conditions in which they will be produced on the island. Destabilizing changes are likely to occur, and in both directions. As the arrival of Netflix portends, the expansion of legally regulated economic exchange will eventually place limits on the circulation of pirated US artistic production on the island. Similarly, Cuban feature films that can now be downloaded through YouTube will likely soon be subjected to licensing requirements, placing a barrier between producers and viewers that previously did not exist. But the US market for Cuban art seems destined to expand dramatically, and Cuban artists living on the island are likely to be exposed to the work of Cuban Americans and their modes of artistic expression.

Relations within the diaspora are a central focus of Chapter 7, by Holly Ackerman, who considers how changes in US-Cuban relations may impact an expanding array of efforts to promote reconciliation between Cubans on the island and in the diaspora, as well as among those living in Cuba. Greater ease of travel in recent years has generated human contacts that inevitably bring about greater understanding, but Ackerman notes numerous initiatives to structure dialogues aimed at healing the divisions that Cuban society has suffered since at least 1959. The speed with which post-17D Cuban national reconciliation will advance may be accelerated, she surmises, thanks to the accumulation of these experiences in recent years. But there are also profound divisions inside Cuba itself, including among opposition factions, some of which have been tainted by receiving US funding under "regime change" programs whose future is uncertain. Ackerman concludes that if these funds were eliminated as part of normalization, it might strengthen the hand of groups, many of which are associated with the Church and the proliferation of informal NGOs in Cuba, who are committed to reconciliation over confrontation.

The logic of confrontation is one theme of Chapter 8, by Marifeli Pérez-Stable, which reflects on the concept of Cuban exceptionalism. Pérez-Stable notes that Cuban Americans played an outsized role during each of several phases of US government efforts to defeat the Cuban revolution, including the regime change programs of the 1990s onward. Echoing Ackerman, she establishes that there have been significant shifts in Cuban American policy preferences in recent years. In particular, young Cuban Americans strongly favor reconciliation. However, for that to occur in a climate of normalcy, the announcements of 17D and the steps taken by both governments during the course of 2015 will not be sufficient. It remains to be seen whether the cessation of hostilities will bring Cuba into the mainstream of countries in which human rights are respected and economic transactions are conducted freely, enabling Cubans to no longer live in circumstances that are oppressively "exceptional."

The degree to which rapprochement between Cuba and the United States improves the lives of everyday Cubans will depend in large measure on how it impacts the economy. The next four chapters analyze some of the principal economic dimensions of reforms underway in Cuba and consider how improved ties with the United States may influence their evolution during the coming years. In Chapter 9, Emily Morris considers a number of the most pressing challenges facing the Cuban economy, and she notes how factors such as the expansion of American tourism, growing remittances from Cuban Americans, and, with the eventual dismantling of the embargo, US investment and access to multilateral financial institutions may impact the financing needs of the Cuban economy. Ricardo Torres addresses in Chapter 10 how the US embargo distorted trade and exacerbated technological backwardness, two frequent problems in centrally planned economies that took on distinctive characteristics in Cuba. He then considers potential lessons from countries that, like Cuba, reformed centrally planned economies after long periods of confrontation with the Americans. Despite differences of history, demography, geography, and scale, not to mention the differing weights of exile and diaspora groups in the United States, he finds that the experiences of both China and Vietnam hold lessons for Cuba as it endeavors to increase its participation in global trade and attract foreign investment to support reforms.

Access to much needed finance is also the focus of Omar Everleny Pérez Villanueva's analysis in Chapter 11. The noted University of Havana economist traces the evolution of Cuban foreign investment policies, particularly following approval of the *lineamientos* (guidelines) for updating the country's economic model, and reviews provisions of key legislation promulgated after the collapse of the Soviet Union and during Raúl Castro's administration. Establishment of the Special Economic Zone and construction of a state-of-the-art port in Mariel constitute an initiative that merits special emphasis in light of the opening to the United States. Pérez Villanueva also reviews preliminary evidence of how US investors are responding to the potential opportunity.

In Chapter 12, Ted A. Henken and Gabriel Vignoli describe the expansion of nonstate employment in Cuba since the reforms associated with the Guidelines. More than half a million Cubans are now working as self-employed *cuentapropistas*, and hundreds of cooperatives are operating, with many hundreds more in the works. Consistent with the argument of Chapter 11, Henken and Vignoli emphasize the need for investment capital. Noting the significance of diaspora support for emerging private entrepreneurs, they speculate on the potential impact of the greater opening for supplying the needs of these new economic actors whose fortunes will be critical to the future of the Cuban economy. American policy can play a vital role in empowering the emerging entrepreneurial sector; however, to do so, they conclude, it must separate its engagement from discourse or practices focused on changes in Cuba's political regime.

In Chapter 13 of this book, Andrés Serbin returns to implications of US-Cuban détente for hemispheric relations. Whereas the focus in an earlier section of Chapter 1 is on the United States standing in Latin America, Serbin considers how détente between Havana and Washington fits within shifting patterns of regionalism in the Americas. He pays particular attention to the fortunes of ALBA, UNASUR, and CELAC, as well as the Organization of American States. Coinciding in many respects with the analysis of the present chapter regarding the Obama administration's concerns about the state of its relations with Latin American governments, Serbin sees the deeper significance of US-Cuban relations in the context of US concerns with its place in a shifting international system. In this reading, 17D is about much more than an eventual normalization of relations between the United States and Cuba: it has everything to do with the role of the United States in the world.

Finally, in the conclusion, the editors reflect on progress made toward normalizing diplomatic relations during 2015, emphasizing that progress has been steady but predictably gradual. While resisting the temptation to forecast the future, the authors sketch a number of variables that are likely to prove influential in determining the scale and scope of change during the years ahead. Beyond diplomatic considerations, the chapter alludes to economic and societal drivers of rapprochement, which they deem likely to outweigh political pressures from those who oppose consolidation of a new cooperative relationship between the United States and Cuba.

References

Armstrong, Fulton, and Eric Hershberg. 2014. "Who Will Attend the OAS Presidential Summit in Panama?" *AULA Blog*, October 2. http://aulablog.net/2014/10/02/who-will-attend-the-oas-presidential-summit-in-panama/.

Brenner, Phillip, and Eric Hershberg. 2014. "Washington and the Hemispheric Order: Explanations for Continuity and Change." *Pensamiento Propio* 39.1: 139–62.

CLALS (Center for Latin American and Latino Studies). 2015. "Implications of Normalization: Scholarly Perspectives on U.S.-Cuban Relations." http://www.american.edu/clals/Implications-of-Normalization-with-SSRC.cfm.

Hakim, Peter. 2012. "La increíble visión menguante de Washington." *Estudios de Política Exterior* 148 (July–August). http://www.politicaexterior.com/articulos/politica-exterior/la-increible-vision-menguante-de-washington/.

Kapcia, Antoni. 2008. *Cuba in Revolution: A History since the 1950s.* London: Reaktion Books.

Perez, Louis A. Jr. 2008. *Cuba in the American Imagination: Metaphor and the Imperial Ethos.* Chapel Hill: University of North Carolina.

Pérez-Stable, Marifeli. 2011. *The Cuban Revolution: Origins, Course and Legacy.* Third edition. New York: Oxford University.

Schoultz, Lars. 2009. *That Infernal Little Cuban Republic: The United States and the Cuban Revolution.* Chapel Hill: University of North Carolina.

Womack, Brantly. 2009. "Recognition, Deference and Respect: Generalizing the Lessons of an Assymetric Asian Order." *The Journal of American-East Asian Relations.* 16.1–2 (Summer).

Chapter 2

Establishing, Not Restoring, Normal Relations between the United States and Cuba

Philip Brenner

When President Dwight D. Eisenhower ended diplomatic relations between the United States and Cuba on January 3, 1961, few imagined that 54 years would pass before his decision was reversed. However, the restoration of diplomatic relations should not be confused with restoring normal relations between the two countries. In fact, Presidents Barack Obama and Raúl Castro cannot restore a normal relationship because one has never existed (see Pérez-Stable 2011 and this volume). Cuban Foreign Minister Bruno Rodríguez Parrilla emphasized this reality at the July 2015 opening of the Cuban embassy in Washington, remarking:

> The challenge [of achieving the normalization of bilateral relations] is huge because there have never been normal relations between the United States of America and Cuba, in spite of the one and a half century of intensive and enriching links that have existed between both peoples.

This chapter provides a brief overview of the abnormal US-Cuban relationship during the past 200 years and then examines what must change for the United States and Cuba to establish a normal relationship for the first time.

A History of Abnormal Relations

Even while Cuba was a colony of Spain, which in itself precluded a normal relationship, the United States debated its future relationship with the island. In 1823, Thomas Jefferson wrote longingly about incorporating Cuba into the United States: "I have ever looked on Cuba as the most interesting addition which could ever be made to our system of States" (Schoultz 2009, p. 19). His dreams were challenged, though, by Secretary of State John Quincy Adams, who feared that the addition of Cuba would strengthen the Southern coalition in Congress. The Massachusetts statesman argued that the United States should bide its time. Like a ripe fruit that inevitably falls to the ground due to the laws of gravity, Adams predicted Cuba "can gravitate only towards the North American Union, which by the same law of nature cannot cast her off from its bosom" (Schoultz 2009, pp. 18–19). Notably, by 1898, US trade with Cuba was greater than Spain's.

At that point, as Cuban independence fighters were about to win their struggle against Spain, the United States intervened to steal away their victory. Denying Cubans permission even to attend the peace treaty negotiations in Paris, the United States proceeded to rule Cuba for five years as an occupied territory. US troops departed only after Cuban constitutional convention delegates agreed to include the Platt Amendment in the new constitution. As the US Department of State's (2015b) history of the Amendment acknowledges,

> The rationale behind the Platt Amendment was straightforward. The United States Government had intervened in Cuba in order to safeguard its significant commercial interests on the island in the wake of Spain's inability to preserve law and order . . . By directly incorporating the requirements of the Platt Amendment into the Cuban constitution, the McKinley Administration was able to shape Cuban affairs without violating the Teller Amendment.

Between 1903 and 1933, the United States sent troops to Cuba three times, including one stint from 1906 to 1909 under Governor General Charles Magoon, who was so overtly contemptuous of Cubans that today they use his name as a synonym for treachery. In 1933, after insurgents overthrew the dictatorship of Gerardo Machado, President Franklin D. Roosevelt refused to recognize the new government, which lasted only one hundred days as a result. The Cuban economy had become so dependent on the United States that Cubans understood their only choice was bending to US political pressure. Although Roosevelt may have eschewed military intervention under his "good neighbor" policy, he was quite ready to intervene in other ways, and subsequent Cuban governments understood the limits of their constrained sovereignty.

Fulgencio Batista's dictatorship tried US patience in other ways—by giving US organized crime syndicates carte blanche to plan global operations based in Cuba and blatantly thumbing his nose at US requests to curtail violence against Cubans and cease human rights violations. Batista's behavior led the Eisenhower administration to seek his ouster in hopes of finding a "third way" in a polarized situation—a favorite US ploy in cases in which its backing of dictators had gone sour. But the January 1, 1959 victory of Cuban revolutionaries removed that option.

Over the next half century, the US-Cuban relationship was marked by both sides contributing to a legacy of fear and mistrust. To be sure, US officials often exaggerated the alleged "Cuban threat." In general, Cuba's support for insurgents fighting against oppressive regimes or colonial rulers challenged US hegemonic ambitions, not the United States itself. But the Cold War perspective of US policymakers encouraged them to apply zero-sum analyses, in which any loss for the United States was a gain for a worldwide communist movement. And the 1962 Cuban missile crisis validated their worst fears, that the existence of a country in the Western hemisphere that did not subordinate itself to US dominance could ultimately confront the United States with a real threat to its very existence.

In contrast, the existential threat Cuban officials perceived had greater validity. The United States organized, funded, and managed the 1961 Bay of Pigs invasion, along with at least seven attempts to assassinate the Cuban leadership (Central Intelligence Agency Inspector General 1967). It engaged in numerous covert operations aimed at regime change. The largest was the multi-faceted Operation Mongoose from 1961 to 1963, which the United States could have reasonably labeled as state-sponsored terrorism if another country had undertaken such a plan.[1] The history of these maneuvers leads Cuban policymakers to envision worst case scenarios even in the twenty-first century. When the most powerful country in the world engages in seemingly harmless clandestine programs—such as the recently unmasked Twitter-like campaign known as ZunZuneo (Sanger 2014)—Cuban analysts worry that US-supported provocations could spiral out of control and lead the United States to use the resulting situation as a justification for military intervention.

With this legacy of tension and hostility, the usually unobjectionable ways in which any two countries engage each other have become problematic for the United States and Cuba. For example, orderly migration or even travel has been compromised by the 1966 Cuban Adjustment Act, which distinguishes Cuban *emigrés* from all others for special benefits that encourage illegal Cuban emigration. Scientific and academic exchanges have been compromised by fears in both countries that scholars might be spies or that the exchanges might be used by the other country for propaganda purposes.

In short, the United States and Cuba have never had a normal relationship to which they can return: not when Cuba was a Spanish colony, not during the occupation of 1898 to 1903, not during the period from 1903 to 1933 when the Platt Amendment was in force, not during the Good Neighbor period, not during the Batista years, and certainly not during the period of hostility since 1959. The two countries need to draw a new map if they are going to travel the road from normal diplomatic relations to normal relations.

From Normal Diplomatic Relations to Normal Relations

Several analysts have well summarized key issues of the US-Cuban negotiating agenda beyond the matter of normal diplomatic relations (Bolaños 2015; LeoGrande 2015). The issues include: the US embargo; US activities that Cuba considers subversive, such as so-called democracy promotion programs and the Cuban Medical Professionals Parole Program, which encourages Cuban doctors working abroad to abandon their obligations and move to the United States ("A Cuban Brain Drain, Courtesy of U.S." 2014; Armstrong 2011); the Cuban Adjustment Act; US opposition to Cuba's membership in international financial institutions; property claims by citizens of both countries; and US occupation of the naval base at Guantánamo. The resolution of differences regarding these issues unquestionably would contribute to the development of a normal relationship. However, the essential elements of fully realizing normality would be the removal of fear and the development of trust between the two countries.

Both countries can take steps to reduce fear and build trust. Consider the US democracy promotion programs. US officials correctly argue that they are required by the 1996 Helms-Burton law (Cuban Liberty and Democratic Solidarity Act) to create and implement such programs. But the State Department is relatively free to determine the programs' nature and how to implement them. It could, as it does with other countries, consult with the Cuban government. There is no certainty that the Cuban government would reject such consultation, if it were undertaken with respect. For example, US officials could interpret the Helms-Burton requirements to mean that training Cubans to use capitalist business practices ultimately would promote democracy. The Cuban government recognizes that insufficient knowledge of ordinary business skills in the country—such as standard accounting practices—undermines its ability to accumulate capital, and it has welcomed the Catholic Church's introduction of extracurricular business classes.

Fears also could be ameliorated in modest ways, such as in the public discourse officials of each country use. For example, Cuba's favorite metaphor is "David and Goliath." It is, fundamentally, a hostile depiction in which the small warrior David kills the giant Goliath. Metaphors are not mere stylistic embellishments. As George Lakoff (1992) explains, they "limit what we notice, highlight what we do see, and provide part of the inferential structure that we reason with" (p. 48; see also Brenner and Castro 2009).

Policymakers in both countries will find that building trust is more difficult than reducing fears because of the legacy of distrust. Even as many Cubans celebrated the December 17 announcements on diplomatic relations, former President Fidel Castro waited more than five weeks to issue a comment. In a letter to the Cuban Federation of University Students on the seventieth anniversary of his matriculation at the University of Havana he wrote, "I do not trust the policy of the United States, nor have I exchanged a word with them, but this is not, in any way, a rejection of a peaceful solution to conflicts" (Castro Ruz 2015).[2]

One might argue that the personal experiences of Fidel and Raúl Castro will soon be irrelevant as they pass from the scene. Yet the senior ranks of Cuban policymakers include several people who have personal memories of numerous times when the United States responded with hostile actions to positive gestures from Cuba (LeoGrande and Kornbluh 2015). From the US side, many diplomats know that several colleagues who attempted to improve relations with Cuba have compiled an unenviable record of failed careers.

Still, diminishing fear and engendering trust are the cornerstones of establishing a normal relationship, because fear and mistrust prevent adversaries from empathizing with each other. Political psychologist Ralph White (1991) helpfully explains that empathy "does not necessarily imply sympathy, or tolerance, or liking, or agreement . . . [E]mpathy implies especially a focus on the other's situation—trying to look out at his situation through his eyes rather than at him as an individual"

(p. 292). While standing in another's shoes is the essential activity in pursuit of empathy, it is insufficient alone. In addition, policymakers must see their own country's behavior as the adversary does.

Empathy is grounded in three requirements. Each adversary must: (1) acknowledge its opponent's understandable anger; (2) recognize the other side's fear of being attacked; and (3) believe that its opponent wants a workable peace (White 1984, pp. 162–63; see also Blight and Lang 2010). Consider how positively Cuba responded when President Obama empathetically acknowledged on December 17 that the United States "tried to overthrow" the Cuban government with the 1961 Bay of Pigs invasion.

Without empathy, two countries are more likely to misinterpret unintended slights or insults as animosity, to perceive bellicose language intended for a domestic audience as a threat, or to treat a minor action, such as a visa denial, as a policy decision, when it may have been no more than a low-ranking official acting in accord with standard operating procedures. Without empathy, behaviors that countries in a normal relationship readily dismiss can become a new source of friction for two former adversaries.

A Jerky Start on the Path to Normalization

The progress toward normalization in the first eight months has been akin to riding in a car whose driver is just learning to use a manual shift. Each new effort seems to begin with a jerk. In going from first to second, the gears give off a noticeable grinding noise. Forward movement frequently comes to an abrupt halt when the car stalls. This pattern should have been expected because both sides had to accustom themselves to a new way of relating to each other. In addition, there are "spoilers" on each side who oppose normalization and have the ability to place obstacles along the path.

Opponents of normalization may have multiple motives for their position, ranging from principled concern about their country's interests to securing their own personal interests. For example, Cuban spoilers include officials who are skeptical about US intentions and worry that normal relations will further encourage a culture of individualism undermining Cuban socialism. Some also may fear their own bureaucratic positions of privilege eroding in the wake of a growing private sector. US obstructionists include those who believe that normalization implies that the United States would be conferring legitimacy to a government they consider illegitimate, which they argue would undermine US moral leadership ("The U.S. Snubs Cuban Dissidents" 2015). Other

US opponents seem to be motivated by narrow partisan objectives, the influence of campaign contributors, or the specter of lost contracts when government funding for anti-Castro activities disappears.

However, both governments have demonstrated an appreciation for acting empathetically and for finding ways to build confidence about the possibility of a normal relationship. Indeed, the list of "constructive" contributions to normalization is longer than the list of "destructive" ones, as Table 2.1 indicates.

Table 2.1 Constructive and destructive contributions to normalization

Constructive	• President Obama removed Cuba from the list of state sponsors of terrorism (Hirschfeld Davis 2015)
	• The United States changed Cuba's designation from Tier 3 to Tier 2 in the State Department's annual report on "Trafficking in Persons" (US Department of State 2015a)
	• The delegations from each country showed appropriate respect and avoided sensitive issues on the occasion of the flag raisings at their new embassies
	• Cuba compromised to allow the free movement by embassy officials
	• President Obama eased several restrictions on travel to Cuba by U.S. citizens (US Department of the Treasury 2015)
	• Cuba released fifty-three prisoners whom Amnesty International had designated as "prisoners of conscience"
	• The two countries tentatively reached an agreement to resume regularly scheduled airline flights
	• The two countries have engaged in new bilateral discussions about property claims, law enforcement cooperation, preparedness for natural disasters, and human rights
	• Cuba has readily granted visas to business executives and members of Congress
	• President Obama has threatened to veto an appropriations bill if it includes provisions preventing new ferry or airline service to Cuba
Destructive	• The United States has continued so-called "democracy promotion" programs that Cuba considers subversive
	• Cuba has insisted on including difficult issues in negotiations, such as the unconditional devolution of Guantánamo Naval Base
	• The United States has continued the Cuban Medical Professional Parole Program
	• The United States has refused to repeal the Cuban Adjustment Act or to end the almost automatic presumption that a Cuban who reaches US territory is a "political refugee" (Sandels and Valdés 2015)
	• President Obama has not submitted to the Senate the nomination of a US ambassador to Cuba, in part because of threats by some Republican senators to stop any nominee's confirmation process
	• The US House included provisions in an appropriations bill (H.R. 2577) that would prevent the start of scheduled airline flights and prevent ferry traffic between the United States and Cuba

Still, the first eight months of détente since December 17 do not provide a secure base for developing a normal relationship. Several changes in US policy have resulted from Executive Orders that could be reversed by the next president. Republican presidential candidates, most prominently Sen. Marco Rubio (Florida), have promised to do just that if elected (Bustos 2015). Moreover, the greatest stumbling block—the US embargo—remains in place. Ending the embargo would require Congress to repeal the Helms-Burton law, which is unlikely to happen soon. Notably, the rationale of Helms-Burton is to change the system of government in Cuba, and the law asserts that "the Cuban Government has posed and continues to pose a national security threat to the United States" (§6021.28). The ongoing embargo undergirds the position of opponents in Cuba who warn that US intentions have not changed, and that the normalization of diplomatic relations is merely a new US tactic to destroy the Cuban revolution (Alarcón de Quesada 2015). Thus, despite the efforts of some in the Obama administration, the United States seems not to have assuaged fears effectively enough for many Cuban officials to trust its giant neighbor.

Empathy and Asymmetry

The effort to appreciate an adversary's fears is difficult when a large country and a small country attempt to empathize, because the calculus of threat for each is so different. A great power tends to not even think about whether it will be swallowed up by another power, whether its identity will be submerged by the interests of a larger state, or whether its internal life will be subject to the whims and dictates of outsiders. In contrast, the Cuban concept of security includes "economic, political, and even social aspects," Cuban political scientist Carlos Alzugaray Treto (1989) explains, "precisely because Cuba, as a small country, is more vulnerable than a big superpower like the United States to all kinds of pressures" (p. 86; also see Brenner 2006). As a result, Cuba pays extraordinarily close attention to every US utterance and every small movement made by US officials, which can readily lead to misinterpretation when taken out of context.

Even the most sensitive US attempt to accommodate Cuba's fears may be unsuccessful because of factors outside the control of the United States. Consider the view from Cuba's Council of Ministers as it watches Venezuela implode, the supportive Brazilian government of President Dilma Rousseff suffer from mounting scandals, and China's economy slide into a period of slow growth. Cuba has sought to diversify its dependence on one foreign supplier as a way of securing its sovereignty. As these three important trading partners become less available for support at the moment that the United States appears poised to replace them, Cuban officials may become fearful of giving too much leverage to its giant neighbor. In general, small powers often perceive an assertive effort to dominate them as the greatest security threat. Indeed, overcoming and not repeating the legacy of US control over Cuba's economy from 1898 to 1958 have been primary concerns for the revolutionaries since 1959. Resistance to US domination was their leitmotif, and they have viewed real independence as a key measure of the Revolution's success.

"Cuba is a small country," political scientist Jorge I. Domínguez (1989) observed near the end of the Cold War, "but it has the foreign policy of a big power" (p. 7). The phrase succinctly captured the frustration that US policymakers felt about Cuba from the very start of the Cuban revolution. Their determination to bend Cuba to the US will—to make it behave like a small country in the US sphere of influence—confronted an even greater Cuban determination not to bend. This confrontation shaped the relationship before and during the Cold War, and continued to condition it after the Cold War ended, even as the two countries negotiated the opening of embassies in January 2015. For example, after US Assistant Secretary of State for Western Hemisphere Affairs Roberta S. Jacobson noted that "we pressed the Cuban government for improved human rights conditions," Josefina Vidal Ferreiro, Cuba's lead negotiator asserted, "Cuba has never responded to pressure" (Klapper and Weissenstein 2015).

As the United States and Cuba move haltingly toward a normal relationship, both countries will need to appreciate that their empathetic skills may not be as finely tuned as they believe. Greater empathy will require US policymakers to discard an arrogance shaped in part by US invulnerability as well as the ideology of American exceptionalism. Cuban officials will need to overcome a tendency to be hyper-vigilant, which, in part, has been a reaction to Cuba's vulnerability and the result of a national security ideology that its vulnerability engendered. Such attitudinal transformations will not come easily. Foreign Minister Rodríguez's observation that the challenge of making these changes is "huge" was apt. But greater empathy will be necessary if the United States and Cuba are going to build trust to establish a normal relationship for the first time.

Notes

1. See "Testimony of Richard M. Helms," U.S. Congress, House, Select Committee on Assassinations, "Investigation of the Assassination of President John F. Kennedy," Hearings, 95th Cong., 2nd Sess., September 22, 25, and 26, 1978, vol. IV.
2. Author translation. Note that the Spanish version reads: "No confío en la política de Estados Unidos," which could be translated as "I do not trust US *politics.*"

References

"A Cuban Brain Drain, Courtesy of U.S." (editorial). 2014. *New York Times*, November 17.
Alarcón de Quesada, Ricardo. 2015. "El mensaje de una ceremonia inolvidable." *CubaDebate*, August 3. http://www.cubadebate.cu/opinion/2015/08/03/el-mensaje-de-una-ceremonia-inolvidable/.
Alzugaray Treto, Carlos. 1989. "Problems of National Security in the Cuban-U.S. Historic Breach." In *U.S.-Cuban Relations in the 1990s*, edited by Jorge I. Domínguez and Rafael Hernández, 86. Boulder: Westview.
Armstrong, Fulton. 2011. "Time to clean up U.S. regime-change programs in Cuba." *Miami Herald*, December 26.
Blight, James G., and janet M. Lang. 2010. "FORUM: When Empathy Failed: Using Critical Oral History to Reassess the Collapse of U.S.-Soviet Détente in the Carter-Brezhnev Years." *Journal of Cold War History* 12(2): 29–74.
Bolaños, Jorge. 2015. "La táctica de EEUU hacia Cuba cambia, pero la estrategia se mantiene." *CubaDebate*, February 6. http://www.cubadebate.cu/opinion/2015/02/06/la-tactica-de-eeuu-hacia-cuba-cambia-pero-la-estrategia-se-mantiene/.
Brenner, Philip. 2006. "Overcoming Asymmetry: Is a Normal US-Cuban Relationship Possible?" In *Redefining Cuban Foreign Policy: The Impact of the "Special Period,"* edited by H. Michael Erisman and John M. Kirk, 280–304. Gainesville: University Press of Florida.
———, and Soraya Castro. 2009. "David and Gulliver: Fifty Years of Competing Metaphors in the Cuban-United States Relationship." *Diplomacy & Statecraft* 20: 236–57.
Bustos, Sergio. 2015. "In speech, Rubio slams Obama's outreach to Iran and Cuba." *Associated Press*, August 14.
Castro Ruz, Fidel. 2015. "Para mis compañeros de la Federación Estudiantil Universitaria." *Granma*, January 26. http://www.granma.cu/cuba/2015-01-26/para-mis-companeros-de-la-federacion-estudiantil-universitaria.
Central Intelligence Agency Inspector General. 1967. "Report on Plots to Assassinate Fidel Castro." May 23; National Archive and Records Administration, JFK Record Series, No. 104-10213-10101, February 3, 1999.

Cuban Liberty and Democratic Solidarity (LIBERTAD) Act of 1996. Public Law 104–14.

Domínguez, Jorge I. 1989. *To Make the World Safe for Revolution: Cuba's Foreign Policy*. Cambridge: Harvard University Press.

Hirschfeld Davis, Julie. 2015. "U.S. Removes Cuba From State-Sponsored Terrorism List." *New York Times*, May 30.

Klapper, Bradley and Michael Weissenstein. 2015. "US, Cuba move toward embassies, disagree on human rights." *Associated Press*, January 23.

Lakoff, George. 1992. "Metaphor and War: The Metaphor System Used to Justify War in the Gulf." In *Thirty Years of Linguistic Evolution*, edited by Martin Pütz, 463–81. Amsterdam: John Benjamins.

LeoGrande, William M. 2015. "Normalizing Relations With Cuba: The Unfinished Agenda." *Newsweek*, January 30. http://www.newsweek.com/normalizing-relations-cuba-unfinished-agenda-303232.

LeoGrande, William, and Peter Kornbluh. 2015. *Back Channel to Cuba: The Hidden History of Negotiations between Washington and Havana*. Chapel Hill: University of North Carolina Press.

Pérez-Stable, Marifeli. 2011. *The United States and Cuba: Intimate Enemies*. New York: Routledge.

Rodríguez Parrilla, Bruno. 2015. "Statement. Ministry of Foreign Relations, Havana, Cuba." July 20. http://www.cubaminrex.cu/en/statement-bruno-rodriguez-parrilla-minister-foreign-affairs-republic-cuba-ceremony-re-open-cuban.

Sandels, Robert, and Nelson P. Valdés. 2015. "The Cuban Adjustment Act: the Other Immigration Mess." *Counterpunch*, August 28. http://www.counterpunch.org/2015/08/28/the-cuban-adjustment-act-the-other-immigration-mess/.

Sanger, David E. 2014. "U.S. Says It Tried to Build a Social Media Site in Cuba, but Failed." *New York Times*, April 4.

Schoultz, Lars. 2009. *That Infernal Little Republic: The United States and the Cuban Revolution*. Chapel Hill: University of North Carolina Press.

"The U.S. Snubs Cuban Dissidents" (editorial). 2015. *Washington Post*, August 14.

US Department of State. 2015a. "Trafficking in Persons" (July). http://www.state.gov/j/tip/rls/tiprpt/2015/.

———. 2015b. "The United States, Cuba, and the Platt Amendment, 1901." Office of the Historian. Accessed August 28. http://history.state.gov/milestones/1899-1913/Platt.

U.S. Department of the Treasury. 2015. "FACT SHEET: Treasury and Commerce Announce Regulatory Amendments to the Cuba Sanctions." Last modified January 15. http://www.treasury.gov/press-center/press-releases/Pages/jl9740.aspx.

White, Ralph K. 1991. "Empathizing with Saddam Hussein." *Political Psychology*, 12(2): 291–308.

———. 1984. *Fearful Warriors: A Psychological Profile of U.S.-Soviet Relations*. New York: Free Press.

Chapter 3

Cuba-US: The December 17 Agreement in the Rationale of Asymmetric Relations

Arturo Lopez-Levy

Disparity is the distinctive feature of Cuban-US relations. Power asymmetry is not limited to differences in capacities but also involves systemic differences in the ways states assess security risks and define their interests and perceptions. As Brantly Womack (2006) explains, "mutual perceptions and interactions in an asymmetric relation will be fundamentally shaped by the differences of opportunity and vulnerability each side confronts. In effect, the relationship of A and B is best viewed as a set of two very different sub relations, A →b and b →A" (pp. 17–18). In the case of Cuba and the United States, the latter country plans and discusses its foreign policy strategy as a Great Power, while the former does so as a small, vulnerable, and developing state.

Although the constitutive rules of international society demand that the sovereignty of individual nations be recognized and the sovereignty of Great Powers be managed (Bull 2012), tensions exist amid these specified principles and their acceptance by respective governments. The English School, some constructivists, and asymmetric relations theorists emphasize the role of history in the advancement of cultural structures (legal, behavioral, and attitude-related) between states (Buzan and Little 2000; Wendt 1999). Even though asymmetry is a source of tension between sovereign states, leaders have the ability to develop stable, peaceful relations through diplomacy and self-restraint. Cultures of interstate relations can change and have changed historically at the bilateral, regional, and global levels.

Interdependence theory expects that mature relations will be cooperative. When countries manage to coordinate their interests and values, the resulting interdependence tends to reduce state-state frictions that are due to misperception and lack of communication.[1] The opening of diplomatic relations between Cuba and the United States over the summer of 2015 is an important watershed because it implied a new direction in the official relations between the two states and the beginning of normalization, which should be understood as a process rather than an event.

Normalization begins when both sides agree that hostility has been too costly for too long and they explicitly or implicitly recognize that the stronger state's imperial-coercive policies have not succeeded at dominating the weaker state. Such an agreement is not permanent. On the contrary, the element of perception leaves open the possibility that a policy may be reversed. If official actors controlling their respective states' strategic calculations later change their perception and modify their positions, or if these officials are replaced by others with different interests and values, then the impetus for rapprochement might diminish and hostility again might become the prevailing logic. Such a reversal occurred in 1980, when the election of Ronald Reagan aborted a previous US-Cuba process of détente.

The first step of normalization consists of replacing hostile images of "threats" and "enmity" with more benign discourses of "countries in transition" or at least a "rivalry" that combines challenges and opportunities. A typical solution to conflicts between a small country with a successful nationalist resistance like Cuba and a neighboring superpower like the United States is an arrangement known as recognition (Womack 2006). In such arrangements, the stronger power acknowledges the sovereign status[2] of the weaker one, and the latter, in turn, expresses deference to the stronger power's prominence in global and regional issues. The essential principle of the arrangement underlying both recognition and deference is *respect*. This has been the case of the United Kingdom with Ireland, France and Germany with Belgium, Russia with Finland, China with Vietnam, and the United States with Canada and Mexico. Such arrangements are not foolproof; "[n]evertheless, for most asymmetric relationships most of the time, managing and negotiating the relationship is preferable to hostility" (Womack 2006, p. 21).

These historic compromises outline power disparities as a cause of tension in asymmetrical relations while placing the interaction between both states in a broader historical comparative framework than do references solely to Cuban exceptionalism. Emphasizing the integral role of domination and resistance in reproducing, escalating, or decreasing conflict helps to outline a constructive, diplomatic approach to addressing mismanaged power disparities. The practices of imperial domination and revolutionary resistance may be changed through negotiations and political will.[3] US imperial-coercive treatment toward Cuba does not have to be a permanent feature of US hemispheric strategy. Rather, it has been determined by associated historical conditions—beginning with the Eisenhower administration's aversion to Latin American nationalism (which it saw as weakening the anti-communist alliance) and encompassing Cuba's alliance with the Soviet Union during the Cold War and the US concern with balancing political power domestically in the post-Cold War era, when Cuba lost priority as a foreign policy issue. Under these conditions, pro-embargo sectors of southern Florida benefited from a previous foreign policy narrative of hostility (Brenner et al. 2008).

A discussion of the history of Cuba-US relations and the attitudes and perceptions of both governments since the foundation of the Cuban republic in 1902 is beyond the scope of this chapter. It is sufficient to say that asymmetry is not a transitional feature in US-Cuba relations. On the contrary, asymmetry has been consolidated over the years as the disparity of power increasingly favored the United States and the disproportionate amount of attention given to the larger country motivated Cuba's nationalist projection of its foreign policy. As Cuba-US interaction increases, a big challenge will be their ability to build a mature nonhostile asymmetry that promotes their mutual interests.

Under these circumstances, the imperial-coercive policy promoted by the United States is not surprising, regardless of how irrational and counterproductive it has proven to be from a foreign policy perspective. As it does with Cuba, the United States approaches other adversaries and world issues with the same combination of emotion, hubris, inconsistencies, and misjudgment about its opponents' ability to resist. Previous conflicts, negotiations, and rapprochement between the United States and Vietnam and China, respectively, are examples of normalization processes in which both sides moved beyond a hostile stalemate and reached a compromise (see Torres, this volume).

Cuban nationalist conviction is not exceptional either. What triumphed in Cuba in 1959 was an authentic revolution with deep nationalist roots in the country's culture,[4] but it was also connected to world trends in the mid-twentieth century, such as decolonization and socialism. Post-1959 Cuban foreign policy has wrestled with the tension—characteristic of revolutionary processes—between nationalism (centered on sovereignty) and internationalism (centered on ideological solidarity). Cuba has struck a different balance on these issues depending on the dynamics of domestic policies and on the international system in which the island operates—and it will continue to have to do so for as long as the revolutionary regime endures domestically (see Halliday 1999).

For decades, Cuba showed tremendous zeal in promoting what Jorge Domínguez (1989) called "a world safe for revolution." Fidel Castro welcomed the challenge of US hostility and insisted on promoting an alternative world order to replace the US-led liberal one. For as long as Cuba's alliance with the Soviet Union continued and resources stayed available, Cuban leadership intervened (on many occasions taking the initiative) in support of their ideological counterparts, acting as "a small country with a policy of a Great Power."

Perception and interactions between Cuba and the United States are in permanent flux. The disparity of power habitually entices the United States to try to force its will on the weaker state. However, Cuba's nationalism has successfully survived almost six decades of the US embargo aimed at imposing regime change from abroad. To understand Cuba's success, one must examine past conflicts in which the disparity of attention given to bilateral relations worked in Cuba's favor and compensated its relative lack of power. Cuban resistance to US attempts to impose its political will on the island, from the 1903 Platt Amendment to the 1996 Helms-Burton law, follows that pattern.

The two countries have, at times, experimented with negotiation and compromise. Great Powers leaders (in this case, the United States) have the choice of self-restraint as a prudent course to build stable relations with weaker neighbors (Cuba). If successful, the United States can enjoy the hegemonic benefits of a peaceful agreement tailored to its liberal values[5] without removing the unpopular embargo that has been condemned by the global society and disrupted American world leadership.

Smaller powers that are zealous defenders of their sovereignty, like Cuba, at times have opportunities to enter into agreements with regional powers based on mutual negotiations, not unilateral impositions. Self-restraint and deference to US status as a Great Power have been, at times, a Cuban choice. US assurances of security can provide Cuba with a more favorable environment in which to concentrate on nationalist goals and harvest the fruits of economic and political development.

The desire of Cuban foreign policy for a mutually respectful relationship with the United States, its neighboring superpower, has been encouraged by various elements of "Lockean" culture in the international system.[6] In such a liberal order, sovereign equality and the prohibition of the use of force are ordinal principles. Paradoxically, in its conflict with the United States, Cuba has demanded respect for the sovereignty of weaker states according to another ordinal feature instated by the US-led coalition that created the United Nations: the principle of self-determination. This is an example of what Bruce Cronin (2001) called the hegemonic paradox. That is, the United States—because of its unilateralism and the disruptive influence of the Cuban-American pro-embargo lobby on its domestic politics—follows policies that undermine the principles of the very same liberal world order established under its hegemony.

The Long Path to December 17

President Obama's announcement on December 17, 2014 that the United States intended to reestablish diplomatic relations with Cuba was the result of an asymmetric stalemate. Despite the enormous disparity of power in its favor, the United States was unable to defeat the political regime brought forth by the 1959 revolution. As the weaker power, Cuba used a strategy of attrition. Havana "wins" just by surviving (notwithstanding the high price it pays in terms of economic development and human rights) and, consequently, increasing the cost of antagonistic US policy in comparison with other available alternatives to Washington.

Cuba's persistence as a sovereign state over the decades of interaction since 1959 has necessitated the search for nonzero-sum solutions to the US-Cuban conflict, solutions fitting the recognition model. The cumulative effect of successive rounds of negotiation and relaxations of tension—starting with the initiatives by Secretary of State Henry Kissinger and including important milestones during the Carter, Clinton, and Obama administrations—is noteworthy indeed. In the diplomatic arena, the opening of Interests Sections in Washington and Havana in 1977 was a watershed event (McCoy 2015) that allowed for a more fluid relationship between both governments and societies than had the nonpeaceful coexistence that prevailed before.

A list of the principal variables that transformed Cuban-US bilateral relations might include several mentioned by Alexander Wendt in his social theory of international relations between countries that have moved from a hostile stalemate to a negotiable one:

a) A spike of interdependence[7] as a result of travel and trade licenses granted through exceptions to the embargo, which have greatly impacted Cuban-American and Midwestern farming communities;

b) Identification of common interests and areas of cooperation (e.g., managing tensions regarding Guantánamo Naval Base, peace in Southern Africa, international cooperation on health issues in the campaign against Ebola in West Africa [Lopez-Levy 2014]) and recognition of common adversaries (international crime, terrorism, drug traffic, pandemics, natural disasters, etc.); and

c) Homogenization[8] of policies (e.g., Cuba's economic reforms and political liberalization since 2008 have reduced the social differences between the island and its neighbors; Cuban acceptance in 1995 of deference to Great Powers according to the 1968 Nuclear Non-Proliferation Treaty made its security policy compatible with a US-led liberal world order on this sensitive issue).

To create space in which those variables could operate, Cuba had to first survive the Cold War by partnering with the Soviet Union. With the Soviet Union, Cuba counterbalanced its power disparity with the United States and was able to project its foreign policy at a global level, increasing the opportunity cost for Washington's imperial-coercive policy.

William LeoGrande and Peter Kornbluh (2014) illustrate the way in which—ever since 1968, when the Working Group on Cuba drafted the first "National Policy Paper"—comprehensive proposals about a transition toward a relation of mutual recognition were formulated by the US foreign policy bureaucracy. The document reflected conventional arguments (some of which already appeared in certain proposals of the Kennedy administration) made by other great powers seeking to change their dynamics of acrimony with a lesser adversary as part of a broader global or regional strategy. It was a vital first step, intellectually speaking, toward mature asymmetry and a potential recognition agreement.

In the aforementioned cases, the nationalism of the weaker states was "appeased" by the great powers. Bilateral asymmetric relations determined by imperial policies and resistance are not mature, even if they achieve some level of precarious stability. In mature asymmetries, the Great Power alters its policies based on the understanding that: (1) responding with imperial-coercive means toward the weaker states has not been worth the cost in terms of regional, global, and soft power; (2) abandoning an imperial logic could be more beneficial in the long-term for achieving hegemony and promoting liberal values; (3) a policy of self-restraint and moderation toward a weaker power guarantees a stable and predictable relationship, thus allowing the Great Power to focus on more significant issues (such as policies toward fellow Great Powers and issues of regional hegemony and stability).

"Appeasing" weak states by acknowledging their sovereignty has required important reciprocal changes in these countries' behavior and attitudes—no simple task for revolutionary states with an internationalist agenda such as Cuba's. For decades, Fidel Castro's foreign policy pursued changes not only for Cuba but also regionally and globally. Cuba's aid to radical leftist movements in Latin America, the Middle East, and Africa in the 1960s and 1970s was a major irritant for Washington, as was Havana's support for the movement for Puerto Rican independence, including for members of armed groups working within this US-controlled territory.

To avoid "unnecessary" conflicts, states in Cuba's position vis-à-vis the United States adjusted their nationalist narrative by acknowledging the advantages of a realistic deference to the neighboring Great Power. These countries did not abandon their revolutionary ideals; instead, they chose to comply with the rules and norms of a world order led by the superpowers. This seems to be the path that Cuba has taken over the past two decades.

Since the 1990s, Cuba has not engaged in antagonistic behaviors toward other governments in Latin America or in the third world. Currently, Cuba carries out its internationalist agenda within the boundaries of international law, mainly with doctors and teachers, not with soldiers. The United States has no security-related reason to reject Cuba's preeminent role in international health issues, for example, even though a byproduct of this role is the promotion of Cuba's ideology and communist values. Health care is simply not a challenge to US power supremacy. In the case of Puerto Rico, Cuba has not aided pro-independence armed groups, recognizing implicit limits on what it can do. Havana has not abandoned its position in favor of Puerto Rico's self-determination (understood exclusively as independence from the United States), but it has carefully avoided provocative actions.

The end of the Cold War was a major change in Cuba-US relations, removing them from an East-West axis and instead placing them in the asymmetrical bilateral relation between the United States and Latin America. In the 1990s, the Castro government was depicted as a "remnant of the Cold War," destined to disappear with the end of Soviet support or, at the very least, with the demise of Fidel Castro. Cuba, nevertheless, did not follow its assigned script. Since its fourth Congress in 1991, the Cuban Communist Party began a long process of political adaptation to the post-Cold War realities.

After Fidel Castro retired due to illness, the government launched parallel processes of economic reform and political liberalization. The Communist Party thus aimed to compensate for the loss of its charismatic leader and to overcome the weaknesses of its unsustainable command economy, which had become unviable in the absence of Soviet subsidies. These processes opened the door to a recognition compromise with the United States because it changed the US political community's perception of Cuba from a Cold War relic to a country in transition.

Cuba's reforms found a positive reception in Latin America and the Caribbean, where most governments have supported the island's gradual transition to a market economy, believing that such a process will eventually bring about deep political transformations. Since the late 1990s, the region has envisaged Cuba as a country in transition, not as a threat. US insistence under President Bush on an imperial policy of harassment and isolation provoked sharply negative responses in Latin America. Ever since the fourth Summit of the Americas in Argentina in 2006, these countries have demanded that Cuba be incorporated into this forum for hemispheric dialogue. It is in this context that the policy change initiated on December 17, 2014 becomes understandable (Lopez-Levy 2014). It was not by coincidence that the rapprochement between Cuba and the United States gained momentum as part of the preparation of the seventh Summit of the Americas in Panama in April 2015. Cuba was reaping the benefits of its strategy to raise the opportunity costs of US policy toward Cuba not only in the bilateral context but also regionally and globally.

From Normalization to Normalcy:
Toward a Stable Asymmetrical Relationship of
Recognition between Cuba and the United States

By the late nineteenth century, Cuban national hero José Martí, who lived most of his adult life in the United States, had clearly signaled the importance of mutual understanding between the United States and Latin America for achieving stable relations. Lack of knowledge about Cuba and Latin America had led US authorities to disrespect the political aspirations of people and politicians in the region. At the same time, Martí exhorted Cubans and Latin Americans to understand the United States and the challenges and opportunities associated with being in the same vicinity as such a powerful country. "The scorn of our formidable neighbor who does not know us is our America's greatest danger. And since the day of the visit is near, it is imperative that our neighbor know us, and soon, so that it will not scorn us. Through ignorance it might even come to lay hands on us. Once it does know us, it will remove its hands out of respect" (Martí 1891).

The events of December 17 were based on an understanding, by political elites in both countries, of the bitter history of confrontation and disrespect that had led to losses for both sides. Cuba has proven to itself and to the hemisphere that it can resist and defend its sovereignty regardless of the consequences. The United States has proven to Cubans that a confrontational approach in the promotion of its revolutionary values has an enormous cost. From that experience, both states can normalize relations on the basis of mutual respect and a realistic approach.

In an agreement of recognition, asymmetrical conflicts do not disappear; instead, they are handled with diplomatic maturity, international standards, and a constructive and inclusive discourse. An essential requirement of this diplomatic compromise is mutual respect. In this sense, it is a frustrating deal for maximalists on both sides. In the case of the stronger power, maximalists resent the fact that disparity of power does not translate into the weaker state's subordination to their own designs. In the case of the weaker power, the most revolutionary sectors resent the implicit acceptance of international hierarchies in which the stronger state remains with a privileged status. They tend to reject a realistic, nonhostile modus vivendi with appeals to a nonhierarchical international order that exists only in their ideological fantasies.

Despite these frustrations, recognition can prevail because it is in the best national interests of both states, given the available alternatives. Engagement in international politics is not a marriage; it is an instrumental arrangement of interests, not love. But instrumental arrangements can grow and transform into dynamics of mutual understanding. The key to such growth is to decrease hostility and examine normalization as a non-zero sum game that offers mutual gains from cooperation.

A recognition deal between the United States and Cuba does not exclude the possibility of the two countries eventually developing strategic trust by habituation, but it begins with a minimal tactical trust to implement specific agreements about concrete topics. Eventually, economic and social ties can displace security concerns and reinforce a history of cooperation and mutual gain that counterbalances the memories of hostility. The logics of engagement are also strengthened when they are grounded in a broader system of regional norms and practices.

A trajectory of cooperation and management of differences serves to reaffirm each country's respect for the other's status as a superpower and a sovereign country, respectively. With time, constituencies will develop that are interested in reinforcing the agreement. Actors in Cuba and the United States who have launched the process of normalization of relations are, to a certain degree, partners—albeit with different dreams. They must acknowledge their differences while working together to defeat spoilers[9] in both societies whose interests and values profit from hostility between the two countries.

For an agreement of recognition to work, the normalization of relations cannot be another means of continuing an existing conflict. The goals are to create a new vision of common interests that should prevail over differences and to handle the latter through diplomatic channels. The key lies in the power of persuasion to demonstrate the convenience of cooperating rather than coercion (by the United States) or disruption (by Cuba). If the United States intends to use the reestablished embassies to repeat the mistakes it committed between 1959 and 1961, when it attempted to oppose Fidel Castro, then Cuba will again entrench itself. If Cuba uses the new relationship with the United States to organize anti-US fronts in Latin America, then it will work in favor of those in the United States who want to return to hostile policies.

A key element to change the dynamics of interaction between Cuba and the United States is the adjustment of official perceptions.

Because the relationship is asymmetrical, it is normal for the stronger partner (the United States) to take unilateral steps in the early stages of the process, given that the impact of its past hostility has been greater. In that sense, taking Cuba off the State Department's list of sponsors of terrorism was a substantial step, not because it lifted sanctions, but because it changed Cuba's image domestically. Cuba now appears in official US discourse as a country in transition, not as a threat.

In a nonhostile context, normalization may lead to a new normality.[10] To that end, it is crucial to take advantage of the final year of Obama's administration to consolidate the exchange structure of recognition with constituencies in both societies who would work to make it permanent. Cuba must feel that its interaction with the United States is an opportunity for its development and not a threat to its sovereignty. The United States must recognize that its role as a Great Power gives it special rights and responsibilities in the regional and global systems. Cuba can use improved relations with the United States to secure a better bargaining position for itself with other international actors such as the European Union, Russia, and China. These relations can constitute a buffer for tensions with or lack of attention by the United States, but Cuba should avoid presenting these ties as threats to Washington's regional or global role as a Great Power. The United States is strengthened, rather than weakened, by a more normal relationship with Cuba.

The two pending tasks for Cuba and the United States will be: (1) the development of conflict management mechanisms capable of neutralizing the possibility that misunderstandings or contradiction may escalate and (2) the creation of joint experts' commissions to enable cooperation and connection regarding issues about which Obama has already initiated the process that will dismantle parts of the embargo. To that end, new routines may be established, as well as institutional procedures and connections, that could engage both societies and create educational, business, humanitarian, and religious communities as well as a critical mass of émigrés committed to normality.

The importance of the symbolic in this process should not be neglected. Normal diplomatic rituals tend to become self-fulfilling prophesies that reinforce virtuous circles of rapprochement because they align bilateral relations with international standards and expectations. Cuba and the United States must aim for their relationship to start working "as if it were normal," including visits back and forth by their foreign relations ministers and even their presidents.

The victory of Cuban nationalism over the embargo is significant for Cubans, but the United States may nevertheless co-opt a sovereign Cuba into a liberal world order under its aegis. Paraphrasing Henry Kissinger, the question to ask the new post-Castro generation of Cuban leaders who will ascend to power in 2018 is whether they see virtue in a permanent conflict with the United States or envision the promotion of Cuba's national interests in a world order in which Washington retains its primacy. If the response is the latter, then bilateral differences will not end, but both countries can enter into a mutually beneficial cycle.

Notes

1. There are conflicts between states that are not due to miscommunications or misperceptions, but rather to incompatibilities of interests and values. The fact that these conflicts are antagonistic does not mean that they cannot be peacefully managed. The Cold War was also called "the Long Peace" because, although it was a conflict between two irreconcilable systems (communism and capitalism), the Soviet Union and the United States never went to war.
2. Brantly Womack uses the term "autonomy" to explain the minimal goal of the weaker state. I prefer to use "sovereignty" because the two terms have different connotations in international law as practical applications of the principle of self-determination. Autonomy of a group or a region can be achieved within a single sovereign state. I look at the compromise of recognition as part of the set of relations within the society of sovereign states (international society).
3. This study tries to distinguish between the questions "Why?" (causal) and "How possible?" (constitutive) in the discussion of the US-Cuba asymmetric conflict. There are many excellent studies about the causes of the clash, but not about how it has escalated to the highest level of hostility. Regardless of the root causes of antagonism between the US-led world order and revolutionary Cuba, certain discourses and practices reproduce and strengthen the logics of hostility.
4. One of the main mistakes of the US diagnosis of Cuba over the past few decades (and one that is typical of greater powers in unstable asymmetrical relations) has been centering the conflict on Fidel Castro as a person and ignoring the mobilizing power of Cuban nationalism as a structural factor.
5. Joseph Nye's discussion (2004) of soft power alerted US policymakers of the importance of combining military and economic power to cope with specific threats and challenges, as well as of the attraction of US values and institutions.

6. Here, I use the concept of culture advanced by Alexander Wendt (1999) at a macro-systemic level. The anarchic condition of the international system is compatible with different logics.

7. Robert Axelrod (1984) has explained how interdependence can generate dominant dynamics of stable and reciprocal cooperation of the "tit for tat" type. The constructivist approach has conducted various case studies in which cooperation is not only the strategic rationale but also social, generating changes in the roles and identities of participating actors (states and societies) (Neumann 1996).

8. On the trend toward homogeneity in international society and the homogenization theme in general, see Fred Halliday (1994).

9. Saul Landau and Nelson Valdez (2010) discussed the role of spoilers within the US government as factors that escalated conflict even within the already hostile policy of the George W. Bush administration.

10. Academic and former Cuban ambassador Carlos Alzugaray (1999) presented a Cuban national view on the issue of normalization of relations between Cuba and the United States.

References

Alzugaray, Carlos. 1999. "Is Normalization Possible between Cuba and the United States after 100 Years of History?" Washington: Latin American Studies Association.

Axelrod, Robert. 1984. *The Evolution of Cooperation*. New York: Basic Books.

Brenner, Phillip, Patrick Haney, and Walt Vanderbush. 2008. "Intermestic Interests and US Foreign Policy towards Cuba." In *The Domestic Sources of American Foreign Policy*, edited by Eugene Wittkopf and James McCormick, 65–80. Lanham, MD: Rowman & Littlefield.

Bull, Hedley. 2012. *The Anarchical Society*. London: Palgrave Macmillan-Columbia University.

Buzan, Barry, and Richard Little. 2000. *International Systems in World History: Remaking the Study of International Relations*. Oxford: Oxford University.

Cronin, Bruce. 2001. "The Paradox of Hegemony: America's Ambiguous Relationship with the United Nations." *European Journal of International Relations* 7.1: 103–30.

Domínguez, Jorge. 1989. *To Make the World Safe for Revolution: Cuba's Foreign Policy*. Cambridge: Harvard University.

Halliday, Fred. 1994. "International Society as Homogeneity: Burke, Marx and Fukuyama." In *Rethinking International Relations*, edited by Fred Halliday, 94–123. London: Macmillan.

———. 1999. *Revolution and World Politics: The Rise of the Sixth Great Power*. Durham: Duke University.

Landau, Saul, and Nelson Valdez. 2010. *Confesiones de Roger Noriega: ¿Diplomacia Muscular o Violación de la Ley?* *Rebelión*, September 22. http://www.rebelion.org/noticia.php?id=113135.

LeoGrande, William, and Peter Kornbluh. 2014. *Back Channel to Cuba: The Hidden History of Negotiations between Washington and Havana.* Chapel Hills: University of North Carolina.

Lopez-Levy, Arturo. 2014. "Fighting Ebola: A New Case for U.S. Engagement with Cuba." *Tampa Bay Tribune*, October 28.

Martí, José. 1891."Our America." *La Revista Ilustrada*, January 1. http://writing.upenn.edu/library/Marti_Jose_Our-America.html.

McCoy, Jennifer. 2015. "Jimmy Carter Paved the Way for U.S. and Cuba Relations." *Time*, August 15. http://time.com/3998306/us-embassy-cuba-jimmy-carter/.

Neumann, Iver. 1996. "Self and Other in International Relations." *European Journal of International Relations.* 2.2: 139–74.

Nye, Joseph. 2004. *Soft Power: The Means to Success in World Politics.* New York: Public Affairs.

Wendt, Alexander. 1999. *Social Theory of International Politics.* Cambridge: Cambridge University.

Womack, Brantly. 2006. *China and Vietnam: The Politics of Asymmetry.* New York: Cambridge University.

Chapter 4

A *Südpolitik* from Washington: How Much of Europe's *Ostpolitik* Is There in the Current US-Cuban Détente?

Bert Hoffmann

Among the few German words that have made it into the English vocabulary, after *kindergarten* and *zeitgeist*, there is *Ostpolitik*: the policy of outreach to Eastern Europe spearheaded by German chancellor Willy Brandt that began in the 1960s in an effort to overcome the Cold War confrontation.[1] However, *Ostpolitik* did not just seek peace and stability, it sought—as its leitmotif postulated—political "change through rapprochement" (Bahr 1963). As the December 17 announcement to restore US-Cuban diplomatic relations heralds "the beginning of the end" of the Cold War in the Caribbean, Obama's policy shift looks like a "*Südpolitik*" *made in Washington*: a "southern policy" of détente and engagement with a communist regime long decried as the perennial foe. How far can this comparison be taken? What lessons, if any, are held by the European experience that could apply to the current course of US-Cuban relations?

Of course, the world has changed since the heyday of Brandt. Today, there is no Soviet Union; back then, there was no Internet, etcetera. *Ostpolitik* engaged with a solidly entrenched, if not petrified, state-socialist bureaucratic regime. In contrast, contemporary Cuban socialism has long since lost its past certainties. Cuban society is in flux, even if reforms are gradual, protracted, and may be driven as much from below as they are directed from above. While Cuba has staged a remarkably smooth succession after Fidel Castro's long tenure (Hoffmann 2009), Raúl Castro will be the island's last head of state from the Revolution's historical generation. Broad generational leadership change is looming large. Moreover, in the United States, foreign policy toward Cuba not only involves Washington and the US citizenry at large but also, in particular, the two-million-strong Cuban American community, which resulted from the migratory processes kicked off by the 1959 revolution. It is this specific sector of US society that has been associated with intense lobbying for an uncompromising stance against the Castro government, but at the same time it has maintained or redeveloped manifold material and nonmaterial ties to the island.[2] In such a context, a US policy of engagement will be felt much more immediately than was the German *Ostpolitik*, with its long-term political horizon.

However, at the core of both policies is depolarization. A timeless African proverb says: "When elephants battle, the grass suffers." To translate into politics, the more a conflict is polarized between two powerful actors, the more it sidelines and paralyzes those in between. When both sides stand in their trenches with guns loaded, those in between keep their heads down. In this sense, the baseline approach of *Ostpolitik* was to depolarize the confrontation, and this is also what Obama's *Südpolitik* seeks to do. Downscaling the military logic of confrontation is also about opening spaces for other actors beyond those in the trenches. When the elephants withdraw, the grass can recover.

In the German case, East Germany styled itself as the anti-fascist Germany while decrying the West's continuity of Nazi elites and revanchist forces.[3] Fascist continuity versus consequent anti-fascism was a very powerful—and a very polarizing—frame of legitimation. It took the *Ostpolitik* to undo it. In brief, in 1966, the West Germans elected a chancellor who unquestionably came from the anti-fascist side of Germany's recent history. In fact, "Willy Brandt" only adopted this name as a *nom de guerre* after he went into exile, fleeing the Hitler regime. Conservative forces found it outrageous that he would keep this name throughout his post-1945 engagement in German politics (Clemens 1989).

Brandt's *Ostpolitik* followed a multi-pronged strategy. In an unprecedented gesture of repentance at the time, he knelt down at the memorial for the Warsaw ghetto victims on a state visit to Poland.

During international negotiations and political treaties, he prioritized recognition: recognition of post-1945 borders (in particular, the acceptance that the formerly German lands to the East of the Oder-Neisse Rivers had become part of Poland) and also recognition of socialist governments, including the East German one, as legitimate interlocutors.

Looking back at Brandt's *Ostpolitik* may help put things into perspective when we refer to the current US-Cuban détente as historic and compare it to Cold War era détente policies. Obama's key policy approach is the same as that of *Ostpolitik*: recognition. The Obama-Raúl handshake at Nelson Mandela's funeral already symbolically conveyed this message of recognition, and the December 17 declaration to restore diplomatic relations sealed the deal, institutionally speaking.

Recognition can be misread as support. According to hard-line Republicans in Congress, Obama has betrayed democracy and extended a lifeline to a moribund dictatorship, "giving away unilateral concessions in exchange for nothing."[4] However, such a perspective overlooks that recognition is a mutual affair. Moreover, the more profound, long-term challenges of normalizing relations are to the Cuban system. Openings to flows of trade, people, and information are not easy to digest for a political system like Cuba's, which had been built on anti-imperialist armed struggle, a state-controlled economy, a state monopoly on mass media, an emphatic notion of national sovereignty, and the militarized political logic of a besieged fortress.

Cuban leaders have legitimized Cuba's single-party system not so much on the writings of Marx and Lenin, but rather as a defense mechanism for a revolutionary regime that required "national unity" and "closed ranks" in the face of US aggression (of which there certainly was plenty). Raúl Castro, who alternates military fatigues and civilian suits according to the occasion, made sure to wear his general's uniform when he read his December 17 announcement to restore diplomatic relations with the United States—thus emphasizing the continued centrality of, in the last instance, military confrontation.

To be sure, the core embargo legislation is still in place. The United States still has overwhelming military capacity and still operates a naval base on Cuban territory. The Helms-Burton Act, which backs the right of emigrated Cubans to reclaim confiscated property under US law, has yet to be lifted, keeping a Damocles sword over the houses currently owned by thousands of Cubans.

Nevertheless, following Obama's policy shift, the United States will start sending tourists, not troops. Instead of conducting military training in the Florida swamps, Cuban emigrants are eager to buy into Havana's freshly opened real estate market through middlemen on the island. Instead of isolating the Cuban market, Amazon, Apple, and company want to ship as many of their goodies as possible to the island, making it just as addicted to their products as is the rest of the world. The more that big, bad Goliath puts away his stick and takes out his wallet, the more Raúl's display of his military uniform looks out of sync with Cuba's actual challenges.

This also marks a key difference between Germany's *Ostpolitik* and Obama's *Südpolitik*. In Willy Brandt's case, the government went boldly ahead of society. Only after he signed the 1970 Treaties of Moscow and Warsaw, and in particular the 1972 Basic Treaty with East Germany, did West and East Germans begin to slowly restore the ties so dramatically cut off by the Wall's construction a decade earlier. In the US-Cuban case, political leaders are trailing behind a process that society on both sides of the Florida straits has been advancing forcefully over the past years. The symbolic announcement of December 17, however, has spurred an avalanche of visits to the island by US politicians, from Congressmen to Governors and State Department officials, and the embassies' opening in July 2015 will further facilitate institutional contacts.

While hardline anti-Castro rhetoric may dominate Miami's air waves, Cuban emigrants have actually been a driving force for the United States to normalize relations. Half a million Cuban Americans visit the island each year; according to estimates, in 2014, as much as US$3 billion went to the island in family remittances. On the Cuban side, insistent pressure from below has arguably led the government to adopt the 2013 migration reform (Consejo de Estado 2013), which allows hundreds of thousands of Cubans to travel to the United States and elsewhere with unprecedented ease (a key restriction being the receipt of an entry visa to the countries of destiny). As a result, on the eve of December 17, the much-cited "people-to-people contacts" were already a social reality, not a goal to achieve through government action.

Washington's turn to a policy of engagement, however, did pave the way for a similar evolution of increased societal links between Cuba and the United States beyond those previously forged by Cuban Americans. The easing of travel restrictions has brought the biggest change for US citizens and residents of non-Cuban origin. Cuba has become a "cool" travel destination. Celebrities, business people, media outlets, and artists have begun flocking to Havana.

Washington's turn to détente thus doesn't invent "people-to-people" contacts, but rather expands them to the US citizenry at large rather than reserving them for Cubans and Cuban Americans only. It should be assumed that, in political terms, this will foster a process of depolarization. For non-Cuban US Americans, passions about Cuba do not run as high as for those with Cuban biographies.

In Cold War times, Western visitors may have smuggled some books or magazines, but their circulation and impact were minimal. Today, informational borders have become highly porous, from cell phones and Internet to USB sticks and *el paquete*, a weekly updated package of digital content (from movies to a Cuban-style Craig's List) that has become widely popular on the island (Hoffmann 2012; Iglesias et al. 2012; Press 2015).

Today Cuban society is more heterogeneous, more mobile, and has more means of communication at its disposal than ever before. Domestically, under Raúl Castro the Cuban government has, albeit reluctantly, accepted society's demands for more diverse media—although it continues to draw a red line where this is seen as "going too far." The key justification for curtailing domestic voices remains external confrontation. But now that the elephants do not appear to be battling as fiercely as they did before December 17, it is likely that demands will increase for what could be a détente toward domestic plurality.

Much of this quest for more voice, respect, and autonomy, which comes from individual citizens as well as from groups or institutions, takes place behind closed doors, but at times some episodes become visible to the public eye. An example is a March 2015 statement by the University of Havana's Scientific Board, which not only strongly pushed for broader Internet access both for academics and for the citizenry at large but also argued that transparency and participation in the debate around these issues should be improved (Consejo Científico de la Universidad de La Habana 2015).

Although change in official media is slow, some outlets have shown signs of a new openness in their online formats. For instance, *Trabajadores* (Workers), the official newspaper of Cuba's trade unions, held an interactive forum on civil society in Cuba, revitalizing a concept that, in the 1990s, had been decried as a Trojan horse of imperialism aimed at subverting the revolution ("Foro interactivo sobre sociedad civil en Cuba" 2015; for the discussion in the 1990s, see Hoffmann 2003). An even more prominent example was an online forum of the Communist Youth newspaper *Juventud Rebelde*, which invited people to discuss the announced reform of electoral law ("¿Qué desea saber sobre el sistema electoral cubano?" 2015). The audience's response was anything but complacent, from a plea to elect the president directly to demands for a clear separation of the executive and legislative branches, and from statements that "nobody wants to go on voting like this" to frank calls for a multi-party system. It may be safe to assume that such demands surpass what authorities will want to implement. Nonetheless, not long ago it would have been unthinkable that *Juventud Rebelde*'s website would even publish such questions without accusing the questioners of being US mercenaries or the like. The genie for voicing these opinions is out of the bottle, it seems, and will not be put back in easily.

Finally, Obama's *Südpolitik* also has important economic implications. The "economics of détente"—as we may call them—are very different from those of the historic *Ostpolitik* experience. In Cold War Europe, people-to-people flows of goods and money were limited. Trade relations with the West as well as the credits extended to socialist countries were made within the central state, which used them in accordance with its priorities. In Cuba, by contrast, people-to-people flows are massive, as much through remittances as through the booming petty trade by travelers. Note that in 2014, despite the ongoing diplomatic freeze between both countries, no less than 350,000 Cuban Americans and another 100,000 non-Cuban US citizens visited the island (Frank 2015).

While the state, through markups on retail prices, tariffs, and other means, taps into the emigrants' remittances and informal credits, these flows are essentially private and linked to family ties. Consequently, they favor those strata of Cuban society from which the emigrants came, that is, phenotypically "white" Cubans rather than those of African descent, urban rather than rural, and pre-1959 middle and upper classes rather than the pre-1959 poor (cf. Blue 2007; De la Fuente 2011; Eckstein 2010; Espina and Rodríguez 2010). The massive increase of petty trade through travel similarly benefits those sectors of society best connected to residents abroad. Moreover, in 2007, Spain passed the "Historical Memory Law," which offers Spanish citizenship to any person who can claim proof of a Spanish parent or grandparent. Since then, approximately 200,000 Cubans have claimed a Spanish passport (Golías Pérez 2014, p. 16), which gives them access to travel possibilities far beyond those of other Cuban co-nationals and to petty commerce associated with travel. Not unexpectedly, most of the individual beneficiaries are phenotypically white.

True, these trends started before the December 17 announcements. Ever since Fidel Castro legalized the US dollar on the island in 1993, having family abroad or not became a key dividing line in Cuban society. Although Cuban Americans have sent amounts of money to their families that far exceed the narrow limits officially imposed by the US government, Obama's 2009 decision to lift the limits on remittances has greatly eased and expanded these flows. Moreover, having access to remittances has taken on new significance due to the internal dynamics of Cuba's economic reform. In the past, remittances from abroad essentially raised a family or individual's consumption levels, but today they can be used to invest in business and housing, leading to a much more profound restratification of society.

Obama's *Südpolitik* will only add to these increasing social inequalities on the island because its economic impact—ranging from increased US travel to Internet services or credit card access—will disproportionately favor precisely those Cubans who are already linked to the hard-currency sector of tourism and migrant remittances. While increased ties, trade, and travel with the United States will help Cuba's economy to reach its 4 percent growth target for 2015,[5] it will also accelerate the underlying process of increasing inequality in Cuban society that accompanies this growth pattern.

In addition, the Cuban state has proposed key investment projects, clearly eyeing the US market in a post-embargo future. Normalization of trade and travel with the United States is indispensable for the economic viability of the ambitious new deep-water container port and free zone of Mariel, as well as for the large marina projected in Varadero (cf. Monreal 2013). Both are located along the northwestern coast, where Cuba is closest to the United States. Given that the foreseeable tourism and real estate surge will also be concentrated in Havana, Cuba's economics of détente will massively shift the island's economic dynamism to the capital and surrounding areas, aggravating the already large development gap with the poorer Eastern provinces.

In the East German case, nothing comparable took place prior to 1989. The German Democratic Republic (GDR) became increasingly dependent on Western credits in the 1980s, but it did not integrate wholesale into a capitalist global economy; it remained anchored in the Comecon's system of a division of labor between the centrally planned economies of the socialist bloc. East Berlin did not establish any export-oriented "Special Economic Zones" as China later did, nor did Western trade and credit deals have any major impact on the East German economy's geographical patterns. The zones that most closely bordered West Germany remained peripheral areas and did not benefit from their location.

In Cuba, the growing economic inequalities and increasing social stratification are, of course, massive challenges for the revolutionary project whose quintessential legitimation had been precisely to overcome social cleavages based on skin color, social pedigree, geographic location, and metropolitan proximity—the markers of pre-1959 Cuba. However, the Cuban elites themselves are part of this restratification of society. Most of Cuba's top party cadres, managers, and army generals have relatives in Miami. As demonstrated by considerable anecdotal evidence, their sons and daughters don't fancy becoming school teachers in Bayamo—not a few of them find it attractive to open posh restaurants in Havana or to enter the import-export business. Alumni of elite Cuban schools like the "Escuela Vocacional Lenin" hold positions of influence both in Havana and Miami, and they easily reconnect to a potentially powerful transnational network.[6]

There is no parallel to these trends in the European *Ostpolitik* experience. In Cold War Europe, the easing of travel and communications in the 1970s did not lead to the emergence of major trans-border networks that would mark the transformation of economy and society under socialist rule. The impact of family or professional ties remained low until after the regime change. In Cuba, in contrast, a societal détente has preceded that between the governments. Barack Obama and Raúl Castro made history with their December 17 announcements to restore diplomatic relations. But all Cubans who in the 1990s began to mend family ties severed in the times of revolutionary fervor, all US citizens who have claimed their right to travel, all Cubans who through words or deeds pressured for travel liberalization, and all émigrés sending remittances to their families on the island have been at the heart of the US-Cuban "grass roots détente" that the government détente belatedly followed.

One of the biggest questions raised by Obama's shift in Cuba's policy is how well this process will endure beyond the end of his mandate in January 2017. Most of the Republican presidential hopefuls have strongly opposed his policy of engagement, and some have vowed to block or undo it however they can. There is good reason to doubt whether, once elected, even the most radical of these voices would live up to their rhetoric. The German experience, however, does not offer unambiguous suggestions for the Cuban case. In fact, mainstream conservative forces who had initially opposed Brandt's policy turn later became "reluctant realists" (Clemens 1989) and eventually accepted and continued the key tenets of the *Ostpolitik* when they came to power in 1982. But such acquiescence occurred 13 years after Brandt was elected chancellor and an entire decade after the signing of the Basic Treaty between the two German states. It took them time. However, the Cuba-US confrontation is different. It is not that of a divided nation. For the United States in the post-Cold War context, Cuba is one foreign policy issue among many. The Cuban American community is a resourceful lobby, but still a small minority within the US population. Strong US business interests have begun eyeing the Cuban market and will not take kindly to upholding a status quo of watered-down opportunities. Hard-line Republicans, it seems, will have to learn how to live with Washington's *Südpolitik* faster than Germany's conservatives had to live with *Ostpolitik*.

Notes

1. For an overview, see Fink and Schaefer (2009), Griffith (1978), and Krell (1991).
2. Mujal-León and Langenbacher (2009, p. 8) have spoken of a "Cuba South" and a "Cuba North," echoing the language of a divided nation. However, despite the size and strong homeland bonds of the Cuban emigré community, the implicit analogy to East and West Germany or North and South Korea is overstating the point. The Cuban case is one of diaspora politics, not of a state divided into two. Miami may be the unquestionable center of the Cuban American community, but it is not the capital—as the authors suggest—and it commands no state-like bureaucracy or foreign policy executive unless it influences Washington.
3. A vivid illustration is the GDR's official wording for the Berlin Wall, calling it the *antifaschistischer Schutzwall* ("anti-fascist protection rampart").
4. For example, Marco Rubio and his reaction to Obama's December 17 announcement, cited in "Politico." http://www.politico.com/story/2014/12/marco-rubio-says-cuba-talks-are-absurd-113639.html.
5. For the first half of 2015, Cuban economy minister Marino Murillo reported a 4.7 percent year-on-year growth rate (Frank 2015).
6. See, for instance, the website lalenin.com or the corresponding Facebook page of the alumni of "La Lenin" (https://www.facebook.com/pages/wwwlalenincom/94127457401?fref=tS).

References

Bahr, Egon. 1963. "Wandel durch Annäherung [Change through Rapprochement]." Speech given in the Evangelische Akademie Tutzing,

Germany, July 15. https://www.fes.de/archiv/adsd_neu/inhalt/ stichwort/tutzinger_rede.pdf. Abbreviated English translation available at http://germanhistorydocs.ghi-dc.org/sub_document.cfm?docu ment_id=81.

Blue, Sarah. 2007. "The Erosion of Racial Equality in the Context of Cuba's Dual Economy." *Latin American Politics and Society* 49.3: 35–68.

Clemens, Clay. 1989. *Reluctant Realists: The Christian Democrats and West German* Ostpolitik. Durham: Duke University.

Consejo Científico de la Universidad de La Habana. 2015. "Resumen de la relatoría acerca de la reunión conjunta del Consejo Científico de la Universidad de La Habana con la sección de ciencias naturales y exactas de la Academia de Ciencias de Cuba y otros invitados celebrada en la Universidad de La Habana el 26 de febrero de 2015." Report presented at the Universidad de La Habana, Cuba, March 31. http://oncubamagazine. com/wmag/wp-content/uploads/2015/04/RELATOR%C3%8DA-con-Resumen-version-5.2-final.pdf.

Consejo de Estado. 2013. "Decreto-Ley No. 302." *Cuba Legal Info.* http:// cubalegalinfo.com/decreto-ley-no-302-modificativo-de-la-ley-no-1312-%E2%80%9Cley-de-migraci%C3%B3n%E2%80%9D.

De la Fuente, Alejandro. 2011. "Race and Income Inequality in Contemporary Cuba." *NACLA Report on the Americas* 44.3: 30–33, 43.

Eckstein, Susan. 2010. "Immigration, Remittances, and Transnational Social Capital Formation: A Cuban Case Study." *Ethnic and Racial Studies* 33.9: 1648–67.

Espina, Rodrigo, and Pablo Rodríguez. 2010. "Race and Inequality in Cuba Today." *Socialism and Democracy* 24.1: 161–77.

Fink, Carol, and Bernd Schaefer. 2009. *Ostpolitik, 1969–1974, European and Global Responses.* Cambridge: Cambridge University.

"Foro interactivo sobre Sociedad Civil en Cuba." 2015. *Trabajadores*, March 8. http://www.trabajadores.cu/20150308/trabajadores-invita-al-foro-interactivo-sobre-la-sociedad-civil/.

Frank, Marc. 2015. "Cuba Economic Growth Rises to 4.7% in First Half–Minister." *Reuters*, July 15. http://www.reuters.com/article/2015/07/15/cuba-economy-idUSL2N0ZV1PR20150715.

Golías Pérez, Montserrat. 2014. "*Los nuevos españoles a través de la Ley de la Memoria Histórica en Cuba y Argentina ¿Oportunidad o identidad?* [The New Spaniards from the Historical Memory Law in Cuba and Argentina: Opportunity or Identity?]" PhD diss, Universidade de Coruña, Spain. http://ruc.udc.es/bitstream/2183/11914/2/GoliasPerez_Montserrat_TD_2014.pdf.

Griffith, William. 1978. *Ostpolitik of the Federal Republic of Germany.* Cambridge, Mass.: MIT.

Hoffmann, Bert. 2003. "Cuba: Civil Society Within Socialism—and its Limits." In *Modern Political Culture in the Caribbean*, edited by Holger

Henke and Fred Réno, 302–21. St. Augustine, Trinidad and Tobago: University of the West Indies.

———. 2009. "Charismatic Authority and Leadership Change: Lessons from Cuba's Post-Fidel Succession." In *International Political Science Review* 30.3, 229–48.

———. 2012. "Civil Society in the Digital Age: How the Internet Changes State-Society Relations in Authoritarian Regimes. The Case of Cuba." In *Civil Society Activism under Authoritarian Rule. A Comparative Perspective*, edited by Francesco Cavatorta, 219–44. London: Routledge.

Iglesias, Benigno, Cecilia Linares, Mario Masvidal, Irina Pacheco, and Rafael Hernández. 2012. "USB: el consumo audiovisual informal." *Temas* 70: 81–91. http://www.temascuba.org/sites/default/files/archivotemas/Temas70.pdf.

Krell, Gert. 1991. "West German Ostpolitik and the German Question." *Journal of Peace Research* 28.3: 311–23.

Monreal, Pedro. 2013. "La era Postpanamax: ¿una oportunidad para Cuba?" *Espacio Laical* (digital supplement) 232. http://espaciolaical.org/contens/esp/sd_232.pdf.

Mujal-León, Eusebio, and Eric Langenbacher. 2009. *Regime Chance and Democratization in Cuba: Comparative Perspective.* Paper presented at the Annual Meeting of the American Political Science Association, Toronto, Canada, September 3–5.

Press, Larry. 2015. "El Paquete and Mi Mochila—sneakernet competitors." *The Internet in Cuba Blog*, March 27. http://laredcubana.blogspot.de/2015/03/el-paquete-and-mi-mochila-sneakernet.html.

"¿Qué desea saber sobre el sistema electoral cubano?" 2015. *Juventud Rebelde*, February 28. www.juventudrebelde.cu/cuba/2015-02-28/que-desea-saber-sobre-el-sistema-electoral-cubano.

Chapter 5

The End of the Bogeyman: The Political Repercussions of the US-Cuban Rapprochement

William M. LeoGrande

The December 17, 2014 announcements that Cuba and the United States had agreed to begin normalizing their bilateral relationship significantly reduced the threat that Washington posed to Cuban national security—a threat that has been acute for the past half century. From 1959 to 2014, except for brief interludes in the mid 1970s, the objective of US policy was to force regime change through diplomatic isolation, economic pressure, and covert subversion. Obama's opening to Cuba is historic precisely because he abandoned coercive diplomacy, replacing it with a strategy of engagement and coexistence. "I do not believe we can keep doing the same thing for over five decades and expect a different result," the president said, explaining his decision to give up on regime change. "Moreover, it does not serve America's interests, or the Cuban people, to try to push Cuba toward collapse. Even if that worked—and it hasn't for 50 years—we know from hard-earned experience that countries are more likely to enjoy lasting transformation if their people are not subjected to chaos" (Obama 2014).

In the months following "17D," as the Cubans call the historic date, Washington took Cuba off the State Department's list of state sponsors of international terrorism, the United States and Cuba resumed full diplomatic relations, and teams of diplomats began working through the nettlesome issues that still divide the two countries. Although some instrumentalities of the old policy remained in place—the economic embargo being the most significant—the new direction of US policy was clear.

Scholars of politics have investigated two effects that a serious external threat has on states: the "rally 'round the flag" effect, in which the threat engenders national solidarity and boosts popular support for the government[1], and the state of siege effect, in which the government responds by repressing domestic opponents, especially those who can be plausibly tied to the foreign enemy (Enterline and Gleditsch 2000; O'Neil 2015; Whitaker 1984). Of course, governments can manipulate these effects. The "diversionary use of force" (Fordham 2005; Miller 1995; Richards 1993) is a well-known strategy for provoking, exaggerating, or even inventing external conflicts to boost flagging domestic support—for example, Argentina's 1982 seizure of the Falkland Islands (Levy and Vakili 1992)—or to rationalize domestic repression—for example, North Korea since the 1953 armistice (Chen and Lee 2007).

But what happens when a long-standing foreign threat that has produced both these effects suddenly disappears? That is the situation Cuba faced after December 17, 2014. Although the normalization of relations with the United States is still at an early stage, the jubilant reaction of the Cuban population to the December 17 announcements clearly indicates that they interpret the new opening as having ended the cold war in the Caribbean. Without the US threat, will national unity be harder to maintain? Will the Cuban public be less willing to accept constraints on political liberties in the name of national security?

Havana's Motives

For Cuba, the principal motivation for normalizing relations with Washington is economic. In 2011, Raúl Castro launched a campaign to "update" the Cuban economy, replacing the Soviet model of central planning followed since the 1970s with a Chinese model of market socialism (Domínguez et al. 2012). For Cuba, this means greater openness to global markets, and the United States is a natural partner for tourism, trade, and investment.

Tourism has become a central pillar of the Cuban economy in the past two decades; this year, the island will host more than three million foreign visitors. But apart from Cuban Americans visiting family, only approximately 4 percent of those visitors will come from the United States because of the ban on tourism (AP 2015b). If the ban were lifted, the International Monetary Fund estimates that as many as three million US tourists might travel to Cuba annually (Romeu 2008, p. 18).

Cuba, partnering with Brazil, has made a billion dollar investment in the new port of Mariel and the Special Economic Development Zone surrounding it in anticipation of normal trade relations with the United States. Mariel can accommodate the large container ships that will transit the new Panamax canal, and the port is a logical transit point for goods headed for the US Atlantic coast and Europe (LeoGrande 2014).

Cuba's Vice President and Minister of Economy and Planning Marino Murillo said last year that Cuba needed to attract $2.5 billion in foreign direct investment annually to attain the rate of economic growth the government envisions (AP 2014). As the largest source of foreign direct investment in the Caribbean, the United States could make a major contribution toward that goal if the embargo were lifted. Before 1959, the United States had more invested in Cuba than anywhere else in the region. Moreover, prominent Cuban American businesspeople, including the sugar baron Fanjul brothers and the Bacardi family, have expressed an interest in getting back into Cuba (Cave 2014). Already, Cuban Americans are sending nearly $3 billion in remittances every year, some of which is serving as the seed capital for Cuba's burgeoning small business sector (Kandell 2015).

Yet the normalization of relations with Washington is a Janus-faced development for Havana. The promise of economic reward comes with heightened political risk. For half a century, nationalist resistance to US hostility has been an important pillar of regime support. As scholar Marifeli Pérez-Stable (2011) has argued, by fusing defense of *la patria* (the homeland) with defense of the revolution, Cuba's leaders have been able to define patriotism as support for the regime in its confrontation with the imperialist north.

Rallying 'round the Flag

One of Fidel Castro's great gifts as a politician was his ability to grasp the core values of Cuban political culture and, through his oratory, reflect them back to the public in ways that resonated deeply. Perhaps the most important of these values was nationalism. Having won independence three-quarters of a century after the rest of Latin America only to have its sovereignty hamstrung by the US-imposed Platt Amendment, Cuba's nationalist sentiment has been especially strong.

Castro appealed to that sentiment during the insurrection against Fulgencio Batista, but even more so after the triumph of the revolution as his new government confronted the United States. Fidel understood very well the political value of mobilizing Cuban nationalism behind his radical program. After one speech featuring especially harsh anti-American rhetoric, Castro encountered the Chargé d'Affaires of the US embassy, Daniel M. Braddock, and said he hoped Washington "had received no hurt [from his speech] as he had intended none," but that it was "necessary in a public rally of that sort to express certain points of view" (Braddock 1959). Predictably, US officials did take offense, whether Castro intended it or not.

Speaking two years later, Castro extolled the virtue of confrontation. "The Revolution has to fight; combat is what makes revolutions strong," he said in early 1961. "A revolution that does not confront an enemy runs the risk of falling asleep, of growing weak . . . Like armies hardening themselves, revolutions need to confront an enemy!" (Castro 1961).

As US-Cuban relations deteriorated in 1959–1960, Washington obligingly provided that enemy. Some Eisenhower administration officials warned that open conflict would enhance Castro's political support. "We cannot expect patriotic and self-respecting Cubans, no matter how distasteful Castro's policies may be to them, to side with the United States," State Department official John Calvin Hill (1960) argued, "if we go so far along the lines of reprisals that the quarrel no longer is between Castro and the real interests of the Cuban people but a quarrel between the United States and their country" (830–32).

In August 1961, during the founding meeting of the Alliance for Progress in Punta del Este, Uruguay, Che Guevara arranged a private meeting with Richard Goodwin, a White House aide to President John F. Kennedy. Che wanted to explore the possibility of a modus vivendi between Cuba and the United States in the aftermath of the Bay of Pigs. But he began by thanking Goodwin for the invasion. "Their hold on the country had been a bit shaky," Goodwin wrote to Kennedy in his trip report, "but the invasion allowed the leadership to consolidate most of the major elements of the country around Fidel" (LeoGrande and Kornbluh 2014, p. 45). The Bay of Pigs enabled Castro to wrap the revolution's socialist agenda in the flag of Cuban nationalism. It was no coincidence that Castro made the first public declaration of the revolution's socialist character during the invasion.

Through the years, Castro proved adept at using confrontations with Washington to mobilize support. In 1964, he made a cause célèbre of Cuban fisherman detained by the US Coast Guard for fishing in US waters. In 2000, he used the campaign to return six-year-old Elián González to reinvigorate flagging revolutionary enthusiasm. For nearly a decade, demands for the release of the "Five Heroes" (the five Cuban spies imprisoned in the United States beginning in 1998) boosted national solidarity. And for half a century, Cuba's leaders have been able to blame the nation's economic problems on the US embargo, although Raúl Castro has resorted to that excuse much less often than his older brother did.

What will happen now that the US threat is diminishing? "*En la calle*" (on-the-street) expectations are running high that rapprochement means the embargo will end, the economy will grow, and daily life will get better. In reality, the new turn in US-Cuban relations is unlikely to have a major economic impact for ordinary Cubans any time soon, so the government has been working to dampen expectations. A long interview with Cuban diplomat Josefina Vidal in *Granma* emphasized that the embargo is still in place (Escobar 2015). But it will be tough to get the genie of heightened popular expectations back in the bottle. If Raúl Castro's "updating" of the Cuban economy does not soon begin to raise the standard of living for ordinary people, then they will be even more apt to blame their government rather than the United States. Or, as US diplomat Roberta Jacobson (2015) put it in testimony defending the new policy to Congress, "The bogeyman of the US being their problem—it's no longer credible."

A recent Bendixen and Amandi International poll (2015) conducted in Cuba after December 17 reveals significant latent discontent and pent up desire for change. Majorities of 79 percent and 53 percent expressed dissatisfaction with the economic and political systems, respectively. When asked what they would like to see the government do to improve things in the next five years, 54 percent wanted better economic conditions and 29 percent wanted political reforms. The Catholic Church had a significantly higher favorable rating than the Communist Party (70 percent positive to 32 percent), and so did opposition groups (46 percent to 32 percent).

The poll showed little evidence that Cubans regard the United States with fear or hostility. When asked whether the United States was "a friend of Cuba," 53 percent said it was and only 10 percent said it was not. Fully 97 percent regarded the normalization of US-Cuban relations as "good for Cuba," and Barack Obama had higher favorability ratings than either Fidel or Raúl Castro (80 percent positive to 44 percent and 47 percent, respectively). A majority (55 percent) said they would like to live in another country, and more than half of those picked the United States. Clearly, ordinary Cubans no longer see the United States as the threatening Colossus of the North that it once was.

State of Siege

States facing existential threats from abroad are notorious for repressing dissent at home in the name of national security, and many constitutions provide for the suspension of basic liberties during national emergencies. In Cuba, the very real threat of attack by the United States in the early years of the revolutionary government, combined with Fidel Castro's intolerance of opposition, produced an authoritarian single-party system justified both by Cuban tradition and by the immediacy of the US threat.

Castro's insistence on national unity was rooted in Cuban political culture. The first war of independence was lost in 1878, when one wing of the insurgent army signed a separate peace with Spain. General Antonio Maceo, the revolutionary commander who refused to accept peace without independence, became a national hero with his "Protest of Baraguá," the anniversary of which is celebrated to this day. The lesson of the need for unity was not lost on José Martí, the father of Cuban independence, who insisted on forging one single revolutionary party in 1895.

At its Fifth Congress in 1997, the Cuban Communist Party (PCC) published a justification for its monopoly on power not by invoking Marx or Lenin, but by invoking Martí. "The great lesson has emerged out of our own historical experience: without unity, revolutionaries and the people can achieve nothing in their struggle," the document declared, and unity required, as in the time of Martí, a single party to prevent the United States from reimposing neocolonial capitalism on Cuba.

Since the earliest years of the revolution, domestic opponents have been branded as agents of the United States and thus as enemies of the revolution. "All criticism is opposition," Castro wrote to compatriot Carlos Franqui. "All opposition is counterrevolutionary" (Bardach 2003, p. 280). Too often, Washington has given the Cuban government a ready-made justification for its intolerance by actively recruiting and supporting domestic opponents as part of its regime-change strategy. The CIA began supporting the opposition in July 1959, providing it with funds, propaganda, and arms. The Bay of Pigs invasion gave the Cuban government an excuse to round up more than 100,000 suspected opponents, approximately 15,000 of whom were held in prison beyond the quick defeat of the invasion force (Nolan and Richmond 1978).

By the late 1960s, US support for Cuban dissidents had subsided for lack of potential recipients. But when the collapse of the Soviet Union produced economic crisis on the island, Washington saw a new opportunity to undermine the Cuban regime from within. To "support democracy in Cuba," the Cuban Democracy Act of 1992 authorized US assistance "for the support of individuals and organizations to promote nonviolent democratic change in Cuba" (CDA 1992, §6004[g]). Four years later, the Cuban Liberty and Democratic Solidarity Act of 1996 (aka Helms-Burton, after its sponsors) expanded the "democracy-building" mandate, authorizing the president to "furnish assistance and provide other support for individuals and independent nongovernmental organizations to support democracy-building efforts for Cuba," including direct financial support for political prisoners and their families, and for opposition organizations (§109). Following the recommendations of his Commission for Assistance to a Free Cuba, George W. Bush increased funding for the democracy promotion programs from an annual budget of $3.5 million in FY2000 to a peak of $45.7 million in FY2008.[2]

In response to these democracy promotion programs, Cuba passed two laws. The Law Reaffirming Cuban Dignity and Sovereignty (Ley de Reafirmación de la Dignidad y Soberanía Cubanas, Ley 80, 1996), which criminalized "any form of cooperation, whether direct or indirect, with the application of the Helms-Burton Act," including providing to the US government information relevant to the law, receiving resources from the US government to promote the law, or spreading information provided by the US government promoting the law (337–38, book's translation). In 1999, the Law for the Protection of Cuban National Independence and the Economy (Ley de Protección de la Independencia Nacional y la Economía de Cuba, Ley 88) made it illegal to disseminate subversive material from the United States, collaborate with foreign mass media for subversive purposes, hinder international economic relations, or receive material resources from the US government, directly or indirectly. In short, these laws criminalized a wide swath of common dissident activity and any involvement with USAID's democracy promotion program (Oppenheimer 1999). In 2003, when the government imprisoned

75 dissidents, they were charged not with dissent per se, but with acting in concert with the United States in violation of these laws. What will happen now that Washington has replaced the policy of regime change with one of coexistence and engagement? To be sure, the US "democracy promotion" programs aimed at stimulating opposition in Cuba have not disappeared and will likely continue for some time. And Obama's policy of engagement explicitly aims to "empower the Cuban people" to demand political change (Obama 2014). But Obama's initiatives are no longer part of a coercive policy of hostility that Cuban leaders can point to as justification for suppressing opposition. Will the reduction of the external threat lead to greater political openness on the island? The dissidents who have endorsed Obama's policy hope and expect that it will, as do many nondissident intellectuals. But after fifty years of top-down politics, it may be a hard transition for Cuba's leaders to make. "It's difficult enough to prepare for a war," said former Cuban diplomat Carlos Alzugaray, "How can you prepare for a declaration of peace? The idea of a siege mentality is embedded here" (DeYoung 2015).

In the mid 1990s, as President Clinton promoted people-to-people programs, Cuban leaders saw the developing linkages between Cuban and US civil society as a threat—heightened, no doubt, by Clinton's explicit rationale that such programs were aimed at undermining Cuban state control. "We believe that reaching out today will nurture and strengthen the fledgling civil society that will be the backbone of tomorrow's democratic Cuba," Clinton (1995) explained.

In a 1996 report to the Central Committee of the Cuban Communist Party, Raúl Castro denounced Cuban intellectuals for having developed dangerously close ties with US groups and foundations. Cuba's economic crisis had created "feelings of depression and political confusion," he acknowledged. He went on to describe people-to-people program efforts to create an independent civil society as internal subversion. "The enemy does not conceal its intention to use some of the so-called nongovernmental organizations (NGOs) established in Cuba in recent times, as a Trojan horse to foment division and subversion here." He extended his critique to every institution of intellectual pursuit. "Within the universities, in film, radio, television and culture in general, both types of behavior exist: behavior which is faithful to our revolutionary people; and the minority with an annexationist orientation, far removed from the patriotic conduct of the majority of our intellectuals." The party would need to "examine" all these institutions, he concluded, to thwart US schemes to turn them into "fifth columnists"

(Castro 1996). In the following months, political commissars conducted inquiries at institutions across the country, including the Party Central Committee's own think tanks, to assure ideological conformity.

But despite the state's best efforts to limit civil society to "socialist civil society"—the mass organizations sponsored and directed by the state and party—the economic and social changes underway that began with the Special Period and have accelerated with the "updating" of the economy are creating new, independent social formations that, even if they are nonpolitical, are social networks with political *potential*. Despite the concerns Raúl Castro expressed in 1996, the state has had little alternative but to tolerate these changes.

In one of his first speeches as acting president, speaking to the Congress of the Federation of University Students in December 2006, Castro even argued for more open, democratic debate. "Argue, analyze, disagree," he urged them, "because the more you argue, the more you disagree . . . out of these disagreements will always come the best solutions" (Castro 2006). He made the same point four years later to the National Assembly. Disagreement was far better than "false unanimity based on pretense and opportunism," he said, adding that the right to disagree was "a right nobody should be deprived of" (Castro 2010).

Cuba's intelligentsia took full advantage of the new openness. Fidel had famously defined revolution as "changing everything that needs to be changed" (Castro 2000)—a phrase frequently invoked by Raúl and others to justify the sweeping changes implied in the Economic and Social Guidelines (PCC 2011). Writers, artists, academics, and an incipient community of bloggers launched a freewheeling debate about just exactly what needed to be changed.[3] Periodicals like *Temas, Palabra Nueva*, and *Espacio Laical*, along with dozens of blogs, provided the venues, sometimes even publishing the views of Cuban American exiles. Although the freewheeling debate made some government officials uncomfortable, First Vice President Miguel Díaz-Canel defended it, acknowledging that in the information age "prohibiting something is an almost impossible illusion. It doesn't make sense." The antidote to bad information, he argued, was "authentic discussion" about "what's good for the Cuban Revolution, and what's not" (Ravsberg 2013).

Yet even as the government has allowed greater space for criticism by what might be called a loyal opposition—those who accept the socialist character of Cuban society and its one-party state but are critical of how it operates—the leadership has remained intolerant of opponents who question the very nature of the system. That intolerance was on display at the civil society forum of the Seventh Summit of the Americas in Panama in April 2015. With assistance from Washington, a delegation of Cuban dissidents traveled to Panama and won accreditation from the host committee. Their appearance at the civil society forum led to bitter protests by the official Cuban delegation, a scuffle between the rival groups, and a walkout by the *oficialistas* (AP 2015a).

In 1961, Fidel Castro famously defined the limits of debate when he declared, "Within the revolution, everything; against the revolution, nothing" (Castro 2008, p. 220). For the past several years, Cuba's intelligentsia has been successfully pushing out the boundaries of debate on economic policy, politics, and culture.[4] As the US threat recedes, they are certain to push harder to expand the limits of what is "within the revolution." Without the bogeyman of the United States, Cuban leaders will have a much weaker rationale for resisting.

Notes

1. Mueller (1973) introduced the concept, focusing on US politics. Others have extended it internationally (Bueno de Mesquita et al. 1992; Bueno de Mesquita and Siverson 1995; Colaresi 2004; Lai and Reiter 2005; Miller 1995; Norpoth 1987; Sirin 2011).
2. The budget fell back to $20 million in FY2009 for lack of opportunities to spend the money (LeoGrande and Kornbluh 2014, p. 359).
3. See, for example, Frank's (2013, pp. 111–112) description of the 2008 Congress of Artists and Writers.
4. On culture, see chapter by Ana Serra in this volume.

References

"Cuban Liberty and Democratic Solidarity (Libertad) Act." 1996. United States Code, Title 22, §§ 6021-6091. http://www.treasury.gov/resource-center/sanctions/Documents/libertad.pdf.
"Cuban Democracy Act." 1992. United States Code, Title 22, §§ 6001-6010. http://www.treasury.gov/resource-center/sanctions/Documents/cda.pdf.
"Law for the Reaffirmation of Cuban Dignity and Sovereignty, Article 8." 1996. In *Cuban Revolution Reader: A Documentary History*, edited by Julio Garcia Luis, 334–40. Enacted 1996, and compiled for volume 2008. Melbourne, Australia: Ocean.
Associated Press (AP). 2014. "Cuba Moves to Attract More Foreign Investment." *New York Times*, March 29.

———. 2015a. "Cuban Dissidents Heckled at Americas Summit." *New York Times*, April 8.

———. 2015b. "US Travel to Cuba Surges 36% Following Thaw in Diplomatic Relations." *The Guardian*, May 26.

Bardach, Anne Louise. 2003. *Cuba Confidential: Love and Vengeance in Miami and Havana.* New York: Vintage.

Bendixen & Amandi International. 2015. *National Survey of Cubans Living in Cuba, April 2015.* Miami, FL.

Braddock, Daniel. 1959. "Telegram 869 from Havana, January 22, 1959." In *Foreign Relations of the United States, 1958–1960, Vol. VI, Cuba,* Doc. 238, compiled by US Department of State, Office of the Historian, 381. Written in 1959, and compiled in 1991. Washington, DC: Government Printing Office.

Bueno de Mesquita, Bruce, and Randolph M. Siverson. 1995. "War and the Survival of Political Leaders: A Comparative Study of Regime Types and Political Accountability." *American Political Science Review* 89.4: 841–55.

Bueno de Mesquita, Bruce, Randolph M. Siverson, and Gary Woller. 1992. "War and the Fate of Regimes: A Comparative Analysis." *American Political Science Review* 86.4: 638–46.

Castro, Fidel. 1961. "Discurso Pronunciado por el Comandante Fidel Castro Ruz, en el Acto de Inauguración de la Ciudad Escolar Abel Santamaría, en la Ciudad de Santa Clara, el 28 de Enero de 1961." In *Discursos e intervenciones del Comandante en Jefe Fidel Castro Ruz,* January 28. http://www.cuba.cu/gobierno/discursos/.

———. 2000. "Speech by Dr. Fidel Castro Ruz … [on] International Labor Day." In *Discursos e intervenciones del Comandante en Jefe Fidel Castro Ruz,* May 1. http://www.cuba.cu/gobierno/discursos/.

———. 2008. "Words to Intellectuals, June 30, 1961." In *Fidel Castro Reader,* edited by Fidel Castro, David Deutschmann, and Deborah Shnookal, 113–19. North Melbourne, Australia: Ocean.

Castro, Raúl. 1996. "The Political and Social Situation in Cuba and the Corresponding Tasks of the Party." *Granma International,* March 27.

———. 2006. "Fidel es insustituible, salvo que lo sustituyamos todos juntos." *Juventud Rebelde,* December 21.

———. 2010. "Speech delivered by Army General Raúl Castro Ruz, President of the Councils of State and of Ministers, during the closing ceremony of the Sixth Session of the Seventh Legislature of the National People's Power Assembly." In *Discursos e intervenciones del Presidente de los Consejos de Estado y de Ministros de la República de Cuba General de Ejército Raúl Castro Ruz,* December 18. http://www.cuba.cu/gobierno/rauldiscursos/index2.html.

Cave, Damien. 2014. "Some Who Fled Cuba Are Returning to Help." *New York Times,* March 4.

Chen, Cheng, and Ji-Yong Lee. 2007. "Making Sense of North Korea: National Stalinism in Comparative-Historical Perspective." *Communist and Post-Communist Studies* 40.4: 459–75.

Clinton, William J. 1995. "Remarks to the Cuban-American Community, June 27, 1995." In *Public Papers of the Presidents: William J. Clinton, 1995, Volume 1,* 953–55. Washington, DC: US Government Printing Office.

Colaresi, Michael. 2004. "When Doves Cry: International Rivalry, Unreciprocated Cooperation, and Leadership Turnover." *American Journal of Political Science* 48.3: 555–70.

DeYoung, Karen. 2015. "As Talks with US Begin, Cubans Anticipate Changes in Their Lives." *Washington Post,* January 25.

Domínguez, Jorge I, Omar Everleny Pérez Villanueva, Mayra Espina Prieto, and Lorenia Barberia, eds. 2012. *Cuban Economic and Social Development Policy Reforms and Challenges in the 21st Century.* Cambridge: Harvard University.

Enterline, Andrew J. and Kristian S. Gleditsch. 2000. "Threats, Opportunity, and Force: Repression and Diversion of Domestic Pressure, 1948–1982." *International Interactions* 26.1: 21–53.

Escobar, Cristina. 2015. "The Blockade Has Not Ended." *Granma International,* February 12.

Fordham, Benjamin O. 2005. "Strategic Conflict Avoidance and the Diversionary Use of Force." *Journal of Politics* 67.1: 132–53.

Frank, Marc. 2013. *Cuban Revelations: Behind the Scenes in Havana.* Gainesville: University of Florida.

Hill, John Calvin. 1960. "Cuba: Suggested Answers to Questions Which Might Be Raised at NSC, March 10, 1960." In *Foreign Relations of the United States, 1958–1960, Vol. VI, Cuba,* Doc 473, Tab D, compiled by US Department of State, 830–32.

Jacobson, Roberta. 2015. "Cuba: Assessing the Administration's Sudden Shift." Hearing of the House Foreign Affairs Committee, Federal News Service, February 4.

Kandell, Jonathan. 2015. "As Cuba-US Relations Thaw Remittances Stoke New Tensions." *Institutional Investor,* April 2.

Lai, Brian, and Dan Reiter. 2005. "Rally 'Round the Union Jack? Public Opinion and the Use of Force in the United Kingdom." *International Studies Quarterly* 49.2: 255–72.

Levy, Jack S., and Lily I. Vakili. 1992. "Diversionary Action by Authoritarian Regimes: Argentina in the Falklands/Malvinas Case." In *The Internationalization of Communal Strife,* edited by Manus I. Midlarsky, 118–46. New York: Routledge.

LeoGrande, William M. 2014. "Cuba's New Foreign Investment Law Is a Bet on the Future." *World Politics Review,* April 2.

LeoGrande, William M., and Peter Kornbluh. 2014. *Back Channel to Cuba: The Hidden History of Negotiations between Washington and Havana.* Chapel Hill: University of North Carolina.

Miller, Ross A. 1995. "Domestic Structures and the Diversionary Use of Force." *American Journal of Political Science* 39.3: 760–85.

Mueller, John. 1973. *War, Presidents, and Public Opinion.* New York: Wiley.

Nolan, Richard, and Frederick W Richmond. 1978. "Representatives Fred Richmond and Richard Nolan, Discussions with Cuban President Fidel Castro." Tab A of Memorandum, Robert Pastor to Zbigniew Brzezinski, January 7, Carter Library, White House Central Office Files, Subj. File Countries, CO-38 (Cuba), Box CO 21, Folder CO-38, 1/1/78–3/31/78.

Norpoth, Helmut. 1987. "Guns and Butter and Governmental Popularity in Britain." *American Political Science Review,* 81.4: 949–59.

Obama, Barack. 2014. "Statement by the President on Cuba Policy Changes." White House, Office of the Press Secretary, December 17.

O'Neil, Patrick H. 2015. "The Deep State: An Emerging Concept in Comparative Politics." Social Science Research Network (SSRN). http://dx.doi.org/10.2139/ssrn.2313375.

Oppenheimer, Andres. 1999. "Cuba: Back to Darkness." *Miami Herald,* March 18.

Partido Comunista de Cuba (PCC). 1997. *El Partido de La Unidad, La Democracia y Los Derechos Humanos Que Defendemos: V Congreso del Partido Comunista de Cuba, La Habana, 8-10 de Octubre de 1997.* Havana: Editora Política.

———. 2011. "Sixth Congress of the Communist Party of Cuba: Resolution on the Guidelines of the Economic and Social Policy of the Party and the Revolution." In *Documentos.* http://www.cuba.cu/gobierno/documentos/index.html.

Pérez-Stable, Marifeli. 2011. *The Cuban Revolution: Origins, Course and Legacy.* New York: Oxford University.

Ravsberg, Fernando. 2013. "El tiro por la culata." *Cartas de Cuba,* BBC Mundo, May 16. http://www.bbc.co.uk/blogs/mundo/cartas_desde_cuba/2013/05/el_tiro_por_la_culata.html.

Richards, Diana. 1993. "Good Times, Bad Times, and the Diversionary Use of Force: A Tale of Some Not-So-Free Agents." *Journal of Conflict Resolution,* 37.3, 504–35.

Romeu, Rafael. 2008. *Vacation Over: Implications for the Caribbean of Opening U.S.-Cuba Tourism.* Washington, DC: International Monetary Fund.

Sirin, Cigdem V. 2011. "Is it Cohesion or Diversion? Domestic Instability and the Use of Force in International Crises." *International Political Science Review,* 32.3, 303–321.

Whitaker, Reg. 1984. "Fighting the Cold War on the Home Front: America, Britain, Australia and Canada," *Socialist Register* 21: 23–67.

Chapter 6

Beyond Revolutionary Chic: How US-Cuba Rapprochement May Affect Cuban Arts

Ana Serra

On December 29, 2014, Cuban artist Tania Bruguera attempted to stage her performance *Tatlin Whisper #6* in the iconic Plaza de la Revolución in Havana. It consisted of a stage on which volunteers from the audience would be given one minute to speak at the microphone about the new US-Cuba relationship. Bruguera had successfully put on a similar performance at the 2009 Havana Biennial, which caused quite a stir because of the intervention of internationally famous Cuban blogger Yoani Sánchez and other Cuban activists. This second performance in 2014, as the hashtag #YoTambiénExijo expressed, sought to provide "ordinary Cubans" on the island with an opportunity to make their own demands before the prospect of renewed US-Cuba relations. According to Bruguera, her intention was to address the discrepancy between the media's ample coverage of the respective presidents' comments on the new regulations versus the silence over the reactions of those to whom the changes might matter the most.

As usually happens when a gradual opening threatens to give way to public expressions of frustration, the Cuban government responded with a show of force. Given Bruguera's reputation as an international artist, the official reaction to her attempted performance was comparatively benign. She was detained and isolated, and her passport was confiscated. Several artists decrying her arrest were also jailed. Although these unfortunate events were more highly publicized in US news and social media than in Cuba, they invite the question: To the extent that the arts in Cuba are a vehicle for self-expression, will a more fluid relationship with the United States provide an outlet for the opinions of island Cubans through the arts? How will renewed relations with the United States impact the production, circulation, and reception of the arts in Cuba? More specifically, what will be the fate of Tania Bruguera and other artists who have at times suffered and at other times benefited from the enmity between the United States and Cuba?

While forecasting the future is risky, significant changes in the relationship between both countries in the past two decades allow for informed predictions. As travel, transportation, and financial transactions become more expeditious, the new regulations may facilitate the circulation and reception of Cuban artistic production in the United States. However, production and reception may be hampered by the removal of what has been variously called "the forbidden fruit" (Rivière 2015), "the nostalgia paradise" (Dopico 2002, p. 464), or the "Post-Soviet exotic" factor (Whitfield 2008, p. 18). Overall, outcomes will differ depending on the type of artistic expression and its development prior to the US-Cuba opening.

Cuban Literature: The Lure of Former Colonial Ties

The Special Period in Times of Peace brought unprecedented economic hardship to the island nation and, most importantly for Cuban literature, a dire paper scarcity. With the exception of educational materials, book publication was nearly stalled and literary production was almost completely reduced to poems or short stories circulating informally in manuscript form. In 1993, a government decree allowed writers to negotiate contracts with foreign publishers independently from state organizations and inaugurated an era of renewed cultural relationships between Cuba and Spain. Major Spanish publishers devoted themselves to printing Cuban as well as Latin American fiction as part of a generalized post-1992—the *Quinto Centenario* or Five-Hundredth Anniversary of the "Discovery of America"—effort to revitalize Spanish presence in the region. Spanish publishers set up literary awards, events, and publications to promote Cuban writers, some of whom published their entire literary production in Spain before they were published in their homeland.

At the end of the 1990s, a vibrant group of exiled Cuban writers established themselves in Madrid and Barcelona. Headed by the influential Cuban writer Jesús Díaz, they founded the literary and culture journal *Encuentros de la cultura cubana*, which became a forum for showcasing artists and promoting debate on Cuban arts from the perspective of the island as well as the diaspora ("Diez años de *Encuentro* de la cultura cubana" 2006). The boom of Cuban literature published in Spain resulted in numerous novels as well as essays and opinion pieces by Spanish writers engaging with Cuban topics and exhibiting varying degrees of accuracy (Serra 2011). As the Cuban writer Ángel Esteban (2011) put it, "¡Madrid habanece!," meaning that the enthusiasm for all things Cuban and the heightened presence of Cubans in the city signified a new dawning of Havana in Madrid.

In light of this close relationship and given the linguistic, political, and economic barriers between Cuba and the United States, Cuban writers have not focused on publishing in the United States. Nevertheless, the novels of popular Cuban writers such as Leonardo Padura—winner of both the 2012 National Award for Literature in Cuba and the 2015 Princess of Asturias literary prize in Spain and a current resident of the island—have been made available in English by British publishers and garnered a following among US readers. Some works by Abilio Estévez, Antonio José Ponte, and Wendy Guerra, among others, have been published in translation, generally by minor publishers in the United States. Similarly, several Cuban short story collections have been printed in English, with the most recent and notable example being *Generation Zero* by Orlando Luis Pardo Lazo. Relatively minor presses such as Arte Público have published Cuban novels in Spanish in the United States but, again, short story collections by multiple authors in their original language seem to have generated more interest. Fiction by Cuban American writers, however, is widely disseminated in the United States, which attests to the popularity of Cristina García, Achy Obejas, and Roberto Fernández, among many others.

Despite the fact that Cuban writers have not published extensively in English in the United States, their works in Spanish published elsewhere have been made readily available to US readers, chiefly by Amazon. Furthermore, the availability of Cuban books in Spanish has aided the development of Cuban Studies in the United States, which has grown considerably in the past decade. To cite one source, at the Latin American Studies Association (LASA) conference, there were 152 panels on Cuba in 2010 versus 410 in 2015. Without a doubt, a more straightforward relationship between Cuba and the United States will facilitate the process of organizing scholarly exchanges.

New regulations will simplify the translation and publication of Cuban works because communication, travel, and royalty exchanges will soon be more predictable.

What remains to be seen is what will happen when the "forbidden fruit" factor is removed for critics and readers of Cuban literature. Will increased freedom in travel, communication, and economic exchange with Cuba result in a loss of interest in the country? Will Cuban literature remain highly appreciated despite the fact that the country is breaking out of its isolation? Once the nostalgia for a simpler past or a communist utopia dissipates and once one can enjoy in Cuba some of the same products one enjoys in the global market, will interest in Cuban literature with its (for some) attractive representations of ruin and scarcity remain strong? Will Cuban literary production change to reflect new realities, or will it cater to the reified illusions of a certain generation in the United States? Where will Cuban Americans stand when they witness changes? Will they crave more of the nostalgic representations of pre-revolutionary times already seen in some Cuban literature? Will more direct exposure to US tourists and products reinstate the once-strong US cultural influence on the island?

Cuban Cinema: Finally Unveiling a "True" Image?

Since the Special Period, when the funding of the Instituto Cubano de Arte e Industria Cinematográfica (ICAIC) was considerably reduced, Cuban filmmakers have had to resort to co-productions with other countries, chiefly Spain, Mexico, France, or Canada. Co-productions have had an impact on the kinds of films made because Cuban directors have had to work with a number of actors and technicians from the co-financing countries and, most importantly, the movies needed to respond to the expectations of European or North American audiences. As Cuban director Pastor Vega put it, co-productions meant thinking about "marketing," "profits," and a more centralized production process, hitherto unfamiliar concepts to Cuban filmmakers (Chanan 2004, p. 480). The decline of ICAIC's influence due to lack of funding and resources has created a climate for recent graduates of Cuban film schools to engage in independent film-making. Made with hand-held cameras and innovative techniques, and focused primarily on documentaries, this new production has redefined filmmaking in Cuba. Most of these films are now made with very low budgets and distributed largely on the Internet or at local festivals in Cuba, but many have received international acclaim in Europe and North America (Burnett 2013; Stock 2009).

While the island was opening itself to foreign filmmakers and audiences, the embargo kept the United States off limits. Significantly, under Obama's recent regulations, documentary film-making in Cuba by US citizens will no longer require special permission from the United States Department of the Treasury. Logistics will be considerably easier once credit card payments are authorized and communications are improved. However, feature-length commercial films are not yet specifically authorized. Granted, documentary film-making in Cuba can be justified under the familiar rubrics of "educational or humanitarian purposes," but these same objectives can arguably be achieved with fictional stories. By authorizing documentary films, the US government seems to succumb to the desire for "realistic representations" of Cuba, to somehow seek "the truth" about the island, as is indeed the premise on which most documentary films rest. The fact that Cuba has been so inaccessible to the United States intensifies the impulse to *document* what is unique on the island and has been well-preserved throughout years of isolation. It is thus not surprising that, according to the Associated Press, actor Matt Dillon is working on a film on Afro-Cuban music and *The Discovery Channel* has prepared a documentary, *Cuban Chrome*, on the creative abilities of Cuban car mechanics to keep their 1950s American cars on the road (Armario 2015). Some of these documentaries made by US filmmakers will likely bring to the forefront some aspects of the exotic Caribbean, the reminiscences of an earlier close relationship with the United States, or the idealization of the Cuban spirit, which satisfy mainstream US audiences.

The relaxation and ultimate lifting of the embargo will paradoxically restrict access to film and television from the United States in Cuba. So far, the Instituto Cubano de Radio y Televisión (ICRT) has been at liberty to pirate entire American series (Padura 2015). Even Oscar-nominated films are watched in private homes in Cuba months before they are exhibited in movie theaters in Europe. While Netflix executives hope for success on the island, it would be far more advantageous for Cubans to continue with their homegrown weekly service of *el paquete*, which—for a couple of convertible pesos—delivers to their home assorted foreign programming and films. Establishing a legal framework for film distribution and reception will make it more costly for Cuban institutions and individuals to access US entertainment, and the island's Internet system will have to be thoroughly strengthened to download on-demand movies. The new regulations, ironically, will also make it more difficult to access Cuban movies in the United States. Despite the fact that Cuba reinstated copyright laws in 1996, most Cuban commercial and even independent films can be watched on YouTube and various pirate sites either for free or for nominal sums.[1] Nevertheless, because of a lack of publicity, these films' audiences seem largely restricted to students of Cuban culture or the larger audience of Cubans/Cuban Americans in the United States. To the detriment of access, after a costly transition, Cuban movies will presumably reach a larger audience when new regulations are put in place, and Cuban film creators will receive long overdue profits for their work.

Cuba's proximity to the United States and the history of love/ dependency and enmity between the two countries, together with the "lush tropical landscapes" as well as "the locations that still look like the 1950s" (as an article by the Associated Press evokes [Armario 2015]) have kept the flame of mutual interest alive. That celebrities such as Sean Penn interviewed Raúl Castro in 2008 and, more recently, Beyoncé and Jay-Z celebrated their honeymoon on the island are only two examples of renewed popularity in mass culture. But what will happen when travel and filming in Cuba, as well as distribution in the United States, become routine for US filmmakers? Clearly, the Cuban film-making industry cannot compete with Hollywood or even US independent films, and it would not be cost-effective for Cuban filmmakers to shoot in the United States. It will be interesting to see how Cuban film-making—which has traditionally been politically engaged and intentionally straightforward in terms of technique—fares when widely distributed because it has to compete against other cinemas in Latin America, such as in Mexico, Argentina, or Brazil, that have adapted more closely to the demands of an international audience. If the relationship between Hollywood and Cuba partly depends on the latter offering the images that US audiences crave, will Hollywood be able to move beyond familiar topics or will independent cinema perhaps take the lead? Can we expect that Cuban American filmmakers will be drawn to the island to get acquainted with an ever-changing environment, or will some persist in trying to rescue landmarks of the past? With new regulations, will availability of state-of-the-art equipment change Cuba's signature *cine imperfecto* (imperfect cinema) and other evolved forms? Promotion, distribution, and exhibition—all of which operate under precarious conditions on the island—will considerably improve, but Cuban filmmakers will have to strive to break stereotypes and resist the formidable temptation to commercialize their films for a foreign audience. As for the

United States, opening to Cuba offers nothing but advantages; American filmmakers will have access to new settings and topics, and American audiences will have the opportunity to enjoy one of the strongest, although least known, filmic productions in Latin America. If watched attentively, these Cuban films will no doubt contribute to foster a deeper understanding of the island nation far beyond what we know about its politics and relationship to the United States.

The 1990s: A True Breakthrough in US-Cuba Relations

The 1990s saw significant changes regarding art production, exhibition, and purchase of Cuban art in the United States. Two key lawsuits against the US Treasury department, the first brought by independent art dealer Ramón Cernuda in 1989 and the second by Sandra Levinson (Director of the Center for Cuban Studies in New York) in 1991, made importation and sale of original art from Cuba to the United States legal but subject to travel, transportation, and payment restrictions. The Cuban regime followed by re-establishing copyright and intellectual property laws on the island at the 1996 Berne Convention and recognizing some forms of *cuentapropismo* (self-employment) among artists. *Cuentapropismo* made it possible for artists to perform and exhibit their work independently, and to negotiate their contracts with foreign companies and individuals without the intervention of the Cuban state. Thus, since the 1990s, artists have become far more independent financially and politically, and their contracts also brought significant revenue to the Cuban government.

As they gained international recognition, so-called cultural producers became an elite class in Cuba—in terms of their wealth, ability to travel and reside abroad, and freedom of expression—particularly visual artists and musicians whose work perhaps lends itself more easily to international consumption. Given historically strong musical ties between the United States and Cuba, and the fact that Cuban plastic arts can arguably convey more directly the kind of images that a US audience craves, it is not surprising that exchanges of visual arts as well as music intensified between the two countries after new regulations on both parts. As a result, since the 1990s, numerous Cuban plastic artists have had a strong presence in US museums such as the Museum of Modern Art and the Chelsea Gallery in New York, as well as in other venues in the city and across the country. In addition, long before the current favorable political climate, Cuban art has graced the walls of the most unsuspected collectors, such as notorious US billionaire and 2016 presidential candidate Donald Trump (Mirabal 2015).

According to the Cuban artist and critic Antonio Eligio Fernández (Tonel), since the Special Period Cuban artists have become "tokenized" and "other" as they have assumed a persona vis-à-vis the outside world rather than their followers on the island (Tonel 2009, p. 13). Cuban artists have been able to establish their presence at international exhibits, especially in the United States, as long as they continue to reside on the island and express criticism of the regime. Artists without an international following have engaged in the progressive theatricalization of art for tourists at public squares, restaurants, hotels, and beaches on the island (Tonel 2009, p. 14). Some visual artists have exploited the allure of nostalgic images of the 1950s (such as American Chevrolets), combining them with revolutionary paraphernalia that has become increasingly more attractive since Fidel Castro ceded power to his brother and many thought the regime was about to expire. It is to be expected that the rapprochement between the United States and Cuba will bring further commodification of revolutionary icons, but as travel to Cuba becomes routine, the wealth of Cuban cultural expression will erode the simplifications of Cold War era souvenirs.

US institutions and collectors are rushing to be the first to strengthen relationships with Cuba in light of improved access. Alberto Magnan, with the Chelsea Gallery in New York, reported that he received 24 calls from collectors on December 17, the day when Obama announced the relaxation of travel restrictions (Burnett 2014). Collectors see in Cuba "a chance to discover the Cuban Picasso or Basquiat before the rest of the world does" (Mogulescu 2015). Sandra Levinson, Executive Director of Cuban Art Space in New York, went as far as stating that "Cuba probably has more artists per capita than any country in the world" and the "arts . . . may be Cuba's greatest exports" (Mogulescu 2015). Although prices of Cuban art have more than tripled since the fall of the Soviet bloc, it is still relatively cheap by international standards (Howe 2009). In addition, Cuban artists have thus far remained extremely accessible on the island, because most of them welcome visits to their Havana studios. The latter is a result of the fact that there are very few galleries in Havana, and they are owned either by the Cuban government or by foreign parties. Although Cuban visual artists have been quite successful in Europe and Latin America, it is to be expected that their long history as "intimate enemies" with the United States will significantly increase their chances of success once travel and business restrictions are eased. But, as was the case with literature and film, the question is how long Cubans on the island will be able to maintain this level of enthusiasm as exhibits and purchases explode in number. Cuban artistic expression, which has denounced the wave of increasing consumerism since the 1990s on the island (Remba 2010), is bound to change as a result of the inevitable mass commercialization of Cuban art.

Numerous challenges remain in the promotion of Cuban art on and from the island. Since the 1990s, the Cuban regime has established a difference between cultural workers in "leading roles," such as "artists, journalists, writers," and those in intermediary positions such as artistic promotion, advertisement, and business with other countries (Partido Comunista de Cuba 1996). Middlemen were subject to unfavorable tax rules and intense scrutiny under accusations of corruption; a socialist society had no place for those involved in commercialization of art in the international market, particularly in a country where artists were asked to serve the Revolution. In addition, the experience of Eastern European countries demonstrated that the emergence of an independent entrepreneurial class posed a threat to the regime (Hernández Reguant 2004). As a result, the Cuban art scene is very disperse: for instance, artists learn by word of mouth of possible sources of funding from foreign companies or grants (Machado 2008). Large exhibits still require the sponsorship of a Cuban government institution, which creates some obstacles; the regime has its own mechanisms of art production and promotion at local levels, which often run separately from the foreign art business. As Cuba renews its ties with the United States, it would behoove the regime to allow the island's art industry to develop and expand considerably, so that the fruits of the Cuban art business are enjoyed on the island. Recent artistic exchanges between the United States and Cuba, however, have evidenced their cultural differences and the gap between their understandings of how art and politics intersect.

The Promise of Cuban Visual Arts: Two Examples

Given the current general appreciation of visual and performative media, and the speed of travel and absorption of visual messages, visual arts hold great potential for stirring controversy and becoming a vehicle for exposing injustice in countries in which freedom of expression is restricted. The ongoing cultural project Queloides and, once again, Tania Bruguera's performances are cases in point.

Numerous Cuban artists such as Belkis Ayón, Pedro Álvarez, René Peña, José Toirac, and others have participated in Queloides since its first two exhibits in Havana in 1997 and 1999. The title refers to Keloids, wound-induced scars that, according to Cubans, are especially prevalent among blacks. The exhibits dealt with stereotypes associated with all Afro-Cubans, such as machismo, violence, poverty, and crime, coupled with the very real problems of discrimination that Afro-Cubans suffer. Scarred black skin is a metaphor for suffering in a society that denies racism and yet continues to practice it, but black skin is not only a symbol of pain—the art reveals its beauty. The exhibits were very controversial at the time of their display because they denounced the fallacy of the regime's presumption that the 1959 revolution had resolved race discrimination. As a result, both the 1997 and the 1999 Queloides exhibits received very little promotion and were hardly seen and appreciated in Cuba (Gates 2012).

In response to this omission, Harvard University Professor Alejandro de la Fuente, together with artist Elio Rodríguez Valdés, curated a third exhibit in Havana in 2010. This third Queloides was fraught with obstacles, culminating in the official decision to let the exhibit take place only on the condition that Alejandro de la Fuente himself would not attend. De la Fuente consented to the arrangement and was later able to hold subsequent exhibits at the Mattress Factory Museum in Pittsburgh (2011) and The 8th Floor gallery in New York City (2011); such exhibits were accompanied by activities that de la Fuente had unsuccessfully tried to organize in Havana, such as conferences and a concert by hip hop artists (Gates 2012).

That Cuban authorities allowed Queloides to take place in Havana, even while they somewhat restricted its content and attendance, is revealing of a stance that remains current: initiatives from the United States are welcome as long as the Cuban officials control their message and impact. The Cuban regime could not forbid Alejandro de la Fuente to hold the exhibit for fear of the negative publicity of this interdiction, preferring instead to enjoy the heartwarming effect of allowing a controversial exhibit to take place on Cuban soil. Subsequent exhibits of Queloides show that the United States is likely to become an outlet for expanded versions of exhibits that were subject to restrictions in Cuba. Further, the incident of Alejandro de la Fuente not being able to attend the exhibit that he himself had curated highlights that intermediaries—curators, art representatives, gallerists—still bear the brunt of accusations of challenging the Cuban regime.[2] After all, according to Elio Rodríguez Valdés, "Things that were not speakable in other realms became possible in the realm of art" (Cuban Art News). But apart from his excellent work as a scholar, de la Fuente played a suspect role in this project; he was a facilitator in creating new paths of expression and dissemination in Cuba and the United States. So far, the Cuban regime has been very careful to control foreign initiatives to develop Cuban arts on the island for fear that they will disseminate unwanted political messages. Further, that de la Fuente is Cuban further complicates his relationship with the art establishment.

In 2010, with travel restrictions still in place and a generalized limitation on Internet access on the island, the impact of a controversial art exhibit in Havana such as Queloides and the contrast with subsequent exhibits in the United States could be reasonably controlled. However, a strengthening of the means of transportation and communications between the United States and Cuba will make this kind of cultural exchange not only more frequent but also considerably more impactful. The cultural offering in the United States is obviously significantly more extended, but given the high degree of engagement of island Cubans, an art exhibit has the potential to foster meaningful conversations on the island and give rise to activism connected to international settings. Conversely, one should not underestimate the effect of an exhibit like Queloides in the context of the movement #blacklivesmatter in the United States, for instance. The lesson of Queloides is that stereotypes of black people persist and discrimination is ingrained at some levels in Cuba, but the population is far more mixed, and there is less animosity and fear toward blacks than in the United States. As relations between the two countries normalize, art viewers in the United States will stop reducing Cuban art to its being for or against Castro and focus instead on its aesthetic, social, and political issues at a more nuanced level. It may be a humbling experience for a US audience to learn that countries like Cuba, which have suffered for decades under totalitarianism, enjoy more freedom and equality than the United States in some respects.

The increasingly common figure of the artist shuttling between both countries uncovers starkly different dynamics in the production and reception of Cuban art on both sides. Tania Bruguera epitomizes an artist who has suffered as a result of the vulnerability of intermediaries, but who has also learned to exploit the possibilities of the volatile relationship between the United States and Cuba. A resident of both New York and Havana, Bruguera has been instrumental in widening the range of freedom of speech in Cuba, chiefly with her numerous performances and installations and her Cátedra de Arte de Conducta (Behavior Art School), which promotes civic action (Schwartz 2012). She describes her latest work as Artivism, or an intervention against the dominant state of affairs in Cuba. Her follow-up to the regime's denying permission to stage *Tatlin's Whisper #6* on December 26 at the Plaza de la Revolución in Havana was a performance using Hannah Arendt's *The Origins of Totalitarianism* (1951). First, Bruguera made a show of abiding by current Cuban laws by obtaining a certificate of *cuentapropista*, or owner of a private enterprise; then, she founded the *Hannah Arendt International Institute for Artivism*; soon after, Bruguera used her permit to become a teacher to conduct a reading of Arendt's work in Spanish for one hundred hours from her own living room. The quiet reading with doors open to the street dramatized the possibility of short-circuiting the habitual disconnect between private and public expression in Cuba, the subversive potential of reading as public performance, and the provocative effect of Bruguera's reputation on the island. The power of the performance was not in the words of the text itself, as it was barely audible from outside, but in the fact that the title of this classic alone evokes the fears and frustration of many Cubans. Most significantly, although many passersby continued with their activities without paying much attention, government officials did their best to interfere with the reading, culminating with a threatening confrontation and a "repudiation act" carried out by a small group of civilians shouting Cold War era political slogans outside Bruguera's home.

The reading of Arendt's text and its aftermath are effective as a performance on several levels. Bruguera demonstrated that it is possible to use current Cuban regulations to create vehicles for protest, which is of course threatening for a regime that is attempting to diversify its economy while also striving for self-preservation. Her provocative act showed that officials respond with censorship and repression against perceived threats, regardless of the actual content of the act: the authorities put on a show of force, with a view to discourage any further defiance. The act of repudiation staged a disavowal of Bruguera's opinions in front of foreign cameras. The ripple effects of the reading and subsequent confrontation, with abundant communications and commentary among the artist and intellectual communities in the United States and to a lesser extent Cuba, complete the performance in which both sides act out their history of mutual aggravation. Moreover, the reading took place during the twelfth Havana Biennial, which is central to the Cuban and international art scene, and after the incident Bruguera was denied entry to an exhibit by Tomás Sánchez and others.

The Biennial's focus for 2015 was "Cuban diaspora artists," and the general theme was "*entre la idea y la experiencia*" (between idea and experience): Bruguera's performance and its aftermath could not be more illustrative of the gap between the *idea* of enhancing artistic and political expression for artists operating both in Cuba and the United States and the actual *experience* of that attempt. Importantly, the white dove that Bruguera released as she was held captive by government officials outside her home reportedly "flew free but . . . hit a house's façade and went down to the pavement where it remained, confused" (Mosquera 2015). The fearful, disoriented, and painful flight of the dove after its release inadvertently offers an apt metaphor for the challenges that some Cuban artists face in this period of transition.

Notwithstanding reactions in the United States, Cuban conceptual artist Lázaro Saavedra (National Award in Plastic Arts in Cuba, 2014) voiced the sentiment of many artists living on the island: Bruguera's performances have exposed what they already know well, that is, that there are restrictions to public expression in Cuba. But considering that Internet access is limited, her act of artivism remains empty for most people in Cuba. Saavedra observed that these performances would surely increase Bruguera's reputation as a provocateur in the United States, which bodes well for other Cuban artists who persevere at her level of political engagement. Indeed, in yet another turn of events, the office of New York City Mayor Bill DeBlasio announced on July 13, 2015, that Tania Bruguera had been offered the position of First-Artist-in-Residence for the Office of Immigrant Affairs, which supervises a new program offering services to undocumented immigrants. Soon after, the New York Museum of Modern Art revealed that that it had accepted Bruguera's "Untitled (Havana 2000)" in its permanent collection. In brief, the installation consists of a large tunnel in which four naked and disoriented men walk on a floor covered in decomposing sugar cane toward a television screen broadcasting footage of Fidel Castro. For some, the installation may resound with the motif of the new man in the context of the historical significance of slavery and the ideology of the Revolution. The acceptance of the piece reveals the extent of the New York museum's commitment to supporting Bruguera's work, given the complexity of the installation. However, the Cuban artist stated that, upon hearing this news, the Cuban authorities immediately returned her passport, which had been retained since the May incident. "They want me out of the country," Bruguera said (Kennedy 2015). As political and economic relations between the United States and Cuba improve, one wonders whether

Bruguera's kind of art will remain attractive in the United States. If, as some argue, relations with the United States will inevitably force Cuba to improve its human rights' record and enhance its freedom of speech, what will be the fate of artivism and other forms of Cuban political art, given that some of them are perhaps less worthy of attention in their own right? With time and more open relations with the rest of the world, can one hope for an improvement on the human rights record in Cuba to the point that artistic exchanges with other countries are not mediated by allegiance or resistance to the revolution on the part of organizers or participants?

"El futuro es hoy" (The Future Is Now)[3]

Once finance, access, travel, communications, and diplomatic relations become smoother between both countries, there is little doubt that cultural production and circulation will be stimulated. Questions remain about the quality and substance of this production, and whether mutual interest is sustainable in the long run. The island nation faces the dilemma of exploiting the attractions that the rest of the world enjoys—images of Cuba as a tropical paradise, socialist utopia, communist apocalypse—or trying to give a sense of its cultural complexity. Since the 1990s, Cuba has opened itself considerably to the rest of the world, but opening to the United States is potentially much more significant, given the prior relationship and the force of US capitalism so close to Cuban shores. Equally important is the question with which this chapter started: if restrictions to free speech in Cuba have been a concern for decades long before the 1959 revolution, will a predicted artistic explosion occur in the context of a willingness to let all manner of Cuban voices be heard? Considering recent history, visual arts can continue to hold the promise of widening the range of free expression in Cuba, as well as being an agent of cultural diplomacy far into the world. In addition, Cuban film and literature seem especially suited to open the rest of the world to the island's rich and complex culture prior to the rapprochement and beyond, and including many aspects besides revolutionary engagement. Exchanges with Cuban students and academics, professional translation of Cuban works, and exposure through dedicated study and frequent visits will lend context and depth to what we learn about Cuba as we enjoy its artistic production. Overall, this is an extremely exciting time to witness how Cuban intellectuals, writers, filmmakers, and visual artists continue to explore new and nuanced means of expression for themselves and an increasingly strong Cuban civil society in the context of improved relations with the United States and the rest of the world.

Notes

1. Before the changes in regulations, small nonprofit companies such as Americas Media Initiative or university-affiliated ventures such as Cuban Cinema Classics had made an effort to preserve, subtitle, and distribute Cuban films in the United States.
2. The United States has also been harsh and fundamentally erratic in the treatment of intermediaries in these exchanges. To give one example, in 2009, the US Treasury denied visas to the philanthropists who financed a concert of the New York Philharmonic Orchestra in Havana (Armengol 2015). However, in May 2015, the Minnesota Orchestra gave two concerts in Havana for which all necessary visas were granted, showing the change of attitude on both sides.
3. This is, significantly, the title of a 2009 documentary by a young filmmaker, Sandra Gómez. As the documentary shows, long before the changes in US-Cuba relations were formalized, the country's youth felt that significant changes were occurring in Cuba, although they were not satisfied with their direction.

References

Armario, Christine. 2015. "Hollywood and Havana Inch Closer with New Cuban Regulations." *The Middletown Press*, February 15. http://www.middletownpress.com/business/20150215/hollywood-and-havana-inch-closer-with-new-cuba-regulations.

Armengol, Alejandro. 2015. "El concierto que no fue." *Cubaencuentro*, May 15. http://www.cubaencuentro.com/cuba/articulos/el-concierto-que-no-fue-322821.

Burnett, Victoria. 2014. "Cuba's Art Scene Awaits a Travel Boom." *New York Times*, December 29. http://www.nytimes.com/2014/12/30/arts/cubas-art-scene-awaits-a-travel-boom.html.

———. 2013. "Digital Technology Is Making Its Mark in Cuba." *New York Times*, January 4. http://www.nytimes.com/2013/01/05/movies/digital-technology-is-making-its-mark-in-cuba.html.

Chanan, Michael. 2004. *Cuban Cinema*. Bloomington: Indiana University Press.

"Diez años de *Encuentro* de la cultura cubana." 2006. *Revista Encuentro de la Cultura Cubana* 40: 203–25. http://www.cubaencuentro.com/revista/revista-encuentro/archivo/40-primavera-de-2006/%28filter%29/index.

Dopico, Ana María, 2002. "Picturing Havana. History, Vision and the Scramble for Cuba." *Nepantla Views from South* 3.3: 451–93.

Esteban, Ángel, ed. 2011. *Madrid Habanece: Cuba y España en el punto de mira transatlántico*. Madrid: Iberoamericana Vervuert.

Gates, Henry Louis. 2012. "Race and Racism in Cuban Art: A conversation with *Queloides* curators Alejandro de la Fuente and Elio Rodríguez Valdés." *Transition* 108: 33–51.

Hernández Reguant, Ariana. 2004. "Copyrighting Che: Art and Authorship Under Cuban Late Socialism." *Public Culture* 16.1: 1–29.

Howe, Linda. 2009. "New Cuban Art Crossing the Accursed Waters." In *Cuban Artists' Books and Prints (1985–2008)*, edited by Linda Howe, 20–28. Winston-Salem, NC: Wake Forest University, The Cuba Project.

Kennedy, Randy. 2015. "Tania Bruguera, an Artist in Havana, Has a Great New York Week." *The New York Times*, July 13. http://www.nytimes.com/2015/07/14/arts/design/tania-bruguera-an-artist-in-havana-has-a-great-new-york-week.html?_r=0.

Machado, Mailyn. 2008. "De boca en boca, de mano en mano, de ordenador en ordenador." In *States of Exchange. Artists from Cuba*, edited by Sebastián López, 32–41. London: Iniva.

Mirabal, Michel. 2015. "Bio." Accessed August 4. https://michelmirabal.wordpress.com/biography/.

Mogulescu, Miles. 2015. "Some of the World's Best Art Is Made in Cuba." *Huffington Post*, July 8. http://www.huffingtonpost.com/miles-mogulescu/some-of-worlds-best-art-i_b_7756648.html.

Mosquera, Gerardo. 2015. "Tania Bruguera: Artivism and repression in Cuba. An Eyewitness Report." *Walker Art Magazine*, June 17. http://www.walkerart.org/magazine/2015/tania-bruguera-artivism-gerardo-mosquera-cuba.

Padura, Leonardo. 2015. "Netflix sueña con Cuba." *El País*, February 15. http://cultura.elpais.com/cultura/2015/02/13/television/1423839577_591144.html.

Partido Comunista de Cuba. 1996. "Political Bureau Report of March 23, 1996." *Granma International*, April 10.

"'Queloides' in New York: An Interview with the Curators." 2011. *Cuban Art News*, April 19. http://www.cubanartnews.org/news/queloides_in_new_york_an_interview_with_the_curators-994/1011.

Remba, Tania. 2010. "La globalización en el mundo del arte contemporáneo cubano." In *Cultura y letras cubanas del siglo XXI*, edited by Araceli Tinajero, 25–38. Madrid: Iberoamericana Vervuert.

Rivière, Melisa. 2015. "What Does the Cuba Détente Mean for the Culture Industries and Ethnographic Praxis?" *EPIC: Advancing the Value of Ethnography in Industry*, January 25. https://www.epicpeople.org/us-cuba-detente/.

Saavedra, Lázaro. 2014. "Tania gana, los derechos civiles continúan perdiendo." *Enrisco Blog*, December 31. http://enrisco.blogspot.com/2014/12/se-abre-el-debate.html.

Schwartz, Stephanie. 2012. "Tania Bruguera: between Histories." *Oxford Art Journal* 32.5: 215–32.

Serra, Ana. 2011. "Desde *El lado frío de la almohada*: La izquierda española imagina la revolución cubana." *Hispanic Research Journal* 12.3: 244–59.

Stock, Ann Marie. 2009. *On Location in Cuba: Street Filmmaking during Times of Transition*. Chapel Hill: The University of North Carolina Press.

Tonel, Antonio Eligio. 2009. "Because of the Increasing Disorder. Notes on Autonomy, Compromise and (Cultural) Politics in Cuban Art." In *Cuban Artists' Books and Prints (1985–2008)*, edited by Linda Howe, 12–16. Winston-Salem, NC: Wake Forest University, The Cuba Project.

Whitfield, Esther. 2008. *Cuban Currency: The Dollar and "Special Period" Fiction*. Minneapolis: University of Minnesota Press.

Chapter 7

Post-17D and Processes of Cuban National Reconciliation

Holly Ackerman

The announcements by Presidents Castro and Obama on December 17 (17D) produced a torrent of media coverage and academic analysis that, understandably, centered on diplomatic negotiations. This chapter examines a less discussed, but equally important, theme: reconciliation among Cubans. Looking at the processes of Cuban national reconciliation from the individual and societal levels, both within Cuba and between the island and diaspora, this chapter identifies likely facilitators and lingering obstacles to processes of accommodation. It complicates the conceptualization of "exile" and "island" by challenging both common stereotypes of a sharply divided nation with an intractably vengeful exile, and of a unified socialist island. It also acknowledges that although the pace of national reunification is accelerating, it is a process that has been in play for almost forty years.

Reconciliation at the Individual Level: A Long-Standing Phenomenon between Island and Diaspora

In 1977, President Jimmy Carter ended the travel ban imposed through the US embargo in 1963, thereby stimulating a process of re-encounter and reconciliation among Cuban families. Despite continued Cuban government stigmatization of those who emigrated and notwithstanding travel restrictions imposed by the Reagan

Administration in 1982, the process of re-encounter continued fitfully. In 2009, the Obama Administration significantly boosted individual contact by allowing unlimited family travel and remittances and authorizing direct flights to Cuba from an increased number of US airports. Cuban Americans could visit relatives more easily and support them more generously. In 2013, 470,732 family visits took place, and an estimated US$2.7 billion was sent as cash remittances from Cuban Americans to loved ones in Cuba (Morales 2014a, 2014b). Travel terms and remittances for non-Cubans were also expanded under Obama in 2011 and 2015 (Sullivan 2015), with total US visitors (family and nonfamily) estimated at 600,000 in 2014 (Rodriguez and Orsi 2015).

From the other side of the Florida Straits, Cuban citizens were empowered by changes in Cuban government travel regulations implemented in January 2013 (Haq 2013). For the first time since the mid 1960s, most citizens can travel to the United States if they obtain a visa and, more importantly, they can be away for up to two years without losing their property in Cuba, with the option of requesting an additional two-year extension. Under the Cuban Adjustment Act, these travelers can obtain a green card in the United States after one year and can leave the United States for up to one year, making it possible for them to have legal status in two places. Consequently, increased numbers of Cubans are multiplying their life chances while simultaneously creating a civic stake in both communities and deepening relationships with family and friends in the exterior. Equally important, diaspora realities can be personally experienced and analyzed by islanders, allowing them to independently formulate opinions without relying on second-hand accounts or government filters. US authorities report a 79 percent increase in nonimmigrant visas granted to Cubans from October 1, 2013 to March 31, 2014 (the first six months of Fiscal Year 2014), and a total of 16,767 visas (eTN 2013) increasing by another 25 percent to 29,700 during the first ten months of Fiscal Year 2015 (Cancio Isla 2014).

This sort of personal connection might be categorized as "informal" or "popular" reconciliation because it is not guided by any ordered process. It simply represents popular will responding to opportunity. When given the chance, Cubans have demonstrated over almost forty years that they support contact between those who left and those who stayed. A 2014 poll of Cuban Americans in southern Florida quantifies the pervasiveness of public support: 68 percent favor normalized diplomatic relations; 69 percent want an end to travel restrictions; and 52 percent support an end to the embargo (Grenier and Gladwin 2014).

Structured individual and small group reconciliations are also taking place in southern Florida as a theoretically informed practice through the pioneering work of Sister Ondina Cortés at St. Thomas University. Sr. Cortés organizes what she calls "Circles of Reconciliation," which include several weekly meetings among voluntary participants who arrived in different waves of migration. Each participant initially tells the story of his or her exit from Cuba, attempting to find forgiveness and reconciliation within themselves in the process—that is, identifying and letting go of trauma, grudges, and rancor. The group then focuses on societal reconciliation by sharing ideas on how to heal divisions within the Cuban nation. Most participants evaluate the experience positively (Cortés 2013).

A variation of this process transpired between 2001 and 2003 in the Cuban National Reconciliation Task Force on Memory, Truth, and Justice: a project sponsored by the Ford Foundation and convened by Marifeli Pérez-Stable at Florida International University (Pérez-Stable 2013). The task force was composed of exile activists with varying political views, scholars, and persons with expertise in other cases of national reconciliation. Political dissidents in Cuba commented on the process as it evolved. Although the task force focused primarily on seeking truth about human rights violations in Cuba, one main conclusion was similar to the Circles of Reconciliation. The Task Force concluded if reconciliation is to succeed at a national and institutional level, then it must begin within each individual and then extend to families and social networks.

Social networks and organizations that bring together small groups of Cubans and Cuban Americans to promote understanding and mutual aid are indeed emerging. For example, the Cuba Study Group (CSG), an organization of Cuban American business people and professionals led by wealthy businessman Carlos Saladrigas, incorporated following the highly emotional Elián González episode in 2000.[1] Their overall goal was to fashion proactive, strategic initiatives that would promote growth among emerging businesses on the island, thus fostering the growth of civil society (CSG 2015a). Successive projects have been grounded in a substantive analysis of how to effectively promote national reconciliation, which was the subject of three years of discussion within CSG (2015b).

Among CSG's projects is the Cuban Entrepreneurial Exchange, which has thus far brought three groups of Cuban entrepreneurs to Miami during 2014–2015—a group of independent small businesswomen; newly authorized "makers" who produce products not previously allowed outside of state facilities, such as paper containers; and some of the best chefs from Cuba's rapidly developing restaurant industry—to meet with successful Cuban American counterparts. It is not hard to imagine the strong identification and continuing bond that must occur between successful Cuban exiles who had to begin with nothing in Miami and those who are just starting out in Cuba. Stereotypes of a greedy Miami monolith are countered, as are notions of islanders who lack initiative. CSG is also preparing a microfinance project that will be ready to assist small businesses as soon as Cuban law allows.

On a more existential level, other Cuban Americans are ending what they call the "Emotional Embargo" as a way of building bridges between diaspora and island. Activist/anthropologist Ruth Behar and poet Richard Blanco, friends for twenty years, are engaging the power of storytelling through a blog titled "Bridges to/from Cuba," which was launched in June 2015, has attracted international attention, and circulates in Cuba hand-to-hand and by USB. Its purpose is to connect Cubans everywhere by inviting testimony on the personal emotional experience of being Cuban over the past 55 years. Behar describes the idea of the blog as their effort to "intervene in a significant historical moment" (Behar, personal communication to the author, July 16, 2015). Following 17D, when the media were featuring politics and the mechanics of diplomacy, Behar and Blanco decided to focus on the hearts and sentiments of Cubans. The blog features monthly posts that "emotionally reconcile the diaspora of our various Cuban identities and claims as we move toward the post-embargo world of tomorrow" (Behar and Blanco 2015).

Speaking about the meaning of his recent poem "Matters of the Sea," prepared for the reopening of the US Embassy in Havana, Blanco expanded on the theme of healing and the importance of the humanistic dimension of reconciliation, saying the poem is about "getting back to our own humanity, the shared humanity beyond the politics. In the end, it's about coming to a place of healing, getting to that place where we can see each other as human beings (Whitefield 2015)." It bodes well for post-17D Cuban national reconciliation that individual and small group levels of understanding are well developed both formally and informally between the island and diaspora.

It should be noted that no parallel process of informal or formal reconciliation at the individual or small group level has been described within Cuba. This is despite evidence that citizens are deeply alienated from each other and from their government as a result of decades of restrictive policies: overzealous monitoring by Committees for the Defense of the Revolution (CDRs) and other mass organizations; violent acts of repudiation taken by CDRs during the Mariel boatlift in 1980; assaults by Rapid Response Brigades at alternative cultural events; and routine aggression against persons deemed to be politically unreliable (Ackerman and Clark 1995; Aguirre 2002; Estado de SATS 2014).

National Reconciliation at the Societal Level

At a recent conference at Florida International University, two well-known Cuba scholars asserted that the present level of alienation of Cuban citizens from their government is broad and deep. They differed sharply, however, on whether the government is aware of the extent of the rift, with one scholar saying, "No one knows better than the Cuban government how deep and wide the discontent of the people is" (Jardines Chacón 2015). Just three hours later, a second scholar asserted, "At this point, the Cuban government itself has no idea how massive the dissent is" (Pérez-Stable 2015). The contrast illustrates how scarce reliable data are that measure both public opinion and the internal government process inside Cuba. Hence, pronouncements on the level of discontent and the need for reconciliation should be considered advisedly.

Nonetheless, pioneering efforts at objective polling are being attempted on the island. Best known is the recent nationwide poll of 1200 Cubans conducted without Cuban government sanction by Bendixen & Amandi International for Univision Television News and *The Washington Post*. Key results show that 97 percent of Cubans think normalization of relations with the United States is good for Cuba, and 58 percent think it favors Cuba more than the United States. Only 39 percent of Cubans said they are satisfied with their political system, whereas 53 percent said they are dissatisfied. Even greater numbers disapprove of their economic system, with 79 percent saying they are dissatisfied and only 19 percent of Cubans saying they are satisfied (Bendixen & Amandi International 2015).

Supporters of the regime point to systematic public consultations, such as the 2010 meetings held nationwide to critique President Raúl Castro's proposed economic plan, as evidence of active debate and continued civic commitment to a national social pact led by the Communist Party (Bobes 2013). They point out that the 2010 consultations resulted in 68 percent of the plan's specifics being altered, thus confirming that the consultations are effective as well as popular. Independent nongovernmental organizations are viewed as divisive and unnecessary (Hernández 2003).

Nevertheless, since the 1990s, hundreds of nongovernmental organizations (NGOs) have developed, attempting to mediate between the people and the state or offering alternative political and social projects. However, even sympathetic observers assert that despite 25 years of organizing, these groups remain almost unknown within Cuba, even though they have won international prizes for their work—the Ortega y Gasset Prize in 2008 and the Sakahrov Prize in 2002, 2005, and 2010 (Ortega and Gasset 2008; Sakahrov Prize 2015), have leaders named among the world's most influential people (Hijuelos 2008), and receive frequent coverage in the world press. Their impact remains largely outside the national borders. They raise foreign awareness, but not the Cuban dissent or reconciliation that is their avowed purpose.

It is illegal in Cuba to form an organizational association without first receiving government authorization (Dupuy and Vierucci 2008; Human Rights Watch 1999). Groups contesting the regime are denied recognition or their applications are simply ignored. NGOs that form in defiance of the law (what I will call "unauthorized civil society") are branded as *grupúsculos contrarevolucionarios* (counter-revolutionary splinter groups). Quite simply, government limits on civil society development are the principal obstacle facing independent citizen-initiated consultation on reform and reconciliation. With the exception of conciliatory accommodations made with the Catholic Church (discussed later), the government continues to insist on state-defined and state-led unity.

Despite being unknown to their countrymen, Cuba's unauthorized civil society has become numerous, diverse, sophisticated in developing and managing support from diaspora and foreign partners, and connected through national and international networks and coalitions. Yet they often remain divided both internally and from one another. Throughout, some have viewed themselves as the protagonists of a future reconciliation among Cubans both on the island and in diaspora.

Rise of Nonviolence

Until the late 1970s, some dissident groups inside Cuba continued to use the violent tactics that had characterized revolutionary armed struggle against the Batista dictatorship (Ackerman 1998). Violence continued in exile into the late 1970s and early 1980s as groups advocating dialogue with the Cuban regime were bombed and socially shunned, and Cuban embassies and passenger aircrafts attacked. By the early 1990s, however, a new strategy of nonviolence arose in response to the following factors: the apparent futility of armed struggle; the death of older, more belligerent exiles; the renewal of family ties with island relatives; and the arrival of a less politicized, post-1980 generation through the Mariel boatlift, the 1994 rafter crisis, and subsequent legal and unauthorized immigration. The post-1980 arrivals wanted to see change in Cuba, but not via violent tactics that might endanger relatives and friends. They were also exhausted by the political mobilization required in Cuba, and most avoided activism of any sort. In response, established activists turned to nonviolent tactics rather than abandoning their hope of a democratic restoration. With few exceptions, an adversarial stance replaced a belligerent one.

Little Growth in Exile: Rising Numbers and Diversity in Cuba

Within the diaspora, political activism has not expanded greatly since the 1990s. Observers can identify a small group of active organizations dominated by long-standing leaders. There are sharp divisions among these groups based on the type of national reconciliation they seek at the societal level. The first oppose any reconciliation with the Cuban government. They view reconciliation as an accounting or truth-telling process that will document the regime's human rights violations. They support the US embargo and any nonviolent tactic that hastens the regime's collapse. Three main groups within this camp include: the Cuban American National Foundation and its related Foundation for Human Rights in Cuba; the Cuban Democratic Directorate; and Madres y Mujeres Anti-Represión (Mothers and Women against Oppression in Cuba).

A second type includes moderates who view reconciliation as a process of dialogue with adversaries to reach accommodation, if not agreement. They focus their work on common goals, seeking consensus while tolerating differences and avoiding debates about issues that divide them. For example, the *Proyecto Demócrata Cubano* (Cuban Democratic Project), the *Partido Socialdemócrata Cubano* (Cuban Social Democratic Party), and the *Arco Progresista* (Progressive Arch) have met both inside and outside Cuba since the 1990s, finding points of agreement. Just prior to 17D, under the auspices of the Konrad Adenhauer Foundation and the Christian Democratic Organization of the Americas, these groups met in Mexico City and attempted to expand their consultation to include a wider range of political views by including oppositionist activists from southern Florida and Cuba. Although the expanded group was able to agree on the need for a transition to democracy, they disagreed sharply on issues such as support for the US embargo. In subsequent meetings held in Miami, oppositionists withdrew their participation. Clearly, the two camps have different visions for post-17D reconciliation.

Despite these differences, a larger assembly of 55 dissident groups (23 from the island and 32 from the exile) once again attempted to find common ground during three days of highly publicized meetings in Puerto Rico in August 2015. This time, right-wing groups packed the meeting, electing a leadership that prioritized wholesale political change in Cuba by incorporating a reactionary 1998 declaration as part of their final statement of purpose ("Declaración de San Juan" 2015; El Acuerdo 1998). The 1998 document presupposes the elimination of the current regime as a beginning and necessary step in democratization. If the previously mentioned Bendixen & Amandi poll is accurate, then the opposition groups continue to focus first on regime change even as the Cuban public believes that economic change is within reach but that political change is unlikely.

In Cuba, there has been an explosion of new activists and a dizzying proliferation of unauthorized NGOs. A directory prepared in 1996 listed more than 360 new organizations (Del Castillo et al. 1996), and hundreds more have organized since then (Álvarez García 2004; Jennische 2015). These groups include political parties, legal reform projects, human rights activists, independent groups of professionals, environmental activists, women's groups, advocates for racial equality, and artists of every sort. During the 1990s, the regime replaced arrest of dissidents and long prison sentences with a combination of harassment, sporadic mob violence, and short-term detention combined with periodic offers to let dissidents emigrate. The 1990s also saw selected dissident leaders given permission for short-term travel, allowing island groups to solicit support and organizational ties with counterparts in the United States, Europe, and Latin America.

As dissidents expanded their organizing to develop nationwide chapters and began to form coalitions of local and national groups, the government cracked down during the so-called Black Spring of 2003, returning to a process of show trials lacking due process, which were followed by long prison sentences for 75 principal leaders. An international outcry followed and in 2010, the Cuban government accepted mediation by the Catholic Church as a means for releasing the members of the "group of 75" who were still imprisoned (Amnesty International 2003; Human Rights Watch 2009). All but twelve chose to leave the country.

The Role of Outside Aid

Any dissident in Cuba can count on being fired from government employment and denied permits for independent work. Consequently, dissidents must rely on outside funding and resources. Salaries, supplies, equipment, and travel costs are generally paid by outside groups. A key debate surrounds whether the dissidents are persecuted patriots worthy of leadership in a process of reconciliation or simply opportunistic creatures of those who give them aid.

In 1996, the United States authorized USAID funds to support such groups (Muse 1996). Similar programs followed in the Department of State and the National Endowment for Democracy (a quasi-independent organization that acts as a conduit for US government funds). The names and funding of aid recipients in Cuba are not publically revealed, adding credibility to the Cuban government's insistence that all dissidents are secret agents of the United States. In fact, many groups operate on a shoestring budget supplied by like-minded individual supporters, relatives in the diaspora, and European political foundations.

Between the late 1990s and the present, a cross-section of dissident leaders traveled widely, establishing relationships with a variety of potential supporters without mediating their requests through exile organizations. Opening of Cuban travel has accelerated this trend. Essentially, island groups now have wider latitude to assess the position of outside groups and to align themselves according to their own preferences rather than immediate need. It appears that, for the first time, some moderate island personalities such as Manuel Cuesta Morua and Leonardo Calvo are widely known and rising in leadership of the overall movement, which speaks well for the evolution of reconciliation.

The taint of US funds and manipulation is a continuing impediment that needs to be addressed in the process of normalizing relations. If US funds are decreased or eliminated, then it would level the playing field between moderate and oppositionist influence. Moving from polarization to pluralism is a slow process, but the repeated attempts to form coalitions show good will. Former belligerents are becoming competitors, if not colleagues.

Divisions Within and Among Groups

In 2013, as he announced the formation of a new coalition of groups, including fourteen victims of the 2003 "Black Spring" round-up, Guillermo Fariñas admitted that "this marked the twelfth time he has participated in launching a 'new opposition' group" ("Top Cuban dissidents launch opposition coalition" 2013). Both the persistence and the failings of the dissident movement are embodied in his comment.

Coalitions seem to falter for two reasons. First, leadership struggles break up national groups and coalitions. The celebrated group Ladies in White is a prime example. Originally a group of women who conducted silent marches in protest against the imprisonment of their loved ones in the Black Spring, the Ladies in White is now composed of political activists, most without relatives in prison since the original political prisoners were released. Just a day before 17D, leadership struggles among the Ladies in White ended with an act of repudiation staged by one founder against another. Organizational control and distribution of scarce funds were blamed. Video recordings of the repudiation show it to be the equal of any government mob attacking democracy advocates (García de la Riva 2013; Yanes 2015). Clearly, in-group reconciliation is an issue, as is the relative stability of commitment to nonviolence. In the case of the Ladies in White, the evolution of organizational purpose is also important. As the group succeeded in negotiating the release of their relatives and leaders left the country, the group purposes were unclear even as their marches became well known and attracted international support and publicity.

A second limiting factor is the continual division between oppositionist and moderate strategies. As with exile groups, island dissidents make repeated attempts to focus on common goals but inevitably seem to come to cross-purposes. The most conservative groups are those receiving US funding. They have pledged to launch a public relations and lobbying campaign to maintain the US embargo. Hence, the expansion of the 17D process and the reconciliation of US and Cuban differences at the state level will be primarily opposed using US government money. The more moderate groups that support normalization were never willing to risk the taint of receiving US funds but, consequently, have fewer resources to advance their position in support of the Castro or Obama initiatives.

The Role of the Church

The only group within Cuba that has emerged with incremental accomplishments and expanding leverage with the state is the Catholic Church. The loss of Soviet aid in the 1990s literally left many Cubans "dispirited," and the Church had the organizational resources needed to promote values clarification as well as social services. The Church negotiated reopening of Caritas to deliver social services, such as disaster relief, daycare programs, and feeding programs for the elderly, at exactly the same time that the Cuban social system was in need of support following the loss of Soviet subsidy. They also published and widely circulated magazines from lay intellectuals (*Vitral* from 1994 to 2007; *Espacio Laical* and *Palabra Nueva* presently) that stimulate debate and provide a forum for citizens to reconcile their individual values, if not their political allegiance.

In 2010, the Ladies in White approached Cardinal Jaime Ortega, head of the Cuban Catholic Church, to attempt mediation with Raúl Castro. The process resulted in the release of a total of 126 prisoners, most of whom chose to accept an invitation from the Spanish government to leave the country together with their family members. Since then, weekly visits to the prisons are a regular part of the Church's pastoral work. Most recently, construction began on the first new church built since the triumph of the revolution, and the Church estimates that more than 80 percent of Cuban children born each year are now baptized in the Catholic Church (Ortega 2012). Oppositionists accuse the Church of accepting small concessions offered by President Castro rather than aggressively advocating for their brand of reconciliation—an accounting of past events and a democratic opening.

Conclusion

In the 1990s, Jonathan Fox introduced the idea of "thickening" as an analytic tool in evaluating social movements. Groups achieve their goals, or "thicken" their influence, by scaling-up their activities, taking advantage of political opportunities, and harnessing social energy through repeated iterations of interaction with internal and external actors (Fox 1996). This does seem to describe the process the Church has enacted, and it may serve as a model for achieving reconciliation.

The bedrock process of informal personal and small group reconciliation that has advanced within the diaspora and between diasporans and the island has been fostered among islanders within the Church. In a parallel move, one of the largest island organizations, the Unión Patriótica de Cuba (UNPACU), announced in 2015 that, having established a network of 5000 members, it will shift its emphasis from political organizing to providing social support (DeYoung 2015; Tamayo 2013). This is an encouraging sign.

Perhaps the best that can be said for attempts by island and exile dissidents to move toward a national reconciliation at the societal level is that things are slowly "thickening," with external recognition and support expanding and island and exile alliances being solidified on terms that favor island leadership. A cadre of younger intellectuals, organizers, and artists is gaining confidence and building social networks. It is a process still in its early stages.

Note

1. In 1999–2000, the Elián González incident involved a struggle between some elements of the Cuban American community and the governments of Cuba and the United States over custody of 5-year-old Elián González, who was the lone survivor of a group of Cuban rafters that included his mother. He was eventually returned to his father in Cuba. The incident made the Cuban American community seem unreasonable to many North Americans and caused some exile groups to revise their methods toward more conciliatory positions.

References

Ackerman, Holly. 1998. "Five Meanings of Cuba's Political Prisoners." *Cuban Studies Association Occasional Papers Series*. Paper 11. http://scholarly repository.miami.edu/cgi/viewcontent.cgi?article=1013&context=csa.

Ackerman, Holly, and Juan Clark. 1995. *The Cuban Balseros: Voyage of Uncertainty*. Miami: CANC.

Aguirre, Benigno E. 2002. "Social Control in Cuba." *Latin American Politics and Society* 44.2: 67–98.

Álvarez García, Alberto F. 2004. "Organizaciones de la sociedad civil cubana no reconocidas legalmente." FOCAL—Canadian Foundation for the Americas, July 29. http://www.offnews.info/downloads/Cuba_organizationsES-Focal.pdf.

Amnesty International. 2003. *Cuba, Massive Crackdown on Dissent*. London: Amnesty International.

Behar, Ruth, and Richard Blanco. 2015 "Bridges to/from Cuba." http://bridgestocuba.com/.

Bendixen & Amandi International. 2015. National Survey of Cubans Living in Cuba, April 2015. Miami, FL.

Bobes, Velia Cecilia. 2013. "Cuban Civil Society During and Beyond the Special Period." *International Journal of Cuban Studies* 5.2: 168–83.

Cancio Isla, Wilfredo. 2014. "Unos 29,700 cubanos recibieron visas para visitar EEUU este año." *Café Fuerte*, September 4. http://cafefuerte.com/cuba/17472-unos-29700-cubanos-recibieron-visas-para-visitar-eeuu-durante-el-2014/.

Cortés, Ondina America. 2013. "Communion in Diversity? Exploring a Practical Theology of Reconciliation Among Cuban Exiles." PhD diss., St. Thomas University.

CSG (Cuba Study Group). 2015a. "Our History." Accessed August 5. http://www.cubastudygroup.org/index.cfm/our-history.

———. 2015b. "The Reconciliation Project." Accessed August 5. http://www.cubastudygroup.org/index.cfm?p=Reconciliation.

"Declaración de San Juan: Primer encuentro nacional cubano." 2015. *CubaNet*, August 15. https://www.cubanet.org/noticias/primer-encuentro-nacional-cubano-declaracion-de-san-juan/.

DeYoung, Karen. 2015. "U.S. Outreach to Cuba Opens Fissures Among Dissidents." *The Washington Post*, February 2.

Del Castillo, Siro, Mercedes Grandío, Andrés Hernández, and Amaya Altuna de Sánchez. 1996. "Lista de organizaciones disidentes, opositoras y de derechos humanos." Comisión de Derechos Humanos, Partido Demócrata Cristiano de Cuba.

Dupuy, Pierre-Marie, and Luisa Vierucci. 2008. *NGOs in International Law: Efficiency in Flexibility?* Northampton, MA: Edward Elgar.

El Acuerdo. 1998. "El acuerdo por la democracia en Cuba." http://elacuerdo.org/.

Estado de SATS. 2014. *Documental Gusano*. Accessed January 29. https://www.youtube.com/watch?v=pW7i48fSCZ4.

eTN. 2013. "Number of U.S. visas issued to Cubans soars." *Global Travel Industry News*, June 30. http://www.eturbonews.com/35802/number-us-tourist-visas-issued-cubans-soars.

Fox, Jonathan. 1996. "How Does Civil Society Thicken? The Political Construction of Social Capital in Rural Mexico." *World Development* 24.6: 1089–103.

García de la Riva, Alejandrina. 2013. "Interview with Alejandrina García de la Riva." Interview by Julio Estorino for Human Rights Oral History Project (HROHP) of the Cuban Heritage Collection, University of Miami Libraries, Coral Gables, FL, September 26. http://merrick.library.miami.edu/cdm/compoundobject/collection/chc5312H/id/11/rec/1.

Grenier, Guillermo, and Hugh Gladwin. 2014. "2014 FIU Cuba Poll: How Cubans in Miami View Relations with Cuba." Cuban Research Institute,

Florida International University. https://cri.fiu.edu/research/cuba-poll/2014-fiu-cuba-poll.pdf.

Haq, Husna. 2013. "Cuba Lifts Travel Restrictions." *BBC*, January 16. http://www.bbc.com/travel/story/20130116-cuba-lifts-travel-restrictions.

Hernández, Rafael. 2003. *Looking at Cuba: Essays on Culture and Civil Society.* Gainesville: University Press of Florida.

Hijuelos, Oscar. 2008. "Heroes & Pioneers. Yoani Sánchez." *Time*, May 12. http://content.time.com/time/specials/2007/article/0,28804,1733748_1733756_1735878,00.html.

Human Rights Watch. 1999. *Cuba's Repressive Machinery: Human Rights Forty Years After the Revolution.* New York: HRW.

———. 2009. *New Castro Same Cuba: Political Prisoners in the Post-Fidel Era.* New York: HRW.

Jardines Chacón, Alexis. 2015. "Ideología y oposición en la era de Raúl Castro." Paper presented at the *10th Conference on Cuban and Cuban American Studies,* Cuban Research Institute, Florida International University, Miami, February 26. Author's notes.

Jennische, Erik. 2015. *Hay que quitarse la policía de la cabeza: Un reportaje sobre Cuba.* s.l.: Editorial Ertigo.

Morales, Emilio. 2014a. "Viajes Desde EEUU a Cuba Empujan Nuevo Escenario Turístico a los Pies de la Nueva Ley de Inversiones." The Havana Consulting Group, LLC, April 8.

———. 2014b. "Emigrados cubanos enviaron más de 3,500 millones de USD en remesas en especie en el año 2013." The Havana Consulting Group, LLC, June 24.

Muse, Robert L. 1996. "A Public International Law Critique of the Extraterritorial Jurisdiction of the Helms-Burton Act (Cuban Liberty and Democratic Solidarity (Libertad) Act of 1996." *The George Washington Journal of International Law and Economics,* 30.2/3 (January): 207–70.

Ortega, Jaime. 2012. *Church and Community: The Role of the Catholic Church in Cuba.* Cambridge: Harvard University, John F. Kennedy Center.

Ortega y Gasset. 2008. Premios Ortega and Gasset de Periodismo. Accessed August 25, 2015. http://www.premiosortegaygasset.com/ediciones-anteriores.html#.

Pérez-Stable, Marifeli. 2013. *Cuban National Reconciliation.* Miami: Latin American & Caribbean Center, Florida International University.

———. 2015. *The United States and Cuba after D17: The Impacts of Diplomatic and Financial Relations.* Miami: Florida International University, February 26. Author's notes.

Rodriguez, Andrea, and Peter Orsi. 2015. "Tourists Flocking to Cuba, Ahead of Expected U.S. Influx, Lifting Travel Ban Could Generate Billions of Dollars." *South Florida Sun-Sentinel,* March 24.

Sakahrov Prize. 2015. "Sakharov Prize for Freedom of Thought." Accessed August 25. http://www.europarl.europa.eu/atyourservice/en/20150201PVL00043/Prizes.

Sullivan, Mark. 2015. *Cuba: U.S. Restrictions on Travel and Remittances.* Congressional Research Service, April 10. https://www.fas.org/sgp/crs/row/RL31139.pdf.

Tamayo, Juan O. 2013. "Cuban Dissidents Change Approach." *Chicago Tribune*, October 10.

"Top Cuban Dissidents Launch Opposition Coalition." 2013. *Tengri News*, February 28. http://en.tengrinews.kz/politics_sub/Top-Cuban-dissidents-launch-opposition-coalition--17382/.

Whitefield, Mimi. 2015. "Poet Richard Blanco Speaks of the Sea and Hope in Cuba." *The Miami Herald*, August 14.

Yanes, Alex. 2015. "Damas de Blanco le dan mitin de repudio a Alejandrina Garcia." YouTube. Accessed January 26. https://www.youtube.com/watch?v=dq41SU4lo90.

Chapter 8

Cuban Exceptionalism

Marifeli Pérez-Stable

Like Americans, Cubans—on the island and in the diaspora—have laid claim to exceptionalism. Although American exceptionalism may be self-evident, Cuba's is not, at least to the outside world. Geographic location, the preeminence of Havana in colonial times, the cane-based economy when sugar meant wealth, the interest of European countries, and the special relationship with great powers like Spain and the United States engendered an uncommon national sense of self in Cuba. When Spain lost her prized colony, "more was lost in Cuba" took hold in the popular imagination of Spaniards as the response to any tale of woe. In 1959–1960, the Eisenhower administration seemed to be at a loss when trying to explain what had happened on the island. Like Spain, the United States had perceived the island to be "ever-faithful."

Well before the revolution, Cubans reveled in their achievements while, at the same time, believing that Cuba could become much more than it was. They felt the same way after 1959, although being exceptional turned into an irreparable tragedy for those who opposed the revolution, went into exile, suffered long imprisonment, and lost their lives for freedom's sake. Still, the revolution raised the hopes of millions on the island and around the world. Although today phrases such as "the Castro-led communist revolution" are commonplace, the historical record shows irrefutably that it was the Cuban revolution. In 1959, most adults in Cuba embraced the revolutionary government. That the leadership turned Cuba into a Soviet ally soured not only the

United States but also many Cubans who opposed what they saw as another dictatorship. Nearly six decades later, the hopes of long ago have largely been dashed, and Cuba is but the largest island in the Caribbean Sea.

The United States and Cuba have never had normal relations.[1] Great powers and their weaker neighbors usually don't. In the early twentieth century, the United States came of imperial age. Mexico, Cuba, and others in the Caribbean Basin faced a neighbor to the North bent on exercising unchallenged hegemony. Although diplomatic relations existed with all countries in the region, relations were not normal in the sense that Washington did not acknowledge the interests of Mexico, Cuba, and other countries.

It was only after 1940, for example, that the United States and Mexico normalized relations when both countries found common ground. Over the decades, the two governments learned to recognize each other's interests. In the late 1940s, under Cuba's last democratically elected president, Washington and Havana took baby steps in the right direction. Havana pursued its economic interests, and Washington—often begrudgingly—accepted Cuba's new assertiveness. In the 1950s, Fulgencio Batista's coup and then the revolution derailed a fledgling normalization that required more than diplomatic relations.

After December 17, 2014, when Barack Obama and Raúl Castro announced that the United States and Cuba would normalize relations, the two neighbors faced the challenge of establishing normal relations for the first time ever. The Cuban government and ordinary Cubans may well start taking baby steps away from exceptionalism. That, too, is part of normalization.

US Policy Regarding Cuba

After 1959, the United States espoused three distinct approaches regarding Cuba. Each reflected Washington's intentions at the time: destabilizing the revolutionary government (1960s); normalizing relations (1970s); and regime change (1980s and, especially, the 1990s until Obama's election in 2008).

- As the revolution radicalized between 1959 and 1960, the Eisenhower administration began to plan for an invasion. As American properties were nationalized, the president cancelled Cuba's sugar quota in the US market. Finally, before leaving office, the president broke diplomatic relations with Havana. After the failed Bay of Pigs invasion, John F. Kennedy took full responsibility and then authorized the CIA to carry out Operation Mongoose to promote a popular insurrection. After the 1962 Missile Crisis, the operation was canceled.

- A second approach crystallized in the 1970s amid détente with the Soviet Union, although it had already been considered by the Kennedy administration in the months before the president's assassination. JFK entertained the possibility of normalizing diplomatic and trade relations with "an independent communist state" in Cuba. Gerald Ford and Jimmy Carter applied Kennedy's template in the 1970s, but neither brought it to a fruitful conclusion.

- Under Reagan, the seeds of a third strategy were planted. While favoring regime change in Havana, the administration pursued ideological warfare, bringing a case against Cuba before the United Nations' Human Rights Commission in Geneva, supporting meetings of anti-communist intellectuals in Europe, and launching Radio Martí. This approach—supported by neoconservatives and the Cuban American community—did not fully mature until the 1990s. The Cuban Democracy Act (1992) and the Cuban Liberty and Democratic Solidarity (LIBERTAD) (1996)—better known as Helms-Burton—embodied the belief that, with the Soviet Union's downfall, a reinforced embargo would, at last, bring Havana to its knees.

For different reasons, none of these strategies worked. The third template, in particular, was built on the premise that Havana would negotiate with the United States about the backbone of its power: the one-party system and the violation of human rights. It failed to bring Cuban leaders to negotiate their demise.

On December 17, Obama jettisoned the post-Cold War template. Ford, Carter, and Clinton had favored a step-by-step process—first in secret, then in open dialogue—to normalize relations. In no small part due to Cuban actions, such as the interventions in Angola (1975) and Ethiopia (1978), and the shoot-down of two Brothers to the Rescue Cessna airplanes over international waters (1996), the piecemeal undertaking did not come to fruition (Domínguez 1989; LeoGrande and Kornbluh 2014; Pérez-Stable 2011).

Cubans/Cuban Americans and US Policy

At every opportunity over the past five decades, Cubans have played a part in US policy toward the island. In 1959–1960, the revolution's leaders chose a path of radicalization: centralizing power, eliminating capitalism, and turning toward the Soviet Union. Notwithstanding, the new government retained deep popular support. Still, not a few Cubans—including many who had joined the armed struggle against the Batista dictatorship—rejected the chosen path; the restoration of democracy had been the driver of their struggle in the 1950s. At home and later from the United States, the opposition saw communism as an affront to long-standing Cuban ideals of independence, sovereignty, and freedom. For their alliance with the United States, exiles were vilified while the international community never brought the same onus on Havana for its relationship with the Soviet Union. In pursuing a free Cuba, exiles and opponents on the island joined or supported the Bay of Pigs invasion and Operation Mongoose. Armed struggle in the Escambray Mountains in Central Cuba (1960–1966), however, was launched and sustained without meaningful US support.[2] In 1963, Marcelina Chacón, a peasant woman, said: "Two of my sons died fighting for Cuba's freedom, one with one idea and the other with another" (Fuentes 1970, p. 26). That is, one died fighting for the revolution and the other died for a democratic Cuba. Even if the revolution thrust Cuba into the Cold War, at heart, the conflict was Cuban.

In the 1970s, the exile community largely opposed the efforts of the Ford and Carter administrations to normalize relations with Havana. Still, a small minority looked favorably on the rapprochement in the making. Influenced by the ideals of the 1960s, some young Cubans who reached adulthood in the United States sympathized with the revolution and traveled to the island after the Carter administration lifted the travel ban.[3] Liberal exiles who had opposed the revolution for its communist turn also started to consider dialogue as an avenue toward a better Cuba. A few Cuban Catholics likewise took their cues from the Church on the island, which had condemned the embargo in 1969 (Secretariado General de los Obispos Católicos de Cuba 1995). In 1977, when Interests Sections were opened in Washington, DC and Havana, the two governments continued their negotiations. In 1978, after a dialogue with Cubans from the United States and other countries, Cuba agreed to free 3000 political prisoners and the United States granted entry to the prisoners and their families—approximately 15,000 people in all. In addition, Havana allowed Cubans abroad to visit their relatives on the island. In 1979, more than 100,000 did so from the United States alone. Whatever the politics involved, exiles were more than willing to overlook them for the sake of embracing their loved ones.

Carter's policies angered powerful sectors in Cuban Miami. In 1979, Jorge Mas Canosa (1939–1997) and other wealthy exiles began laying the groundwork for the Cuban American National Foundation (CANF). With Ronald Reagan in the White House, Mas Canosa crafted a strategy of influencing those in power. Between 1981 and 1997, their contributions to Republican and Democratic candidates who advocated a hardline toward Havana totaled $3.2 million (Kiger 1997, p. 2).[4] Radio Martí was CANF's most significant achievement. The foundation also cooperated with the Reagan administration in helping the Nicaraguan *contras* and Jonas Savimbi's guerrillas in Angola. At the end of the 1980s, CANF engineered a program to bring to the United States Cuban exiles who had been stranded for years in Panama, Costa Rica, Peru, and Spain. The Cuban Democracy Act and, especially, Helms-Burton codified the embargo, giving Congress the sole authority to end it. Neither would have been possible without Cuban Miami's political heft. Mas Canosa and the CANF showed the exile community the efficacy of lobbying in Washington, DC and of making campaign contributions. Politics—not terrorism against Cuban officials, Cubana Airline flights, and moderate exiles—was the way to go.

Cuban American Public Opinion

After Jewish Americans, Cuban Americans are the second most over-represented group in the US Congress, with three senators (two Republicans, one Democrat) and four representatives (three Republicans, one Democrat).[5] All oppose Obama's policy changes regarding Cuba. Although these elected officials may remain in Congress for a long time, Cuban Americans in Miami do not necessarily share their hardline stance. An overview of public opinion polls conducted over the past 25 years follows the changing—if sometimes conflicting—opinions (Florida International University Cuban Research Institute 2014).[6]

- Early in the 1990s, nearly 87 percent supported the embargo; by 2000, that support declined to 62.4 percent. In 2014, 52 percent opposed its continuation. At the same time, whatever their position on the embargo, growing majorities of Cuban Americans in Miami thought it worked badly or not at all.
- In 1993, almost 50 percent said US companies should be allowed to sell medicines to Havana; by 2000, more than 66 percent did.

Regarding US companies selling food to Cuba, just less than 25 percent approved at first, but by 2000 this proportion had more than doubled to 56.1 percent. Support for US companies selling food and medicine increased between 2004 and 2011 from 55 percent to 65 percent (food) and from 60 percent to 75 percent (medicine).

- In 1991, 40 percent favored a national dialogue that included the government, opposition, and exile; in 2000, nearly 52 percent did. By 2011, a solid 58 percent strongly or mostly supported such a dialogue.
- Although travel to the island and sending remittances to their families always garnered majority support, by 2014 an overwhelming 80 percent of Cubans in Miami favored them. Sixty-nine percent supported unrestricted travel to Cuba by all Americans.
- In 2014, 68 percent of Cubans living in Miami-Dade County favored diplomatic relations with Cuba. Three-quarters supported continuing or expanding trade with Cuba.
- In the 1990s, support for a US invasion of Cuba remained constant (63 percent versus 60 percent). By 2007, it had declined to 51 percent.
- Sixty-three percent of Cuban Miami believes Cuba should remain on the State Department's list of countries designated as sponsors of terrorism.
- Eighty-six percent support the Cuban Adjustment Act.

The most significant findings of these polls are the opinions of Cuban Americans younger than 44 years old and Cubans who arrived after 1998. Both groups—especially the latter—hold views on normalization of relations, trade, national dialogue, unrestricted travel for all Americans, and the embargo more intensely than older cohorts and earlier exiles on the same issues. Cuban Americans younger than 44 and post-1998 immigrants constitute a majority of Cuban Miami. Even though Obama in 2012 and then Charlie Crist in 2014 (defeated in Florida's gubernatorial race) narrowly won their vote, younger Cuban Americans and the newer immigrants do not yet account for a majority of Cuban American voters. Still, as life's course takes its toll and new generations reach adulthood, these trends are likely to continue. Similarly, as long as 20,000 or more Cubans arrive in the United States annually under the Cuban Adjustment Act and the immigration accords of the 1990s, recent arrivals—who have family members on the island—will tend to feed the same attitudes of moderation that older exiles still reject.

These findings also highlight the emotional pull among Cubans in Miami. While attitudes toward the embargo have shifted over time, even when support was at 87 percent, most Miami Cubans did not think it worked well or at all. Even when most probably knew that the likelihood of a US invasion was almost nil, a slight majority nonetheless supported the idea in the 2000s. Significant majorities today favor normalization of relations with Havana, yet two-thirds say that Cuba should remain on the list of countries sponsoring terrorism. Even though the Cuban Adjustment Act will at some point be rescinded, solid majorities favor it. There is, in fact, nothing particularly unusual about individuals holding contradictory views. That the emotional pull no longer determines attitudes toward changing US policy is more telling. All the same, a few days after December 17, 48 percent of Cuban Miami opposed Obama's announcement while 44 percent supported the president—even though in June 2014 most favored an inclusive national dialogue, normalization of relations with Havana, and continued or expanded trade (Caputo and Flechas 2014). After so long, when change finally came to Washington regarding Cuba, many Cuban Americans initially did not know what to make of it. Still, the 48–44 percent split suggests that 44 percent is the floor of support for Barack Obama's announcement that the normalization of relations with Cuba is now the goal of US policy. In March 2015, a second poll indicated 51 percent supported Obama's policy in Cuban Miami and 67 percent among Cubans living elsewhere in the United States did as well (Bendixen and Amandi International 2015).

Cuban Exceptionalism?

Normalization of relations will take a while. How could it not after nearly six decades? Now that the embassies are open in Washington and Havana, both governments will need to find a modus vivendi that establishes basic trust. The United States will continue to uphold human rights and the right of Cubans to live in a democracy. Cuba rightfully insists that the United States should lift the embargo, and the Obama Administration has been undermining it through federal regulations and executive actions. The power to lift the embargo in its entirety lies with Congress. Havana also wants back the territory occupied by the Guantánamo Naval Base and calls for the United States to pay Cuba US$181 million for the damages attributed to the embargo. Seeing each other as neighbors will certainly help, but no one should be surprised if old habits across the Florida Straits occasionally resurface.

Cuba has many challenges ahead, including the exceptionalism that sometimes comes across as self-entitlement. After 1959, Cuba became nearly as dependent on the Soviet Union as it had been on the United States. After the USSR disintegration, Cuba was left adrift amid a special period that saw the economy decline 35 percent. In the Communist Party Congress, Fidel Castro (1991) read a long list of all that Cuba lacked due to the precipitous fall in Soviet imports. No Cuban leader before him ever gave such a testimony of dependence. From Havana's perspective, the United States should compensate Cuba for the embargo. Who will pay the Cuban people for the decades of erratic economic policies followed by their own government? In the late 1990s, Cuba found a new ally in Hugo Chávez's Venezuela. Subsidized oil in exchange for medical personnel and military advisors once more placed politics at the center. Rarely did Havana pursue a viable economic program to lessen dependence.

At a meeting in January 2015 of the Community of Latin American and Caribbean States (CELAC), President Raúl Castro, after going through the list of Cuban demands for concessions from the United States, said: "It wouldn't be ethical, just or acceptable for Cuba to be asked to give anything in return." Given the power differentials between the United States and Cuba, there is some logic to Castro's statement. Yet, his words—reflective of a mindset among Cuban leaders—also highlight an inability to accept even the slightest responsibility for the long-standing enmity or for the economy's poor performance over decades. Of course, there will be give-and-take in the process of normalization between the two neighbors. Ethics, justice, and acceptability have little bearing on the matter, but realpolitik does.

Take two issues of interest to Cuba and to the United States. In 2014, Cuba enacted a new Law on Foreign Investment. The previous law in 1995 anticipated a hefty flow of investments that did not materialize, in part because investors considered the law to be unfavorable. The 2014 law cut taxes on profits in half (from 30 to 15 percent), eliminated the 25 percent tax on labor costs, and allowed 100 percent foreign ownership (see Pérez Villanueva, this volume). Investors in joint ventures receive an eight-year exemption from taxes on profits, real estate investments are permitted in private housing, and other changes offer investors greater incentives (Asamblea Nacional del Poder Popular 2014). Uncertainties, nonetheless, remain. Is the Cuban government fully committed to foreign investments? Is it willing to further loosen state control over the economy? Would it allow foreign investors to hire labor directly and pay workers in convertible pesos (Valdés-Fauli 2014)? These are no small matters. While the new law is a step in the right direction, the country's needs for foreign investments demand a more liberal environment. Whatever the economic imperatives, Havana prefers a slower tempo.

A short-term lens may advise Havana to go slow. Even so, rapid economic reforms—such as those advised by China and Vietnam—are in order. First, to attract the full influx of capital to promote growth and increase productivity, Cuba must modernize an infrastructure long in disrepair. Internet connectivity should similarly be upgraded to international standards. In June 2015, Google executives proposed a quick and massive expansion through Wi-Fi connections and cellular phones, and even offered to pay for it. Cuban officials reacted with skepticism (Gámez Torres 2015). Second, Cuba needs American tourists. Although the travel ban is still in effect, the number of non–Cuban American US residents traveling to Cuba since January 2015 under relaxed regulations increased by 35 percent. Havana, Trinidad, Varadero, and other tourist destinations are experiencing economic boomlets, but not most of Cuba. Third, Cuba needs access to the World Bank and the International Monetary Fund. Under Helms-Burton, US representatives at these institutions are compelled to deny Cuba's entry even if, for now, their votes would be pro forma. Cuba, in turn, has to ask to join them and, if it does, to submit documentation on the state of the economy to the World Bank and the IMF for their consideration. Normalization extends well beyond relations with the United States.

Raúl Castro is a cautious man who puts the highest premium on political stability and, hence, the slow tempo. There is, however, a counterargument. Unless the Cuban government accelerates economic reforms, ordinary men and women will not improve their lives. Those who are self-employed or host tourists and other foreigners in their homes, for example, have convertible pesos that get them into well-stocked stores. Most Cubans, however, earn in plain pesos and average approximately $20 a month. Despite the burdensome regulations and high taxes, the emerging private sector is doing well. It is also generating some employment, but only up to a point. If the self-employed hire five or more workers, then taxes increase. The state cares more about regulating the private sector than creating opportunities. And, yet, political stability may also suffer if the majority living with pesos sees their living standards decline as a privileged minority, especially the elite and their children, continues to do well without tangible benefits for most citizens.

In 2009, Cuba signed the International Covenant on Civil and Political Rights (United Nations Office of the High Commissioner for Human Rights 1966). In Latin America and the Caribbean, almost all countries have signed and ratified the Covenant. Cuba has yet to ask the National Assembly to ratify it. Upon signing, Havana appended the following Declaration:

> The Republic of Cuba hereby declares that it was the Revolution that enabled its people to enjoy the rights set out in the International Covenant on Civil and Political Rights. The economic, commercial and financial embargo imposed by the United States of America and its policy of hostility and aggression against Cuba constitute the most serious obstacle to the Cuban people's enjoyment of the rights set out in the Covenant. The rights protected under this Covenant are enshrined in the Constitution of the Republic and in national legislation. The State's policies and programmes guarantee the effective exercise and protection of these rights for all Cubans. With respect to the scope and implementation of some of the provisions of this international instrument, Cuba will make such reservations or interpretative declarations as it may deem appropriate.

This declaration—a standard option on UN documents—is, in part, outdated. The United States and Cuba are now neighbors. It also reflects what Havana calls different views on human rights and democracy, which remain a point of contention between the United States and Cuba.

The Covenant reaffirms "the equal and inalienable rights of all members of the human family" and that these rights derive from the "inherent dignity" of all people. Human rights are ours without distinction for "race, colour, sex, language, religion, political or other opinion, national or social origin, property, birth or other status." By the early 1970s, the Soviet Union and its Eastern European allies had signed and ratified the Convention. In 1982, Vietnam did the same, even while ostracized by the international community for its 1979 invasion of Cambodia. Like Cuba, China signed, but has not ratified, the Covenant. Cuba should ratify the International Covenant on Civil and Political Rights. While ratification carries the obligation to modify some laws to comply, the United Nations knows how to look the other way. Cuba, moreover, is extraordinarily adept at working with the Human

Rights Council. Ratification would signal Cuba's disposition to be treated under the same rules as most of countries in the Western Hemisphere. Asking for special treatment is another manifestation of exceptionalism.

Obama's change toward Cuba carries other consequences. Restoring diplomatic ties, chipping away at the embargo, and, perhaps, a presidential visit to the island may well allow the Western Hemisphere to have fully normal relations with Havana. Cuba will no longer be the exceptional focus of US enmity, and will no longer have an excuse for being the exception to the Hemisphere's commitment to democracy. The emerging context may likewise lead some countries—Brazil, Mexico, Panama, and Chile, for example—to exert discreet pressure on Havana regarding human rights. Why shouldn't Cubans be entitled to free speech, peaceful assembly, and free and competitive elections? The Cuban government long ago exhausted the legitimacy initially bestowed upon it by the revolution. Like young people everywhere, Cubans younger than 44 may also see the world differently than their parents and grandparents.

At some point, Cuba may well be a normal country. By this I mean one whose political leaders put human rights for all citizens and the improvement of living standards at the center of their mandate. Should it come to pass, such a government would start restoring the long-squashed hopes of ordinary Cubans. If at that point they choose to claim exceptionalism, I wouldn't object.

Notes

1. See Pérez-Stable (2011). In this book, I developed the idea that the United States and Cuba had never had normal relations. I originally introduced the idea in 1993 with *The Cuban Revolution: Origins, Course, and Legacy*, now in its third edition (2012).
2. Although the CIA air-dropped supplies, these were not meaningful enough to sustain the guerrillas until 1965. Havana, in fact, underscored the insurrection's homegrown character. Beginning in 1966, the military forcibly relocated thousands of peasants and their families to *pueblos cautivos* (captive towns) in Pinar del Río and other provinces. Escambray has never recovered its pre-1959 agricultural productivity.
3. Full disclosure: I was one of those young Cubans at the time and went to Cuba often between 1975 and 1991. After 24 years, I returned for the August 14, 2015 ceremonies at the American embassy and the ambassador's residence.
4. By current standards the sum is meager, but it wasn't then.

5. Senators are Ted Cruz (R-Texas), Bob Menendez (D-New Jersey), and Marco Rubio (R-Florida). House members are Carlos Curbelo, Mario Díaz-Balart, and Ileana Ros-Lehtinen, all South Florida Republicans, and New Jersey Democrat Albio Sires.

6. Links to earlier polls can also be found on this page.

References

Asamblea Nacional del Poder Popular. 2014. "Texto de la Ley No. 118 de la Inversión Extranjera." *Granma*, April 16. http://www.granma.cu/cuba/2014-04-16/asamblea-nacional-del-poder-popular.

Bendixen and Amandi International. 2015. *Special Session: Polling Results on Cuban Americans' Viewpoint on the Cuba Opportunity*. https://www.american.edu/clals/upload/Bendixen-Amandi-Poll-Cuban-Americans-Viewpoint-2015-03.pdf.

Caputo, Marc, and Joey Flechas. 2014. "Poll: Cuban-Americans Split on Obama's Cuba Policy." *Miami Herald*, December 19.

Castro Ruz, Fidel. 1991. "Discurso pronunciado por el Comandante en Jefe Fidel Castro Ruz, Primer Secretario del Comité Central del Partido Comunista de Cuba y Presidente de los Consejos de Estado y de Ministros, en la inauguración del IV Congreso del Partido Comunista de Cuba." Speech given at the Teatro "Heredia," Santiago de Cuba, October 10. http://www.cuba.cu/gobierno/discursos/1991/esp/f101091e.html.

Domínguez, Jorge I. 1989. *To Make the World Safe for Revolution*. Cambridge: Harvard University.

Florida International University Cuban Research Institute. 2014. "2014 FIU Cuba Poll: How Cuban Americans in Miami View U.S. Policies toward Cuba." https://cri.fiu.edu/research/cuba-poll/.

Fuentes, Norberto. 1970. *Cazabandido*. Montevideo: Libros de la Pupila.

Gámez Torres, Nora. 2015. "Sources: Google Offered Cuba Expansion of Web Access." *The Miami Herald*, July 2. http://www.miamiherald.com/news/nation-world/world/americas/cuba/article26186836.html.

Kiger, Patrick J. 1997. *The United States, Cuba and the Helms-Burton Act*. Washington, DC: Washington Center for Public Integrity.

LeoGrande, William M., and Peter Kornbluh. 2014. *Back Channel to Cuba: The Hidden History of Negotiations between Washington and Havana*. Chapel Hill: University of North Carolina.

Pérez-Stable, Marifeli. 2011. *The United States and Cuba: Intimate Enemies*. New York: Routledge.

———. 2012. *The Cuban Revolution: Origins, Course, and Legacy*, 3rd edn. New York: Oxford University.

Secretariado General de los Obispos Católicos de Cuba. 1995. *La voz de la Iglesia en Cuba: 100 documentos episcopales*. México, DF: Obra Nacional de la Buena Prensa.

United Nations Office of the High Commissioner for Human Rights. 1966. "International Covenant on Civil and Political Rights." Adopted and opened for signature, ratification, and accession by General Assembly resolution 2200 (XXI) of December 16 and entered into force on March 23, 1976. http://www.ohchr.org/en/professionalinterest/pages/ccpr.aspx.

Valdés-Fauli, Raúl J. 2014. "What the New Foreign Investment Law Means." *Law360*, August 11. http://www.foxrothschild.com/raul-j-valdes-fauli/publications/what-the-new-cuban-foreign-investment-law-means/.

Chapter 9

How Will US-Cuban Normalization Affect Economic Policy in Cuba?

Emily Morris

The US-Cuban rapprochement announced on December 17, 2014 will have profound effects on the Cuban economy and, therefore, on economic policy. To begin to understand how policy is likely to change and the probable timing and sequence of any adjustments, we first need to look at the direct economic effects of measures introduced so far and those that are likely to follow in the near future. This provides some indications concerning the more far-reaching repercussions of the change in bilateral relations for the Cuban economy and economic policy over the longer term.

Direct Economic Effects of Measures So Far

In economic terms, the most significant normalization measures announced to date will increase the number of US citizens "licensed" to travel to Cuba, allow them to buy a limited amount of goods to bring home (with credit cards making the purchases more convenient), permit some two-way trade between the US and Cuban private sectors, and enable Cuba to improve its international telecommunications links. Some approximate calculations can indicate how strong the direct effect on the economy is likely to be in the short run, providing some pointers to the likely short-term impact on economic policy.

It is relatively easy to estimate the increase in Cuban earnings from international travel. Before the changes, the number of US visitors traveling on licenses—excluding around 400,000 Cuban Americans and those traveling illegally through third countries—was approximately 100,000 per year, and travel operators suggest that this number could increase quickly by as much as five-fold. Reports to date suggest a 50 percent increase in US visitors in the first half of 2015, with the pace of growth accelerating. If we make the generous assumption that the number trebles in the first full year (and that the number of Cuban American visitors and US visitors traveling illegally stays constant), Cuba would receive an extra 200,000 visitors in 2015. The total number of international visitors in 2014 was 3 million, so this would increase total international arrivals by around seven percent. If we make the further assumption that the average spending per US visitor (including their purchases of rum and cigars) is the same as the overall average spending per existing visitor (ONEI 2015),[1] then this would bring in additional gross foreign exchange earnings of approximately US$170 million. To put that in broad context, total Cuban earnings from exports of goods and services in 2014 were around US$17.5 billion.[2] Therefore, the additional US visitors would boost Cuban foreign exchange earnings by something in the order of one percent. Although there is no consensus on how to measure Cuban gross domestic product (GDP) in US dollar terms, a plausible estimate based on World Bank data[3] would suggest that this amount of stimulus would represent roughly 0.2 percent of the estimated GDP in 2015: a perceptible but hardly transformative boost.

In the near term, the legalization of US-Cuba trade involving the Cuban private sector (both the export of goods from the US to Cuban nonstate businesses and US imports of goods and services from the Cuban nonstate producers)[4] is likely to have a similarly modest direct impact on Cuban GDP for three reasons. The first is that this type of activity has already been flourishing, albeit mostly in the informal economy.[5] Second, residual US restrictions and requirements continue to create legal, logistical, and payment obstacles for Cuban private sector business hoping to export to the United States, so that only a few niche activities might be expected to turn a profit. And third, the existing small private sector in Cuba is focused on the internal export market—mainly tourism and associated activities—rather than on goods or services that could contribute to cross-border trade. The most important exception in terms of value in the short term might be the sale of Cuban art in the US market. These sales were already permitted before December 17, but greater communication between the two countries might stimulate more sales. There also appears to be strong potential for the development of trade in information technology (IT) services, judging by the speed with which Cuba's new army of programmers (many created by recent state investment in computer education, including the creation of a new IT university, but also plenty of self-taught young computer enthusiasts) have jumped at the opportunity to develop business. In line with the pattern of new IT business, the revenue stream from the successful Cuban IT entrepreneurs is likely to be small in the first year, although it could well pick up over time to reach significant amounts.

Although the short-term impact on the economy as a whole might be modest, for some private individuals and businesses in Cuba the changes will greatly increase earnings, and to the extent they improve the availability of equipment and spare parts for nonstate enterprises they could result in an increase in productivity and in the pace of the sector's expansion.

Taking into account these effects, a plausible estimate of the impact of the initial changes on Cuban national income in the short term would therefore be a boost of approximately one percentage point of GDP. On its own, this might not seem to be enough to radically improve Cuban lives, but it is enough to be felt by individuals and to provide a noticeable upturn in fiscal revenue. The changes will also raise new policy challenges by exacerbating inequality within Cuba, because the first to enjoy the benefit will be those with private (registered or informal) businesses, mainly those catering to the new visitors. Among this group are the most successful private sector operators, who are already relatively privileged in terms of real incomes in Cuba.

Next Moves on US Economic Sanctions

There seems to be little doubt that the process of normalization of economic relations will continue, and the only uncertainty now is the pace of change. The initial moves have served to create a momentum for change that seems to picking up strength. By opening up the debate and relaxing travel restrictions, the US government has fostered the rapid development of networks between US-Cuban families, businesses, research institutes, cultural organizations, and policy institutes, and each of these groups is improving mutual understanding and opening up new possibilities for engagement, ensuring an increasing rate of growth in bilateral economic—as well as "people-to-people" and official institutional—relations. With each week that passes, the foundations of US sanctions against Cuba seem to become shakier. In January 2015, it appeared that President Obama's scope for making any further moves toward liberalizing bilateral economic relations were restricted by the impossibility of pushing through the legislation required through a Republican-dominated US Congress, but the swift turnaround in public and business opinion since then has raised the possibility that the process of normalization might be more rapid than initially expected. However, with a host of legal obstacles remaining and opponents still determined to resist, a complete removal of economic sanctions in the near future remains unlikely.

The next stages will include measures to improve telecommunications links and facilities for processing financial transactions and further moves to ease restrictions on US travel, direct flights, and shipping routes. Discussions on these are already underway, and the first results are emerging. Further significant changes to come are the restoration of Cuban access to international capital markets and, finally, access to direct trade with the United States. Given the legal complexities surrounding US obstacles to Cuba's access to finance and trade, it seems likely that dismantling the restrictions on trade and finance will be the hardest. The US president seems to be preparing to use his executive powers to introduce specific exceptions, which in turn could set the scene for subsequent step-by-step progress before the restrictions are fully removed. Although setbacks are likely and the pace of change is contingent on the outcome of the 2016 presidential and congressional elections, the possibility of a reversal of the process of normalization is becoming increasingly remote as the expectations of citizens, officials, and business actors adjust to the trajectory of normalization.

Cuba's Policy Response

These developments—both the immediate impact of the removal of the limited range of obstructions to bilateral economic relations so far and the expectation that a new process toward eventual normalization is underway—present new economic policy challenges for the Cuban government. To understand the impact on Cuban economic policy of the moves so far, it is necessary to examine how they interact with existing policy shifts. These include important turning points in fiscal and monetary policies that were already underway before December

2014, as well as the moves toward expansion of the private sector and rationalization of the state sector that have been widely interpreted as a process of economic "transition to capitalism."

The fiscal and monetary policy turning points have received little attention from external commentators, whose focus has persistently remained on the question of whether Cuba is making adequate progress in its process of "transition." However, they provide important indications of the nature of the broader policy approach and will have a more direct impact on economic performance in the short term to medium term than "transition" policies. Regarding fiscal policy, the modest boost to GDP resulting from the lifting of some US restrictions came at the same time as a shift from a very cautious and restrictive approach to a markedly more expansive stance. The new fiscal stance was announced in December 2014, when the Cuban National Assembly's Economic Commission reviewed the year's results and—independently of the developments in the secret negotiations—decided to move decisively away from the retrenchment of the past five years to an expansionary phase.[6] The planned fiscal deficit for 2015 was set at 6.1 percent of GDP, a clear departure from the previous two decades, when the average deficit was 3.1 percent of GDP. An important contributor to the expansionary stance was a budgeted 29 percent increase in public investment. The fiscal deficit is to be financed through the issuance of government bonds, a new policy departure since 2013 that replaces the former practice of monetizing the deficit.

There is insufficient published data to be able to pinpoint exactly how the fiscal stimulus and lifting of restrictions on US travel and trade have been transmitted to national income growth, but the reported acceleration of real GDP growth—from 1.3 percent in 2014 to 4.7 percent year in the first half of 2015—owed more to the Cuban fiscal stimulus than to the US moves. Nonetheless, the vigor of the fiscal stimulus can only be enhanced by the extra lift to government revenue arising from the relaxation of sanctions so far. This will come from sales tax revenue from sales in state-owned stores, income tax receipts from nonstate businesses, and net profits (and therefore taxes and dividends) from state enterprises. Given Cuba's record of disciplined adherence to fiscal deficit targets,[7] it seems probable that higher tax receipts will feed through to a similar increase in public spending.

Any additional revenue could also contribute to a process of adjustment of basic salaries, another policy shift that was already underway. Average nominal state salaries were raised by 24 percent in 2014

(ONEI 2014, p. 13), with state employees in public health, sugar, mining, and scientific research having received increases of more than 40 percent over the past two years. This follows two and a half decades of severe pay restraint—which seems to have been tolerated, at least in part, because it has been suffered most acutely by public servants and the older generation, the social sectors that have tended to be the least critical of government policy to date. The relaxation of US sanctions has improved the Cuban government's ability to lift the pay and benefits of state employees by boosting tax revenue at the same time as it has made such an adjustment more necessary by adding to income inequality in which state employees and pensioners have been the losers. An approximate calculation can serve to obtain an idea of the modest magnitude of the effect of the changes: if 25 percent of the estimated US$400 million additional foreign exchange (from the increase in US visitors plus the other changes, using the most generous assumptions) were to find its way to government coffers (lifting revenue by US$100 million), and if that amount were shared equally between approximately 4 million state employees and 2 million pensioners, then it could finance an increase in annual income of approximately US$17 per person. The complexities of Cuba's price system make it impossible to give a meaningful figure for how much of an increase this might be in percentage terms but, like the boost to GDP, it would seem to be perceptible but not dramatic.[8]

Even with these pay increases, income inequality will remain high and the real disposable income of public sector workers will remain very low. The removal of the "bifurcation" (Ritter 1995) of incomes, and of the economy more broadly, will only be possible when a long-awaited reform of the exchange rate system is finally introduced. By easing the foreign exchange constraint, progress toward normalization of US-Cuban relations may facilitate this crucial reform.

The dual currency system, in place since the early 1990s, has entrenched extreme distortions in the Cuban economy, obstructing integration between the domestic and external sectors and causing severe damage to economic efficiency and incentives, as well as widening the gap between the haves and have-nots. Although the removal of US sanctions is a necessary condition for Cuba's opening to the international market to reach its potential, the process will not be complete without the reform of the currency system.

Neither of Cuba's two exchange rates—the "official" rate or the "Cadeca" rate—provides the price signals required to incentivize efficient economic decision-making. The "official" rate, which values the

Cuban peso (CUP) at par with the convertible peso (CUC, which is, in turn, valued at par with the US dollar), hugely overvalues the CUP. This is the rate applied to Cuban state enterprises. The overvaluation of the CUP makes it impossible for exporters to be competitive while flattering the reported profitability of importers. Consequently, foreign exchange (required by exporters to pay for inputs and by importers to make purchases) has to be allocated by the central planning authorities rather than by price. A more realistic official exchange rate would allow enterprises to allocate their own resources and thus make meaningful decentralization of enterprise decision-making possible.

However, the Cadeca rate of CUP24:CUC1 undervalues the Cuban peso. This rate was originally used for personal transactions, which meant that it also applied to the informal sector, and now it is the rate available to the new private sector. The undervaluation of the CUP at the Cadeca rate means that a person working in the private sector who earns just over CUC 1 per day (that is, US$1, the absolute poverty threshold as measured by the World Bank) can match the purchasing power of the average monthly state sector salary (CUP 584 in 2014). Thanks to Cuban citizens' entitlements to state subsidies for basic goods, the real purchasing power of the average monthly wage is far higher than the paltry US$24 for which it can be exchanged at the Cadeca rate, but the ability of nonstate workers to earn multiples of the nominal state salary even at very low levels of productivity inevitably generates deeply pernicious effects on incentives in the state sector and productivity in the private sector.

The economic damage caused by exchange rate distortions grows with time, but the urgent need for reform has been set against the authorities' fear of the economic upheaval that adjustment will cause. Exchange rate unification has been an official policy objective for two decades now. It was clearly restated as one of the five-year "guidelines" for policy approved in April 2011 (PCC 2011, p. 15), and plans for the day of the change (referred to as "*día cero*") were published in March 2014 by the Ministerio de Finanzas y Precios. A nationwide process of preparation and training ensued, and the intention was to make the change by the end of 2014. However, it seems that the more the planners studied the disruptive impact of unification on the price system and threat to foreign exchange reserves, the further they have postponed *día cero*. In the meantime, there has been an ongoing process of realigning the "official" exchange rate used by state enterprises. Few details of this process have been published, but the available information suggests that within enterprises, new accounts are being prepared using more realistic exchange rates of approximately CUP10:US$1. This is happening alongside a general move toward the decentralization of economic management and increase in enterprise autonomy and management accountability.

The Cuban process of gradual transformation, in which state enterprises are converting from organs of a centrally planned economic system to more autonomous enterprises (required to generate profits or face takeover or bankruptcy) while the exchange rate and relative prices are being adjusted toward their market level, represents profound changes in the system of economic management. The approach to reform is in line with a pattern that has been established since the crisis of the early 1990s: first a period of analysis, then pilot programs to test new proposals, review, adjustment, and, finally, rollout, followed by more review and adjustment.[9] This super-caution is designed to minimize risk, but the gradualism has costs. In the case of the exchange rate, every month of delay further entrenches distortions and therefore adds to the cost of adjustment as economic actors make decisions based on existing relative prices.

All the efforts by the Cuban authorities to prepare for exchange rate reform cannot prevent some amount of monetary instability as relative prices and wages (both market and state-controlled) adjust, creating a major coordination challenge and risks of inflation; in the absence of sufficient international foreign currency reserves or access to support from the IMF as "lender of last resort," a resultant loss of confidence in the currency could create the danger of an inflation/depreciation spiral. Given the degree of risk-aversion shown by Cuban planners, it is still possible that the move will be postponed further. In this context, the boost to Cuba's foreign exchange reserves that results from the additional earnings from US changes could make a positive contribution to the process by mitigating the risk of a currency crisis. And to the extent that the easing of US sanctions might contribute to bringing the currency reform forward, it thus might provide a crucial contribution to Cuba's economic opening. This effect would be greatly strengthened if Cuba were to regain access to funding from international financial institutions (IFIs), including the World Bank and International Monetary Fund, and US investors were permitted to enter the Cuban market. These changes would also have a major impact on the growth potential of Cuba's investment-starved economy, not only by directly providing additional financing for investment but also by reducing the financial risk of doing business with Cuba and therefore boosting investor confidence and cutting the price (and improving the availability of) other sources of international finance.

Longer-Term Repercussions and Reverberations

If the moves toward normalization of US-Cuban relations contribute to currency reform, then they will have profound indirect economic repercussions for the longer term. Exchange rate unification will at last allow the integration of Cuba's two economies: the domestic one, which has operated in Cuban pesos (CUP), and the external one, which operates in foreign currency or convertible pesos (CUC). By doing so, it will increase the integration of Cuba's economy as a whole into the global economy. This, in turn, would provide a spur to the economy's efficiency and dynamism and create the conditions for the decentralization of economic management. In this sense, it will arguably be a greater step toward the transformation of economic decision-making from the state planning system to the market than the much-vaunted opening of the formal nonstate sector, which still accounts for only 25 percent of national employment.

The other major change for the longer term concerns expectations. Since December 2014, we have already seen a startling pace of change in perceptions, not only in the United States and Cuba, as discussed, but also in third countries. US-Cuban networks have already been crafting new initiatives at an impressive pace. New ideas for tours, flights, telecoms contracts, TV shows, and cooperation in cultural, sporting, research, and conservation activities are being reported daily, and this process seems set to accelerate. For Cuban policymakers, the growth of networks and renewed third-country business interest represent new policy challenges. Each new opening will invigorate innovation within Cuba in all areas, including the already-enlivened economic policy debates.

Until the December 17 announcement, potential private investors from third countries had been deterred by both the lack of movement on US sanctions and threat of penalties for violating them—particularly international banks and multinationals with important US interests. The change in the US posture has already begun to weaken the deterrent, as evidenced by an increase in business interest. Although approval by the US Congress is needed to remove the most important measures that affect third-country businesses (particularly the 1996 Cuban Liberty and Democratic Solidarity [Libertad] Act, known as Helms–Burton), the removal of Cuba from the US list of

"State Sponsors of Terrorism" and from the blacklist for human trafficking so far in 2015 serve as encouragement to potential economic partners. The fact that US legislation continues to block their US rivals provides an added incentive for third-country businesses to move quickly to gain a foothold on the island while they can. Fearing a return to overdependence on the United States, the Cuban government is also keen to strengthen ties with other countries and has already stepped up its effort to attract potential investors. This, in turn, is giving US businesses greater impetus to lobby for legislation to remove obstacles to their participation in Cuban markets. Cuba's pointed insistence that there will be no discrimination against US investors seems designed to encourage this.

The initiation of normalization of US-Cuban relations has therefore ignited processes that are likely to accelerate. Cuba's reform process will continue to widen the opening to international markets, particularly if the obstacle created by the dual currency system is removed. Its system of economic management will need to adapt and become more flexible in response to the direct impact of recent changes and subsequent indirect effects on networks and expectations. Meanwhile, the contradictions between a policy of moving toward diplomatic normalization and the US laws that continue to block free travel, bilateral trade, US investment, and financial flows to Cuba are likely to become increasingly untenable.

Transition?

The discussion of the impact of normalization on Cuban policy among external commentators has centered on the question of whether it will precipitate "transition." However, the economic meaning of the term has altered since the initial certainties of the period immediately following the fall of the Berlin Wall, as economists have sought to understand the difficulties experienced by some of the postcommunist countries of Eastern Europe and acknowledge the range of outcomes that are possible for formerly state-controlled economies.[10] In light of these considerations, the term "transition" and its application to the case of Cuba are arguably uninformative. The idea of a "market" economy versus a "state" one was always a caricature: the state clearly plays a crucial role in all capitalist economies (unless failed states are included in the definition), and markets have always existed within communist economies, including Cuba.

To understand Cuban economic policy, it is more useful to examine the specific drivers of change and responses than to try to measure "progress on transition." The demise of the Soviet bloc forced Cuba's economic system to change fundamentally, and it has been evolving constantly since then. The reform process instigated by Raúl Castro has been part of this process, and normalization of relations with the United States will herald a new phase of its ongoing process of transformation. This will make the Cuban economy more open and probably more prosperous while also creating major challenges in terms of maintaining monetary stability and responding to growing inequality and comprehensive institutional adjustment. The most likely outcome is that Cuba will remain a mixed economy with its own unique features—including, for the foreseeable future, a comparatively large and interventionist, but often inefficient and unusually effective, state.

Notes

1. ONEI (2015) shows 2014 gross earnings of US$2.55 million from 3 million international tourists, or an average of US$848 per person.
2. Author's estimate, based on ONEI (2015) data for goods export earnings in 2014 and estimate of services earnings, assuming a reduction from the *Anuario Estadístico de Cuba 2013* (ONEI 2014) figure of US$13 billion.
3. Using the World Bank (2015) estimate of the US dollar value of Cuba's GDP for 2013 (the latest available) adjusted for US inflation and real Cuban GDP growth to 2014.
4. Amendments to the Cuban Assets Control Regulations (CACR) and Export Administration Regulations (EAR) introduced by the US Department of the Treasury and the US Department of Commerce published on January 16, 2015 included the US export of materials, tools, equipment, and supplies to the Cuban nonstate sector and "the commercial importation into the United States of certain goods and services produced by independent Cuban entrepreneurs" (http://www.state.gov/e/eb/tfs/spi/cuba/).
5. Informal trade and financial flows between Cuban Americans and their families on the island have been expanding since restrictions on travel and remittances were lifted in 2009. Along with informal flows from Europe and elsewhere, they have been playing an important part in providing start-up capital and equipment to establish new enterprises on the island.
6. The targets approved in the December National Assembly meeting (Lee et al. 2014, p. 3) were in line with the draft budget approved by the Council of Ministers at the end of November. The fiscal

policy shift therefore predates the announcement of the US-Cuba agreement. Fiscal policy had been tight since the mid 1990s, when the stabilization program launched in 1994 to halt the sharp decline in the value of money (reflected in black market prices and exchange rates) in the wake of the collapse of the Soviet bloc. From 1995 to 2007, the fiscal deficit averaged less than three percent of GDP. When Raúl Castro first took over, he faced the task of renewed fiscal adjustment in the wake of a collapse in the nickel price and the costs of three hurricanes that widened the deficit to 6.7 percent of GDP in 2008. This, combined with state retrenchment linked to economic reform, kept the average increase in real government consumption to just 0.4 percent between 2010 and 2014, and the average deficit restricted to just 2.2 percent of GDP.

7. Apart from the noted exceptional circumstances of 2008.
8. The dual currency system and state control of prices for basic goods and services make it impossible to calculate the percentage increase in real terms. State sector wages averaged 584 Cuban pesos (CUP) per month in 2014, or CUP 7008 per year (ONEI 2015), which at the "official" exchange rate (currently being phased out) converts to US$7008. US$21 would represent a 0.3 percent increase. At the "unofficial," but legal, Cadeca rate used for nonstate transactions, the same amount would be just US$280, so the extra US$21 would represent a more significant increase of 7.5 percent. The real value of the Cuban salary is somewhere in between, because many basic goods and services are sold in CUP at highly subsidized prices. After currency unification and a comprehensive price reform that is likely to ensue, it will start to become easier to evaluate real relative incomes.
9. A feature of Cuban policymaking described more fully in Morris (2014).
10. Roland (2000), Campos and Campos and Corricelli (2002), and the World Bank (2002) show the development of economists' understanding of the transition process, which is clearly evident in the annual *Transition Report* published by the European Bank for Reconstruction and Development (EBRD) during the 1990s. Between the 1992 and 1999 EBRD reports, economists were chastened by the unexpectedly poor performance of some transition economies and high social costs. The initial optimism (when "progress in transition" was characterized as simply a process of replacing state control with free markets) was replaced by greater emphasis on the importance of state institutions and governance for the development of efficient markets and adequate social protection.

References

Campos, Nauro F., and Fabrizio Coricelli. 2002. "Growth in Transition: What We Know, What We Don't, and What We Should." *Journal of Economic Literature* 40.3: 793–836.

EBRD (European Bank for Reconstruction and Development). 1995. "Transition Report 1995."
———. 1999. "Transition Report 1999."
Lee, Susana, Lissy Rodríguez Guerrero, and O. Fonticoba Gener. 2014. "Presupuesto del Estado con los pies en la tierra." *Granma*, December 20. http://www.granma.cu/impreso/2014-12-20.
Ministerio de Finanzas y Precios. 2014. *Gaceta Oficial No. 12 Extraordinaria de 6 de marzo de 2014*, Resolución No. 19/2014, Resolución No. 20/2014. http://www.cubadebate.cu/wp-content/uploads/2016/01/unificacion-gaceta-marzo-2014.pdf.
Morris, Emily. 2014. "Unexpected Cuba." *New Left Review* 88: 5–45.
ONEI (Oficina Nacional de Estadísticas e Información). 2014. *Anuario Estadístico de Cuba 2013*. Havana, Cuba. http://www.one.cu/aec2013.htm.
———. 2015. *Anuario Estadístico de Cuba 2014*. Havana, Cuba. http://www.one.cu/aec2014.htm.
PCC (Partido Comunista de Cuba). 2011. *VI Congreso del Partido Comunista de Cuba: Lineamientos de la política económica y social del partido y la revolución*. Lineamiento 55. http://www.cubadebate.cu/wp-content/uploads/2011/05/folleto-lineamientos-vi-cong.pdf.
Ritter, Archibald. 1995. "The Dual Currency Bifurcation of Cuba's Economy in the 1990s: Causes, Consequences and Cures." *CEPAL Review* 57: 113–31.
Roland, Gérard. 2000. *Transition and Economics: Politics, Markets, and Firms*. London: MIT Press.
World Bank. 2002. *Transition—The First Ten Years: Special Report*. Washington, DC: The World Bank. http://siteresources.worldbank.org/ECAEXT/Resources/complete.pdf.
———. 2015. "World Development Indicators." Accessed September 11. http://databank.worldbank.org/data/.

Chapter 10

Cuban Economic Reforms and Rapprochement with the United States: A Comparative Perspective

Ricardo Torres

Introduction

It is widely acknowledged that by the second half of the nineteenth century, the United States—by then an emerging industrial power—had become Cuba's main trading partner and a critical driver of its economy. Following US intervention on the island in 1898, and during the founding of the Cuban republic, wide-reaching new laws codified US influence[1] and extended its reach further into Cuba's political, military, and cultural sectors. The 1959 Revolution, within a matter of years, destroyed a relationship that, although long-standing and close, had always been asymmetric. In many respects, Cuban economic development had languished because of the extensive commercial and investment privileges granted to large US corporations in the domestic Cuban market.

After more than a half-century of estrangement, the two countries have now entered into a period of cautious rapprochement. This chapter analyzes the impact of US economic sanctions on Cuba over the past five decades, with a particular focus on how these sanctions have intersected with and exacerbated the weaknesses in Cuba's own centralized planning model. It also examines Cuba's current economic reform process through a comparative study of experiences in other countries, establishing parallels and divergences with similar cases in China and Vietnam. The final section addresses details of the Cuban economic reform process and considers how the recent rapprochement with the United States may affect Cuba.

Central Planning Problems in Light of US Sanctions

US economic sanctions have been highly controversial both within and outside of Cuba. In the United States, opponents have objected to them for various reasons since their enactment, and the opposition case has been significantly strengthened since the mid 1990s. Virtually no sovereign state defends the sanctions, much less does anything to support them directly. In Latin America, they became a constant source of contention, exacerbating headaches for US policymakers faced with an already beleaguered US policy toward the region. It was the US sanctions and policy of isolating Cuba, for example, that until the December 2014 announcement of rapprochement had threatened to completely derail the 2015 Summit of the Americas in Panama, a meeting considered essential to US diplomatic standing in the region.

Without a doubt, the Cuban people[2] are the ones who have suffered the most from the sanctions due to their harsh effects on the island's economy. The sanctions have also accentuated many of the weaknesses in Cuba's system of central planning. In light of the fact that the Cuban model is now undergoing its biggest transformation in half a century and the sanctions regime appears to be nearing an end, it seems fitting to emphasize precisely how the embargo has interacted with the shortcomings in Cuba's economic model.

Literature on centrally planned economies (CPEs) highlights particular characteristics that have essentially developed into stylized facts. These characteristics are of great interest considering the diverse nature of the countries that have used central planning at some point or another during contemporary history. One such characteristic associated with CPEs is their relatively low level of openness to foreign trade, even when the volume of trade is controlled for the size of the economy (Weill 2008). In relative terms, trade has been less important for centrally planned economies, an especially noteworthy fact given the rapid growth of international trade after World War II (Fouquin et al. 2012). In Cuba's case, trade has remained well below expectations given the size and level of development of the island's economy. Until 1989, the ratio between its trade and gross domestic product (GDP) grew because of increased imports, but exports remained stagnant

(Figueras 1999). The subsequent decades continued this general trend with few modifications, although the volume of Cuba's trade with the rest of the world increased.

After the United States imposed punitive sanctions on Cuba, the island's trend toward high levels of imports worsened at the same time that international transactions became more costly. This was especially true in the case of Cuba's relations with the West, which had developed in keeping with the usual practices of international trade. Cuban trade was dependent on the availability of foreign currency for carrying out transactions and, consequently, on the ability to access abundant credit. Credit was, in turn, linked to the tone of political relationships with Western countries that were always sensitive to US pressure when choosing allies. For example, key trading partners like Canada cut ties to Cuba after the Cuban military intervened in the war in Angola during the mid-1970s.

In the 1980s, the debt crisis and the tightening of sanctions under the Reagan administration curtailed Cuban access to credit and prompted the island to declare an indefinite moratorium on payments. The move further damaged Cuba's international standing, which in turn negatively impacted its economic performance over the ensuing few years. As an open economy, Cuba was highly susceptible to changes in the external environment, and plummeting trade with the Western bloc limited its growth. In addition, Western countries could obtain products and equipment that were unavailable to their socialist counterparts, the lack of which hindered Cuba's industrial capacity. The effects of these developments of decades ago continue to be felt to the present day, as evidenced by Cuba's persistent difficulties in accessing credit for trade and development and by the paltry financial support that the island has received from Official Development Assistance (ODA).

For socialist countries in the 1980s, these economic barriers made them more dependent on trade even as they were heading toward collapse and suffering through their worst periods of economic crisis. Note that during the mid to late 1980s, several states, including the Soviet Union, had begun to relax certain economic controls to increase their share of international markets. Various Eastern European countries already maintained strong trade ties with developed capitalist countries,[3] and Vietnam enacted a radical economic reform in 1986. All of this better-positioned these countries to withstand the collapse of the Eastern bloc at the end of the decade. In contrast, Cuba faced an enormous adjustment because of its already weak economy (its GDP barely grew between 1986 and 1990) and its disproportionately high commercial and financial dependence on the USSR (Pérez Villanueva 2010).

This distorted trade pattern (Montenegro and Soto 2000) undermined Cuba's economic development in three principal ways. First, the island's pre-1959 production, in particular its commercial and logistical systems, had been designed to accommodate Cuba's ties to the nearby United States, where two-thirds of its trade was concentrated. With the imposition of sanctions, Cuba was abruptly forced to divert the bulk of its trade to much more distant countries, particularly to the socialist bloc and, more recently, to Eastern Europe, Asia, Canada, and Latin America. The new trading pattern substantially raised transportation and storage costs, necessitating multi-million dollar investments to maintain Cuba's own merchant fleet.

Second, and probably with even more pernicious ongoing effects, Cuba's isolation from the United States (and to a lesser degree from other large, developed countries) has reduced the economy's growth threshold due to the country's continued reliance on outdated technologies. During the first 30 years after the Revolution, Cuba imported the majority of its capital goods from the Council for Mutual Economic Assistance (COMECON). This meant that its imports primarily came from the Soviet Union, with increasing Chinese participation from the 1990s onward. Cuba purchased more equipment through COMECON than did any other comparable country (Eaton and Kortum 2001). Yet the Soviets' means of production were of lower quality than those of the advanced capitalist economies, as evidenced by its international pattern of specialization. Although the Soviet Union successfully produced large quantities of machinery domestically, it exported insignificant amounts of such goods to countries that had a comparable level of development (Myant and Drahocoupil 2011).[4]

At the same time, equipment designed to meet Soviet demand was characterized by limited variety and product modification, maximum product standardization, and a preference for quantity in lieu of quality. All of these principals were consistent with the prevalence of the "Fordist model" and supply-driven economics (Kornai 2014). The inferior quality of Soviet goods limited Cuba's already diminished capacities to expand and diversify its exports and to penetrate new markets outside of COMECON. Consequently, Cuba was often forced to return to the same trading bloc, deepening an already vicious cycle.

Another significant impact of Cuba's isolation from the United States had to do with the shortage of spare parts for an industrial system largely based on US-made equipment. Worn out equipment was replaced when it was feasible, but Cuba also began to develop the capacity to produce its own spare parts. However, inasmuch as Cuba's technical obsolescence continued to worsen, its industrial plants permanently operated below capacity (Rodríguez 1990), due to both general wear and tear and recurring interruptions and breakdowns.

Finally, the excessive concentration of trade within COMECON significantly contributed to the slow rate at which Cuban enterprises engaged in foreign trade and adopted new business practices and marketing techniques. Intergovernmental policies and agreements had previously guaranteed sales to socialist countries, but once this preferential framework disappeared, Cuban trade suffered accordingly.

From the perspective of important sectors of the Cuban state, ongoing aggression from a powerful neighbor has been thought to reinforce the need for centralized and vertical governance. Such a response is common in extreme situations, including cases of armed conflict. Here, it was fostered by the US sanctions, which helped to legitimize the belief in the utility, and indeed the necessity, of a centralized Cuban model that extends beyond the purely economic sphere.

In general, US policies served to isolate Cuba and push it toward its COMECON allies. The government was left with virtually no other alternatives, and the sanctions handed an argument to those seeking to justify the orthodox policies enacted in the mid to late 1990s. Much the same has happened since the end of that decade. Faced with an unfavorable international environment, Cuba has concentrated its trade again with countries that offer the island certain special arrangements or advantages, among them Venezuela, China, Russia, and Brazil.

Vietnam and China as Points of Reference?

A recurring theme in the literature on Cuba's economic and geopolitical situation has been the attempt to compare its experience with those of other, presumably analogous, countries. The thinking goes that these countries may offer potentially useful lessons for analyzing Cuba's situation and provide examples of viable paths for it to follow during the transition from central planning. In particular, many scholars have identified China and Vietnam as indispensable points of reference. Perhaps the most obvious reason for this comparison is because both of these nations have chosen—in word if not always in deed—to undertake widespread reforms to their CPEs while still preserving other elements of this model. This makes their cases broadly comparable to Cuba's process of "updating" its economy.

However, Cuba's process differs from these countries at the political level. While China and Vietnam have openly adopted (though at different rates) economic models with significant free-market mechanisms, Cuba has begun to reform its model considerably while denying that the goal of these changes is to establish a market economy. In fact, Cuban authorities explicitly distance themselves from the prevailing notion of "reforms" in China or Vietnam, preferring instead to use the term "updates."

Cuba's distinctive rationale for its changes creates particular dynamics for its integration into the global system of accumulation, a system that is dominated by capitalism in the era of globalization and has a marked US influence. In Asia's case, the very nature of reforms implies the need to normalize, over the medium and long term, these countries' relations with the United States, the axis of the global system. This overarching need negates the historical and ideological forces that are incompatible with the new direction. For China and Vietnam, economic imperatives drive these processes, and success requires engaging with the world's foremost contemporary power. Cuba, however, still assumes that it must open itself to the world *with caution*, in part due to perceived US aggression. As a result, Cuba moves toward integration at its own pace and seeks many counterbalances depending on the trade partner in question: Europe versus the United States; Latin America versus other regions; China and Vietnam versus other strategic partners, and so on.

There are other differences between Cuba and its Asian counterparts. China's growing importance in the global economy has granted it much freedom in managing its relationship with the United States; it can negotiate its ties with the Americans aware of the advent of a situation of bilateral dependence. Vietnam's rise on the international stage also increases its relevance, which is related to its differences from China and its active participation in regional coordination and integration mechanisms like the Association of Southeast Asian Nations (ASEAN). On the other side, Cuba's situation is unique. Its relevance in international politics far surpasses both its territorial and demographic dimensions and its economic potential. Cuba's influence in Latin America is largely due to the social assistance it has provided on multiple occasions, its political harmony with progressive governments that have emerged over the past decade and a half, and the sympathy that it evokes from being perpetually bullied by such a powerful neighbor. While the practical effect of rapprochement with Cuba may be insignificant for the United States, its symbolic value is great given that Cuba is a geographically close, unexplored market that has been virtually untouched by international investment and market forces.

Additionally, the origins, triumph, and trajectory of the Cuban Revolution were more closely linked to a rejection of US influence than was the case in Asia. In fact, US foreign policy toward Cuba has been significantly influenced by the establishment of a large section of the Cuban bourgeoisie in the United States that strongly oppose the Cuban government and its policies. Although Cuban political action groups in the US share some similarities with those of other diaspora groups (Chinese or Vietnamese), their longevity and reach in North America is such that they have become an influential caucus within the US Congress.

The relative size of the three economies also varies significantly. China and Vietnam are large countries with young, growing populations and notable economic potential in the medium and long term. Both countries are fortunate to have substantial productive resources (labor, natural resources) that give them important assets to operate effectively within the system of international capitalism. These resources allow the option, for example, of exploiting cheap labor while also reaping the benefits of educational systems that are constantly being improved. These factors favor development in the most dynamic sectors of global trade and investment, like electronics, automobiles (in the case of China), and textiles. Cuba, in contrast, is a small economy with relatively scarce natural resources whose advantages do not situate it advantageously in global systems of accumulation. Because of this, large corporations do not perceive Cuba as essential for their insertion into key circuits in the global economy. Simply put, the business sector has placed stronger pressure on the US political elite to normalize relations with China and Vietnam than with Cuba.

Cuba does, however, share some similarities with China and Vietnam, two Asian allies with which it has maintained close political relationships over the past five decades. These relationships were notably strengthened after the collapse of European socialism, a time that also coincided with the maturation of Chinese and Vietnamese reforms and their ascension onto the international stage as countries with high economic growth.

Although the three countries differ in size, all of them are countries in development—and in transition[5]—that are united by several key elements of their international agendas. First, as underdeveloped nations, international trade represents a critical source of their growth and productive transformation in a century in which linkages between growth and productivity have become especially intricate and varied. Enabling trade to proceed without substantial setbacks has become a key objective of each country's global aspirations. Furthermore, a substantial part of their transitions involves creating new frameworks for relationships with entities such as foreign stakeholders, multilateral financial institutions, businesses, suppliers, and markets. The success of each country's transformation rests, to a large degree, on its ability to skillfully manage these relationships. Ultimately, these three countries will transform, at their own pace, into more open and globally interdependent economies. However, to do so, they will need to understand, and very pragmatically accept, many international rules that fundamentally operate in tension with certain ideological stances prevalent in their governments.

Second, these three nations maintain political systems far removed from the preferred US model. Although the Asian countries have made significant transformations in their economic models, they have done so amid relatively stable institutional contexts, without radically breaking away from their preexisting political institutions. Such a move has allowed the United States to keep on the agenda traditional issues of Western discourse—such as democracy, rule of law, and human rights—which may be taken up again at will during negotiations or disputes.

Another interesting parallel among the three countries comes from the fact that they all have experienced significant political-military conflicts with the United States, albeit with varying implications and levels of intensity. Vietnam is an extreme example. Its protracted war with the United States, along with its alliance and intelligence collaboration with the USSR, took a high human toll on both sides and left lasting consequences for the Vietnamese people. Yet Vietnam's reforms and economic success, clearly oriented toward creation of a market system, have ultimately helped it turn the page in its once antagonistic relationship with the United States. China, in contrast, continues to disagree vehemently with the US position on Taiwan and its maintenance of a military enclave in South Korea (China supports the North Korean government). It has, however, learned to manage these topics pragmatically, in such a way that they do not impede cooperation in other areas.

Cuba has had numerous points of contention with the United States, from radical politics at the beginning of the Revolution that directly affected North American interests, to the island's eventual Cold War alliance with the Soviet Union (which prompted several unpleasant episodes, such as the missile crisis), and finally to its intervention in the war in Angola and support for popular movements throughout Latin America and beyond. The sheer number of disagreements that have built up between the United States and Cuba over the course of five decades would suggest that, out of the three countries evaluated here, Cuba's bilateral conflict will likely be the most challenging to resolve. Further complicating this daunting task are structural questions related to Cuba's proximity to the United States, the Cuban diaspora[6] that lives there, and the "imaginary" that Cuban Americans and others in the United States have created that equates transformation on the island with a transition toward a market economy and a Western-style democracy.

Economic Reform and 17D, What Now?

This discussion explains the distinctiveness of Cuba's path in times of wider economic reform. Four years after the official launch of the transformation process (2011) and eight years after President Raúl Castro first spoke about the need for "structural change," it is now possible to outline some of the essential characteristics of this process (Torres 2014). An initial topic reveals a contradiction. The government has been abundantly clear about the urgent need for substantial changes to the long-standing Cuban model of central planning, which is understood to be untenable. Nevertheless, the government has proposed to "update" its model, as if it were simply a matter of gradually improving an already successful system to bring it into the present. But this is not the case for Cuba's system. However, although the Cuban government emphatically declares that it is not starting a transition toward capitalism or a market economy, it does not specify an alternate model that it will follow, imbuing the changes with a large dose of uncertainty and experimentation. It also seems unclear where Cuba wants to go or how it hopes to get there. It is amid this climate of uncertainty and ambiguity that the current reforms are unfolding.

The dramatic announcements on December 17, 2014, together with the Cuban government's stated willingness to engage in a respectful dialogue with the United States, seem to indicate that the island's leaders have tacitly accepted the fact that a prosperous economy requires a radical shift in its relations with its northern neighbor. China and Vietnam—larger countries that are farther from the United States—came to the same conclusion in their own time. For Cuba, an eventual rapprochement will be an even greater departure from the status quo ante, given the intensity and significance of past US-Cuban hostilities.

Interestingly, Cuba's current reforms, which have been presented as a strictly economic move, are now also seen as necessary and desirable for the country's internal cohesion and strategic thinking. The economy itself is a major headache for the government. However, the inevitable generational shift in leadership demands that Cuba advances as much and as quickly as possible in sensitive areas, including relations with the United States. It is reasonable to expect that a leader who enjoys the legitimacy of Raúl Castro would want to draw on that political capital to make peace sooner rather than later and, at the same time, decisively contribute to improve Cuba's prospects for economic advancement. One of the flagship projects of foreign investment— the Mariel Special Development Zone—is a clear demonstration of this desire. Due to its location and reach, the Mariel initiative would never have been completed without the prospect of integrating North American enterprises and gaining direct access to the US market (see Pérez Villanueva, this vol.).

Cuba's improved ties with the United States could contribute significantly to its reintegration into the international monetary and financial systems. Reintegration could generate significant benefits for the island by improving its access to resources, reducing the cost of foreign financing through a lower "country risk" ranking, and providing support in the form of valuable technical assistance in key areas of macroeconomic management. With regard to the latter, the experience accumulated by multilateral institutions through their assistance to other economies in transition would be extremely valuable to Cuba. Financial reintegration would also lessen third-party fears, both from countries and businesses, regarding the risks of active participation in Cuba's reform process. Additionally, compared to China and Vietnam at the start of their reform processes, Cuba is better placed (as a smaller country that is fairly educated and relatively stable financially) to bridge the gap more quickly. This would contribute to the success of Cuban reform and therefore strengthen the government's position in the short term.

The literature on transitional economies has demonstrated that the state plays an essential role in guiding these inherently uncertain processes, which generate innumerable conflicts and notable short-term costs. An entity with sufficient legitimacy—usually the state—should manage the process if it hopes to maintain support for continued trans-formations (Ahrens 2008). In turn, the legitimacy of the state itself can also be affected by reforms. The re-establishment of diplomatic rela-tions, for example, has had a clear, positive effect on the Cuban gov-ernment because, during this process, the United States has formally recognized that the current government represents the Cuban state. It follows, then, that the Cuban state should participate in discussions sur-rounding many issues of mutual interest. Furthermore, for the Cuban people, the recent turn of events strengthens the narrative that normal-ization has resulted from the failure of a misguided US policy of isola-tion, a contention that the Cuban government had long espoused.

In other areas, evaluations of possible impacts of normalization are more ambiguous. Increased interaction between a wide variety of Cuban individuals and businesses and the outside world, operating under market rules, could intensify demands for greater economic independence for economic actors seeking to accelerate access to finance and trade, as well as for a political opening that would create new models that would provide for the interests of distinct social strata within the Cuban population (Feinberg 2013). Some sectors within Cuba may interpret this as a threat. For example, the reforms carry immediate costs for employees in the public sector who lack the neces-sary organization to clearly articulate their interests and demands. The reforms significantly cut the government's social spending and reduce unnecessary public sector jobs, but they fail to provide equivalent short-term compensation (such as new economic opportunities) for those who lose out in the process. Some influential segments of Cuban society could object to changes on ideological-political grounds, insist-ing on state-directed economic reforms without radical modifications to the political structure. Such concerns would prompt an, at best, ambivalent attitude toward both the current economic transformations and the rapprochement with the United States.

Another factor to take into consideration—one that was also import-ant in Asia—is the role of the Cuban diaspora. The size, socioeconomic status, and political influence of the Cuban American community have made it one of the most powerful diaspora groups in the United States. Cuban Americans have participated in the transformation of the island's economic playing field since the 1990s through their growing transfer of remittances and increasingly frequent visits to the country. Now, new and bigger opportunities have arisen. The Cuban American community provides much of the financing for businesses in Cuba and has also established initiatives to offer educational and advisory services. As Cuban foreign investment laws have become more flexible and US government policies have shifted, many Cuban American business people have begun to imagine participating in this process, not only to turn a profit but also to contribute to Cuba's "national development."

Perhaps it should be emphasized that, although Cuba's resumption of normalized relations with its northern neighbor is clearly positive on the whole, the rapprochement process itself cannot substitute for the changes necessary in the island's productive environment and social reproduction. It would be a strategic error, and an unforgivable delusion, to consider that the primary obstacle to Cuba's prosperity lies beyond its borders. In this context, it is worth summarizing lessons learned from China and Vietnam.

Reform in Cuba is not necessary because of a need to improve relations with the United States, but rather because of the need to overcome the weaknesses in the Cuban model and create lasting prosperity (Torres 2013). Along the pathway of change, integration with foreign markets is a key vehicle for development. For this reason, over the long term, Cuba must normalize its ties to the United States, the leading power in the world today. Doing so requires managing these ties with great pragmatism to prevent disagreements from affecting the achievement of strategic objectives. As painful as history has been, there is space to begin a new chapter of US-Cuban relations. Compared to China and Vietnam, the impacts of normalized relations for Cuba will be especially strong because the island is much smaller, closer to the United States, and culturally and idiosyncratically very western.

Notes

1. This was primarily made up of the Platt Amendment (included in the Cuban constitution of June 12, 1901), the Cuban-American Treaty (May 1903), Trade Reciprocity Treaties of 1903 and 1934, and the Treaty of Relations of 1943.
2. This has also become one of the preferred rationalizations of those against the embargo. That is, this policy has not weakened the Cuban government, but it has punished the same Cuban people it claims to defend.
3. Especially Czechoslovakia, Poland, Hungary, and Yugoslavia.
4. The same occurred in other socialist countries such as Czechoslovakia, the Democratic Republic of Germany, or Poland.

5. Transition in this context is used to signify the process of change from a central planning economy to another where the market plays a much more important role.

6. It is worth mentioning that this community has constituted a much more diverse and pluralized space in the present, observing clear positions favorable to rapprochement between the two countries, with few conditions. The current community has been a key to shaping the political capital that President Obama used to implement substantial change in the policy toward Cuba.

References

Ahrens, J. Joachim. 2008. "Transition Towards a Social Market Economy? Limits and Opportunities." *Ordnungspolitische Diskurse*, No. 2008.05. http://www.econstor.eu/handle/10419/55411.

Eaton, Jonathan, and Samuel Kortum. 2001. "Trade in Capital Goods." *National Bureau of Economic Research Working Papers* 8070. http://www.nber.org/papers/w8070.pdf.

Feinberg, Richard. 2013. "Soft Landing in Cuba? Emerging Entrepreneurs and Middle Classes." Brookings Institution, November 8. http://www.brookings.edu/~/media/Research/Files/Reports/2013/11/cuba-emerging-entrepreneurs-middle-classes-feinberg/cuba-entrepreneurs-middle-classes-feinberg.pdf?la=en.

Figueras, Miguel. 1999. *Aspectos estructurales de la economía cubana*. Havana: Félix Varela.

Fouquin, Michel, Houssein Guimbard, Colette Herzog, and Deniz Ünal. 2012. *Panorama de l'économie mondiale*. Centre D'Études Prospectives et D'Informations Internationales, December. http://www.cepii.fr/PDF_PUB/pano/monde.pdf.

Kornai, János. 2014. "The Soft Budget Constraint." *Acta Oeconomica* 64: 25–79.

Montenegro, Claudio E., and Raimundo Soto. 2000. "How Distorted Is Cuba's Trade? Evidence and Predictions from a Gravity Model." Universidad Alberto Hurtado Facultad de Economía y Negocios Working Paper, January 21. http://www.economiaynegocios.uahurtado.cl/wp-content/uploads/2010/07/inv87.pdf.

Myant, Martin, and Jan Drahocoupil. 2011. *Transition Economies: Political Economy in Russia, Easter Europe and Central Asia*. Danvers: Wiley.

Pérez Villanueva, Omar Everleny. 2010. "Estrategia económica: medio siglo de socialismo." In *Cincuenta años de la economía cubana*, edited by Omar Everleny Pérez Villanueva, 1–24. Havana: Ciencias Sociales.

Rodríguez, Jose Luis. 1990. *Estrategia del desarrollo económico en Cuba*. Havana: Ciencias Sociales.

Torres, Ricardo. 2013. "Algunas contradicciones del desarrollo económico cubanocontemporáneo." In *Miradas a la economía cubana. Entre la eficiencia económica y la equidad social*, edited by Omar Everleny Pérez Villanueva and Ricardo Torres, 29–40. Havana: Editorial Caminos.

————. 2014. "Transformations in the Cuban Economic Model. Context, General Proposal, and Challenges." *Latin American Perspectives* 41.4: 74–90.

Weill, Laurent. 2008. "On the Inefficiency of European Socialist Economies." *Journal of Productivity Analysis* 29: 79–89.

Chapter 11

Foreign Direct Investment in Cuba: A Necessity and a Challenge

Omar Everleny Pérez Villanueva

Introduction

Foreign investors, absent since the 1959 Revolution, returned to the Cuban economy at the beginning of the 1990s in the context of the so-called Special Period. In certain spheres, such as tourism, foreign capital was very dynamic and propelled fundamental structural change. In general, however, the isolation of external investment projects from the overall economy—and the persistence of administrative bottlenecks that fostered this separation—created idiosyncrasies that converted the Cuban case into a sui generis for the absorption of international capital. This was evident in the government's insistence on considering each investment proposal separately, as well as in the use of a currency other than the Cuban peso to implement all agreements. As a result of these obstacles, after a period of steady expansion until 2003, foreign investment in Cuba stagnated despite various measures targeted toward its stimulation.

This chapter considers the prospects for foreign investment in Cuba from 2013 onward. This is a period in which foreign investment has been prioritized to accelerate economic growth rates in a context in which fiscal constraints have severely reduced public investment. Describing potential foundations of this takeoff, the chapter addresses the consequences of Law 118 of 2014, which altered the framework governing foreign investment. The analysis suggests that this measure takes on special importance in light of the 2013 enactment of a decree-law permitting the creation of a Special Development Zone in Mariel, which may contribute meaningfully to improving Cuba's insertion into advantageous economic niches in the Caribbean and beyond. Finally, and above all, the analysis considers the potential for investors from the United States after the restoration of diplomatic relations in July 2015.

Analysis of the Evolution of Foreign Direct Investment from 2003 to 2013

Cuban policies designed to attract foreign investments and contracts have been far from stable during the past quarter century. While there was a foreign investment boom in the 1990s, dictated by the extraordinary challenges facing the Cuban economy during the years subsequent to the collapse of the Soviet Union, its trajectory declined radically in 2003, with only a modest recovery achieved in 2010 and 2011 (Figure 11.1).

Foreign investment has largely been concentrated in a few sectors. The largest percentage involves agreements in tourism, petroleum, and agro-industry. To a lesser extent, it has been linked to other spheres such as construction, transportation, and commercialization. Significantly, foreign investment has been minimal in areas of greater added value

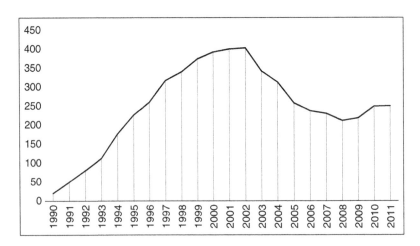

Figure 11.1   Number of associations with foreign capital in Cuba
Source: Peréz Villanueva and Vidal Alejandro (2012).

or in high-tech fields, despite the fact that some of the most valuable assets in Cuba are its human resources, given the qualifications of its workforce. It is important to note that the business investments that the Cuban government approved during this period made little use of this asset, with the exception of mixed Cuban enterprises created outside the country, particularly in health or biotechnology. Joint ventures and hotel administration contracts were predominant, as depicted in Figure 11.2.

Despite the decrease in the quantity of businesses that were functioning after 2003, those that remained in operation exhibited positive results. The contributions of so-called International Economic Associations (AEI by its Spanish acronym) consistently increased Cuba's total sales of goods and services, which reached more than US$5.2 billion in 2013 (Figure 11.2). Exports grew to more than US$3.4 billion, whereas direct income into the country generated by foreign-owned enterprises was estimated at approximately US$600 million.

In nearly all of the productive areas where Cuba has achieved favorable overall performance or high export rates, foreign capital has had a presence in some form or another. This should serve as an encouragement to the authorities to attract further investment, including in

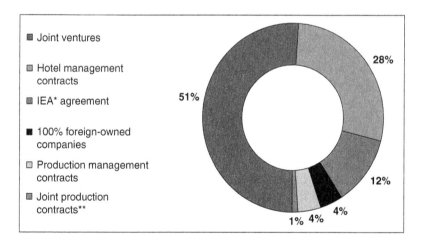

Figure 11.2   Foreign-invested enterprises by category (2013)

Note: *Cuba's Foreign Investment Act defines an International Economic Association (IEA) as a "partnership of national and foreign investors within the national territory for the production of goods, the rendering of services or both, for profit" (ANPP 2014).

**In Spanish, *Contratos para la Producción Cooperada*.

Source: MINCEX. "Cuba: Cartera de Oportunidades de Inversión Extranjera." November 2014.

areas that directly impact the population, such as the production of food, household products, and consumer goods.

The unfavorable macroeconomic situation, the deterioration and technological obsolescence of Cuba's productive capacities, and the need to advance toward sustainable future development motivated policymakers to renew efforts to attract foreign direct investment (FDI). The guide to economic changes in Cuba, known as the Guidelines of the Economic and Social Policy of the Party and the Revolution, or *Los Lineamientos* in Spanish, insists on this in twelve of its 313 proposals. The *Lineamientos* considered that attracting FDI could satisfy diverse objectives such as supporting access to advanced technologies, improving the quality of management, expanding and diversifying export markets, and import substitution. In the medium and long term, the contribution of external financing could also increase productivity and create opportunities for new sources of employment, particularly in high-skilled fields.

To attract external investments in the quantity that Cuba needed, greater liberalization and a new foreign investment law were necessary to grant greater incentives to foreign capital. This was deemed especially critical in areas, such as those related to infrastructure, with long recovery times for invested capital. Therefore, it was necessary to implement tax exemption policies for a defined period or for businesses that were 100 percent foreign-owned. It has also been understood that the use of administrative discretion in approving individual investments should be limited. Moreover, bids submitted to implement projects should be made public given that specific solicitations may result in receipt of multiple proposals.

The 2014 Foreign Investment Law

As the World Bank (2013) suggested in its "Doing Business 2014" report, a good measure of the ease of doing business is the degree to which the regulatory environment is "business-friendly." This evaluation coincides with that of the Cuban state, which therefore prepared and introduced a new foreign investment law reflective of its need to attract additional resources to the country. That it is imperative to attract such resources is beyond doubt. In recent decades, successful social and economic development processes around the world have involved annual growth rates of more than 7 percent that are sustained during a prolonged time period, as was experienced by the emerging Asian economies (Lee, forthcoming). And for this growth to be possible, the increase in the availability of physical capital for productive activities has been an important factor. The dynamic economies from East Asia have had rates of capital accumulation between 30 and 40 percent of their gross domestic products (GDPs); Latin America, by contrast, has achieved average rates of only approximately 20 percent (Foxley, forthcoming).

Yet from 1990 to 2013, Cuba achieved relatively low rates of GDP growth as well as low as rates of capital accumulation, with averages below the rest of the Latin America and Caribbean region. Cuba had a significantly low gross fixed-capital formation; for example, in 2012, it was only 13.6 percent at constant 1997 prices, whereas at current prices it was even lower (less than 8 percent). Had Cuba decided in 2012 to commit to achieving a growth rate of 5 percent, then it would have had to dedicate 30 percent of its GDP to investment, which could only have been achieved through a reduction in consumption of more than 10 percent. Given how badly reduced consumption affected the quality of life for the general population throughout the years of economic crisis, transferring such a high level of resources into investment would have been a difficult decision for Cuba to make. It would also have been detrimental to labor productivity.

To fulfill both requirements for the Cuban economy—consumption and investment—the only viable option is to turn to external sources of savings, such as credit financing, FDI, portfolio investment, or international aid and transfers (remittances, donations, and other types). FDI is among the most important of these means of accessing external resources. However, because such investment is difficult to attract, favorable conditions should be provided to maximize inflows. Cuban authorities have determined that an annual rate of accumulation between 25 and 30 percent would be necessary to increase its GDP growth rates to between 5 and 7 percent. And this leads to an attempt to access annual FDI inflows between US$2 to 2.5 million—at least initially, with the possibility of requiring larger volumes over time (Murillo 2014).

To have a remote possibility of achieving these levels, it was necessary to reformulate existing legislation regarding the inflow of foreign capital, especially to modify Law 44. To this end, a new law was approved in March 2014, reflecting a set of policy principles that External Business and Foreign Investment Minister Rodrigo Malmierca articulated in his presentation of the law to the National Assembly of People's Power (ANPP by its Spanish acronym). These highlight the fact that FDI contributes to solving structural problems in the economy through its links to Cuba's long-term development plan. FDI is crucial to the success of the plan because it can incentivize integral development projects to generate production chains, contribute to the change in the country's energy grid by harnessing renewable energy sources, and allow for access to advanced technology that can increase labor productivity.

The law permits, although on an exceptional basis, the participation of legally incorporated nonstate economic organizations as well as companies financed by Cuban capital. It also supplies significant tax incentives. The Council of Ministers approved the foreign investment policy on October 19, 2013. Afterward, it was analyzed in meetings of the Commission of the Political Bureau for Agreement Control of the VI Congress of the Communist Party of Cuba (PCC for its acronym in Spanish), which were held on January 6 and February 24, 2014. Some of its key elements are worth noting (ANPP 2014):

Primary Principles of the Policy
- Foreign investment is an *active and fundamental element* toward the growth of particular sectors and economic activities.
- *Foreign investment is promoted on the basis of a wide-reaching and diverse project portfolio*, by phase and potential sectors, prioritizing the Mariel Special Development Zone.
- The development of *comprehensive projects that generate productive linkages* will be incentivized.
- Foreign investment will be oriented toward export and import substitution sectors, as well as toward the elimination of bottlenecks in production chains, the prioritization of modernization, the creation of infrastructure, and technological change.
- The establishment of completely foreign-owned enterprises may be authorized for the execution of complicated investments, especially to develop industrial infrastructure.
- Investments may be able to contribute to change in the country's energy grid.
- Cubans will always maintain majority participation in natural resource extraction, public service lending, biotech development, wholesale trade, and tourism.
- The system of labor contracting through the Cuban state shall be maintained and its fundamental objective will be to supply and monitor the workforce.
- On an exceptional basis, foreign investment can be oriented toward the development of activities by legally incorporated nonstate economic actors.

There exist many obstacles to increasing FDI in Cuba that should not be underestimated. These include the continued US embargo and the external debt situation, although a recently completed renegotiation process has resulted in favorable debt-forgiveness agreements from several countries, including Japan, Mexico, and, in particular, Russia, which forgave 90 percent of Cuba's debt. Others obstacles include policy errors committed in the past, for example, suspensions on payments to investors who have thus been constrained in efforts to repatriate profits. And, crucially, there are restrictions caused by the scarcity of foreign currency.

Legal Framework for Foreign Investment
The new legal framework generally establishes guarantees, destination sectors, methods, authorization rules, and regulatory norms relative to the protection of the environment, such as the use of natural resources. It also establishes conflict resolution mechanisms and special systems governing areas such as banking, labor contracting, export and import, reserves and taxes, and insurance. Also maintained is the principle that the government will review and authorize foreign investments on a case-by-case basis. The most significant modifications with regard to the earlier Law 77 can be summarized as follows (ANPP 2014):

- Regarding the three methods of foreign investment that are recognized in the new legislation (mixed enterprises, completely foreign-funded enterprises, and international economic association contracts), the latter has been extended to incorporate the administration of production and services, hotel administration, and professional services.
- The approval system has redefined the levels of approval for businesses in line with their characteristics, allowing a decentralized approval process for some projects. The procedure for evaluating and approving investments has been modified, making it more agile. It stipulates 60 business days from the presentation of an approval document and 45 days when decisions come from the OACE.
- The State Council will approve investments in nonrenewable natural resources, management of public services and public works projects, or those that involve the use of goods in the public domain.
- The Council of Ministers will approve transactions when a completely foreign-funded business transfers a property or other state-owned good or when a public foreign enterprise is participating. It will also

approve cases regarding renewable energy sources, cases in which nonrenewable resources are at risk, and investments in the health sector, education, and armed forces.

- The Council of Ministers may delegate approval authority to the heads of Central State Administration Agencies (OACE by its Spanish acronym).
- Details of the conflict resolution system are spelled out, with particular emphasis on the role of national courts.
- Provisions are put forth for treating foreign investments at the time of future currency unification.
- Taxes on profits will be set at zero percent during the first eight years; in exceptional circumstances, the exemption will persist for a longer period. Subsequently, taxes on profits will be fixed at 15 percent. Reinvested profits also will be taxed at zero percent. In Law 77 they had been at 30 percent, which could increase to 50 percent for profits involving the use of natural resources (ANPP 1995).

The recently approved body of laws offers investors full guarantees of protection and security. Their holdings cannot be expropriated, except for considerations of public utility or social interest motives in line with Cuba's Constitution, international treaties to which Cuba subscribes, and prevailing legislation, with all due compensation for its value to be established by mutual agreement. The state also guarantees investors *the freedom to repatriate convertible currency* without having to pay fees or other encumbrances from dividends or benefits that the foreign investor obtains in Cuba. Thus, the foreign investor may sell or transmit his or her rights to the state, to parties in the association, or to a third party, as authorized by the government. The new regulations apply to foreign investment established for Special Development Zones with adaptations that authorize special rules that are available as long as they do not run contrary to the zone's functions. The former notwithstanding, the special rules conceded in the law will be applicable to investments wherever they provide the most benefit.

Mariel Special Development Zone:
A Crucial Initiative for the Future

The Mariel Special Development Zone (ZEDM by its Spanish acronym) was created in 2013 through one of the approved guidelines that contemplated the promotion of Special Development Zones to increase exports, substitute imports, foster high-tech projects, and provide new sources of employment. The ZEDM has been an especially high priority for the Cuban government, which outlined its objectives in Decree-Law No. 313 of September 23, 2013 (ANPP 2013). Beyond its role in generating exports and promoting import substitution, the ZEDM was a means to develop critical infrastructure and create a highly efficient logistics system for imports, exports, and distribution. The initiative sought to promote the establishment of national or foreign firms, generate employment, and facilitate the transfer of advanced technology and know-how, along with business management skills. Appropriately, the decree-law also considers ZEDM's articulation with the rest of the economy.

As a component of this Special Development Zone, the Port of Mariel was inaugurated with a modern container ship terminal, involving what is today one of the largest investment projects ever undertaken in Cuba. This undoubtedly has to be understood in light of the broader context of reconfigurations in the international economy and Cuba's efforts to link its fortunes to dynamic areas of economic activity. Because of Mariel's advantageous geographic position, which will become all the more attractive to investors once the new locks of the Panama Canal are completed and give way to a new generation of container ships from the *Ultra Post-Panamax* series, Cuba aims to become a key logistics hub and a site for the accumulation of capital. The success of this venture will be critical to the country's future.

Among the most noteworthy elements of the ZEDM is the fact that Cubans employed there will receive 80 percent of the wages that are agreed on between state employment agencies and the contractors or licensees ("Régimen de contratación en Zona Especial de Mariel beneficia a trabajadores" 2014). Those wages, in turn, will be set at levels that take into account prevailing rates in the Caribbean and Central American region and the specific characteristics of the Cuban workforce. This is meant to serve as a stimulus for both workers and investors, and it addresses one of the primary demands that have long been voiced by foreign investors operating in the country.

Decree-Law 313 contains numerous tax incentives, as summarized in Table 11.1.

Article 20 of Chapter III of the decree-law is also appealing to investors, allowing that "concessions can be granted for a term of up to 50 years and are renewable." That is a very advantageous time period and, more broadly, the approved legal framework and the government incentives that have been introduced for this development zone may attract investors drawn by the many favorable conditions

Table 11.1   Taxes payable by Cuban or foreign entrepreneurs in the ZEDM

Type of tax	Mariel Special Development Zone Decree-Law 313
Payroll	Exempt
Profits	0% during the first 10 years of operation (exceptions may be made for a longer period); subsequently taxed at 12%
Tariffs on equipment and inputs for investment	Exempt
Sales and services	0% during the first year of operations; subsequently taxed at 1%
Contribution for social security	14%
Contribution for local development	Exempt

Source: Prepared by the author based on Decree-Law 313.

that it offers. In the immediate future, the ZEDM should become a particularly attractive zone for US investors due to its state-of-the-art transport facilities.

Economic Potential for US Businesses in Cuba

The restoration of diplomatic relations between Cuba and the United States on July 20, 2015, should bring about a gradual normalization of relations between the two countries. This has caused a widespread debate in the media and the business sector about the possible conditions in which economic links may now be developed. In this regard, it is still premature to arrive at definitive conclusions about what the future might hold. Of course, strictly speaking, Cuba has had economic relations of various types with the United States for many years, especially from 2001 onward. It is worth keeping in mind that between 1995 and 2012, US institutions paid approximately US$1.6 billion to Cuba for telecommunications services. This figure can only grow given the Obama administration's broad licensing of US telecommunications companies to provide both goods and services to Cuba. Despite the impasse in relations and the US embargo, the United States has played a significant role in the Cuban economy, and its importance is certain to grow in the near future.

The US government has authorized raising the official maximum remittance amount from non–Cuban Americans from US$2000 to $8000 per year. In this regard, it is worth noting that remittance statistics

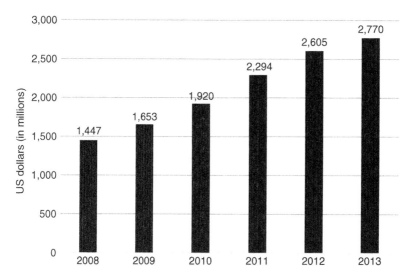

Figure 11.3   Remittances to Cuba from abroad (2008–2013)
Sources: The Havana Consulting Group (THCG), 2014, 2013. Cited by Paolo Spadoni (2015).

are based on estimates that take into account that the majority of funds are transferred through individuals as opposed to institutions. This peculiarity has resulted in the existence of considerable speculation around the actual quantity of remittances and their impact on Cuban society. To illustrate this point, while I question the arguments used to get these estimates, consider the estimates put forth by The Havana Consulting Group (THCG), which count all types of transfers to Cuba—from medicine packets to cell phone charge cards (Figure 11.3). Their estimates are based on very limited samples for the volume of passengers who move between the two countries. THCG provides a 2013 estimate of remittances at US$2.77 billion, but it adds on another US$3.5 billion in kind, according to its calculations, representing what each passenger carries in luggage and packages (Spadoni 2015). Taking into account that these are unidirectional transfers, these flows are significant regardless of their precise levels.

Potential for US Investment in Cuba

Future steps by the Obama administration and, eventually, the US Congress to facilitate business, investment, and arrival of tourists to Cuba will undoubtedly open business opportunities for important

North American enterprises with interest in the island. Many of these firms have already expressed clear interest. From the Cuban perspective, economic ties with the United States present business opportunities and also significant challenges that will have powerful impacts on the country's development strategy. There is a wide range of scenarios for both the short-term and long-term reactivation of commercial and financial ties between Cuba and the United States, and much will depend on the pace with which North American restrictions are lifted. In this context, numerous initiatives are being considered in the Congress, following a trend that began well before December 17, 2014. As some of them begin to take effect, they will serve to benefit economic interests on both sides.

Of all the dimensions underlying the July 20, 2015 re-establishment of relations between Cuba and the United States, the possibility that FDI from the United States may flow to Cuba is especially interesting, and there are scenarios in which it could play a valuable role in the ZDEM and in the rest of the country. In the short term, US businesses will be most interested in sectors related to tourism, hospitality, and travel services. Additionally, they will be interested in maritime transit, telecommunications, the construction materials industry, and agriculture.

In tourism, the need to expand lodging capacity in cities such as Havana and other provincial capitals is obvious. There is also the need for new investments to accommodate cruise ships and ferries—as the Office of the Historian of the capital has been doing—as well as new initiatives that will allow for rapid growth in cultural and entertainment sectors that serve an expanding tourism industry. Other potential considerations for Cuba include biotech pharmaceutical products, along with software development work for Communications and Information Technology Services (TICS by its Spanish acronym). There is also the possibility to develop high-quality agricultural exports, among other exports, for the US market.

In a recent report, Anamary Maqueira (2015) identifies additional activities in which US investors could be present, distinguishing likely phases of engagement. In the short term, the report highlights tourism, biotechnology, and petroleum extraction. For the medium term, and in part due to multiplier effects and the increased demand of the previously mentioned sectors, Maqueira identifies telecommunications, agriculture, and port infrastructure. Later, in the long term, there is potential in consumer goods and medical device fields, as well as in the production and sale of construction materials along with air cargo and airline passenger services, among others.

Of course, Cuba must confront the enormous challenges that come along with the potential of possible FDI from North America. The most logical approach is to properly orient projects toward national development objectives while remaining attractive and viable for investment projects. The risks for US investors must also be recognized, given that Cuba lacks a solid banking system, its physical infrastructure is deteriorating, and the embargo remains in effect, thus blocking investment in Cuba by US firms beyond the telecommunications sector. Companies also do not have authorization to enter into contractual relations with the Cuban government, which the latter's mixed-capital investments regime currently requires.

However, the Cuban government has sent a clear welcome message to US investors, even as Cuban decision-makers have been quiet on many aspects of the measures announced in January 2015 by the Obama administration. These include direct exports to private enterprises, permissions for ferry services, and proposals for information technology services such as Google, among others. Recently, Jorge Pérez, Executive Director of The Related Group (a construction company), commented on the possibility of luxury tourism in Cuba, which he believes could displace other Caribbean markets if US companies are able to invest in this line (Gámez Torres 2015). Jones Lang LaSalle (JLL), a Fortune 500 company specializing in commercial real estate, also evaluated business opportunities for the state of Florida that could benefit from the possible increase in demand for offices handling financial and legal services on Cuban topics on the assumption that diplomatic relations and business transactions between both nations advance (JLL Florida 2015).

It would be too extensive to list all of the large transnational companies that have visited Cuba during the course of 2015, among them Caterpillar, Cargill, Marriot International, and others. However, just to illustrate the breadth of interest that US business has demonstrated in establishing a presence in Cuba, the following is a list of corporations that have openly announced intentions to conduct business with the island:

- *American Express* and *MasterCard* plan to allow US credit cards to be used in Cuba.
- *IDT Corp.* announced an agreement with *ETECSA* to establish direct communications between the United States and Cuba.
- *Netflix* began to offer its services in February.
- *Apple* reported that its software and products will be sold officially in Cuba.

- *American Airlines* announced direct flights.
- *Delta Airlines, United Airlines,* and *Jet Blue Airways* are interested in direct flights (not charters) to Cuba.
- *Airbnb* (a web portal to rent houses) is now available in Cuba for US travelers.
- *Google* announced interest in the country, and its executives visited the island.
- Ferry companies set to serve Cuba were approved by the US Office of Foreign Assets Control (OFAC).
- A luxury yacht business from Florida was authorized to establish a presence in Cuba.
- *Carnival,* the world's largest cruise ship operator, received approval from the US government to travel to Cuba beginning in May 2016.

Conclusion

It can be said that in an initial phase there was an effort to attract foreign investment to Cuba that would focus on leveraging Cuba's idle capacity, industrial plants, and its surplus workforce. This was the case until the mid 1990s, when mining and petroleum sectors were also opened up to outside investment. Tourism received an influx of external funds, but these did not exceed US$250 million because there already were 5500 rooms in joint venture hotels. The Cuban telecommunications company ETECSA received approximately US$700 million in outside investments, and in petroleum the figure may have surpassed $2 billion, whereas cigar manufacturer Altadis (*habanos*) received upwards of US$600 million. Between 1991 and 1994, nearly all sectors of the national economy gradually incorporated the practice of seeking out foreign "partners" who could facilitate access to capital, technology, and markets.

Enactment of Law 77 for foreign investment in 1995 marked a qualitative shift to the AECE's formation process. This was primarily because it defined the legal and institutional roles that each party would play. Additionally, it allowed for the acceptance of foreign payments in the real estate sector, formulated duty-free zone policies, and accepted entirely foreign-invested businesses when they could be considered beneficial for the country. However, the Helms-Burton Law obstructed a particular inflow of international investments in Cuba. Although the law did not paralyze possible investor interests and, practically speaking, brought about only a few occurrences of contract cancellations or complicated investor negotiations, it represented a barrier above and beyond the economic embargo that had already been imposed on the country. Until 2003, despite the ups and downs in new business approval, FDI enjoyed institutional guarantees. Its economic results were sufficiently acceptable—it had dabbled in new external markets—and exports had increased as a result of increases in production. But then state policy shifted away from its welcoming stance toward foreign investment because of a combination of ideological resistance and diminished sense of economic crisis. Efforts to stimulate the influx of new foreign partners were put on hold, and rigorous controls were instituted along with changing the de facto rules of the game for foreign enterprises. This reduced the number of foreign firms operating in Cuba by more than 50 percent.

Recent legislation confirms a sharp departure from these measures that diminished the significance of foreign investment in Cuba. Most notably, Law 118, approved in March 2014, contains novel aspects in comparison to Law 77 of 1995 (ANPP 2014). Although in essence it is not a completely new law, it makes the process more transparent and tends to minimize bureaucratic discretion. It also contains important tax incentives, accelerated and decentralized approval for new ventures, and special provisions for priority areas, among other provisions. Combined with this new domestic regulatory environment, the thaw in US-Cuba relations since December 17, 2014 could mark a relaunch of economic links between the two countries in both the short term and the medium term.

It goes without saying that the re-establishment of relations between Cuba and the United States makes the international setting more favorable to Cuba, making attraction of foreign capital all the more important. As outlined in this chapter, several important policy initiatives in Cuba have created conditions more favorable to foreign investment, although much remains to be done. For example, although this is not the first priority, because it is necessary to stimulate the inflow of foreign capital to small and medium private Cuban enterprises from Cubans living abroad, those enterprises should also be permitted to associate with foreign firms. During an initial phase, this might take the form of collaborations with urban cooperatives. This and other challenges confirm that deploying foreign investment to enhance Cuba's economic performance will be plagued by uncertainties marked by different aspirations and conflicting interests. But if the work of economic rapprochement between the United States and Cuba is done rapidly and with good sense, then the final balance should be beneficial to both economies.

References

ANPP (Asamblea Nacional del Poder Popular). 1995. "Ley de la inversión extranjera en Cuba (Ley 77)." *Gaceta Oficial de la República de Cuba*, September 6. http://www.cubagob.cu/rel_ext/cpi/ley.htm.
———. 2013. Decreto-Ley Número 313. "De la zona especial de desarrollo Mariel." *Gaceta Oficial de la República de Cuba*, September 23. http://www.zedmariel.com/DOCUM/Decreto-Ley%20No.%20313(ESP).pdf.
———. 2014. "Law No. 118—Foreign Investment Law." *Cámara de Comercio de la República de Cuba*. http://www.camaracuba.cu/index.php/es/negocios/inversion-extranjera-en-cuba.
Foxley, Alejandro. Forthcoming. "Inclusive Development: Elements for a Shared National Strategy." In *Innovation and Inclusion: How to Avoid the Middle Income Trap in Latin America*, edited by Alejandro Foxley and Barbara Stallings. New York: Palgrave Macmillan.
Gámez Torres, Nora. 2015. "After Trip to Cuba, Jorge Pérez Talks Art and Business." *Miami Herald*, June 28. http://www.miamiherald.com/news/business/biz-monday/article25650241.html.
JLL Florida. 2015. "In Business with Cuba." *Jones Lang LaSalle Florida Blog*, June 3. http://www.jllblog.com/florida/2015/06/03/navigating-uncharted-waters/.
Lee, Keun. Forthcoming. "Industrial Upgrading and Innovation Capability for Inclusive Growth: Lessons from East Asia." In *Innovation and Inclusion: How to Avoid the Middle Income Trap in Latin America*, edited by Alejandro Foxley and Barbara Stallings. New York: Palgrave Macmillan.
Maqueira, Anamary. 2015. "Potencialidades de la Inversión Extranjera Directa de Estados Unidos Cuba." *Revista Oncuba*, January 7.
MINCEX (Ministerio de Comercio Exterior y la Inversión Extranjera). Various years. *Annual Reports*. Havana, Cuba.
Murillo, Marino. 2014. Intervention during the National Assembly of the People's Party. Havana: Radio Cubana, March 29. http://www.radiocubana.cu/audios-radio-cubana/78-intervenciones-y-discursos/1843-intervencion-de-marino-murillo-jorge-en-la-asamblea-nacional-del-poder-popular-parte-1.
Peréz Villanueva, Omar Everleny, and Pavel Vidal Alejandro. 2012. "La Inversión Extranjera Directa y la actualización del modelo económico cubano." Presentation given at the Centro de Estudios de Economía Cubana de la Universidad de Habana, Havana, March 16.
"Régimen de contratación en Zona Especial de Mariel beneficia a trabajadores." 2014. *Cubadebate*, April 14. http://www.cubadebate.cu/noticias/2014/04/14/regimen-de-contratacion-en-mariel-beneficia-a-trabajadores/#.VurFO-IrKUl.

Spadoni, Paolo. 2015. *El Descongelamiento de las Relaciones entre EEUU y Cuba: Impacto Potencial en la Economía Cubana.* Augusta: Georgia Regents University.

World Bank. 2013. *Doing Business 2014: Understanding Regulations for Small- and Medium-Size Enterprises.* 11th edn. http://www.doingbusiness.org/~/media/GIAWB/Doing%20Business/Documents/Annual-Reports/English/DB14-Full-Report.pdf.

Chapter 12

Entrepreneurial Reform, Market Expansion, and Political Engagement: Risks and Opportunities for Cuba Today

Ted A. Henken and Gabriel Vignoli

After consolidating his new government once becoming president in 2008, Raúl Castro made a series of unprecedented moves in late 2010 to encourage the re-emergence of private self-employment (known as *trabajo por cuenta propia* or *cuentapropismo*)—explicitly reversing Fidel Castro's policy that, according to Raúl's own bold assessment, had "stigmatized" and even "demonized" it (Castro Ruz 2010b). Subsequently, the number of legally allowed private occupations grew from 178 to 201, and the number of Cuba's *cuentapropistas* (self-employed workers or micro-entrepreneurs) more than tripled, from less than 150,000 in 2010 to more than a half-million by mid 2015. Additionally, hundreds of new nonagricultural cooperatives have been authorized to operate since their legalization in 2012. Moreover, on December 17, 2014, as part of a momentous diplomatic thaw between Washington and Havana, the Obama Administration announced a new policy of engagement targeted explicitly at "empowering" Cuba's new class of private entrepreneurs by allowing US companies to trade with "the emerging Cuban private sector."[1]

How might Washington's new policy of "empowerment through engagement" and the larger bilateral move toward normalization impact the island's emerging entrepreneurs and the rest of the "non-state sector" of its economy? Although there are many potential economic benefits of US private sector engagement with Cuba's *cuentapropistas*, new US policy also poses potential risks for US businesses. The US embargo remains in place, which means that companies doing business in Cuba must adhere to complex Commerce and Treasury Department regulations. Moreover, the monopolistic Cuban government poses significant challenges to those who want to do business on the island, reach out directly to island entrepreneurs, and hire Cuban workers—as many European and Canadian companies can attest. How will this work in practice, who will be the likely winners and losers (both in Cuba and abroad), and how can the Cuban government deal effectively with the growth in socioeconomic inequality that will inevitably follow an expanded private sector?

Direct US engagement with Cuban entrepreneurs is likely to grow as a result of freer travel and increasing remittances. US businesses will be able to export badly needed inputs to island *cuentapropistas* and import private or cooperatively produced Cuban goods and services. Technology and know-how transfers have already begun. These are all encouraging elements of Obama's new Cuba policy, changes that have the potential to both "empower" individual entrepreneurs—the stated goal of US policy—and incentivize the initial, exceedingly cautious, private sector reforms begun by the Cuban government.

The goal of US policy should be to increase Cubans' economic independence and the island's overall prosperity by focusing on the economic needs of entrepreneurs, rather than trying to effect "regime change" by other means. Given the need to build bilateral diplomatic trust after more than fifty years of mutual antagonism, Washington should eschew any "Trojan horse" approaches to entrepreneurial engagement that aim to empower the Cuban people by undermining the government. Such an antagonistic and divisive approach has not worked in the past and could derail Obama's promising effort to encourage the incipient pro-market reforms already underway.

At the same time, a US policy based on empowerment through economic engagement—even when motivated by the best and most transparent of intentions—will be a dead letter if the US Congress insists on clinging to the outdated and counterproductive embargo and if the Cuban government stubbornly refuses to ease its own *auto-bloqueo* (internal embargo) against island entrepreneurs. As it implements a self-described economic "updating of socialism," will Cuba continue to hold fast to its monopolistic "command and control" economic model—one that *"ya no funciona ni para nosotros"* ("no longer works even for us"), as Fidel Castro himself famously admitted in a rare moment of economic candor in 2010 (Goldberg 2010)?

A "Cuban Moment" and the Cuban Model

December 17, 2014—"*Diecisiete-D*" as the date is now referred to in Cuba—is often understood as a "Cuban moment" in the United States, representing a seismic shift in hemispheric relations. However, the change that took place on that now historic date had much more to do with the US decision to reverse its longstanding and uniquely unsuccessful isolationist policy toward the island than it did with any changes on the island itself.

Change in Cuba began earlier. In the second half of 2010, and under the leadership of Raúl Castro, the government began a series of unprecedented economic reforms. On September 13, Cuba's Communist Party newspaper *Granma* published a communiqué from Cuba's Central Workers' Union, informing its rank-and-file that half a million state workers would be laid off over the next six months, with hundreds of thousands of other state sector jobs to be eliminated over the coming years ("Pronunciamiento" 2010). Then, toward the end of the month, *Granma* published a second article that celebrated private microenterprise as "much more than an alternative" to the state sector, publicly banking on it to both absorb laid-off state workers and lead the reversal of the economy's long-standing inefficiency and poor productivity. "We aim," the article boldly declared, "to distance ourselves from those concepts that condemned self-employment to near extinction and stigmatized those who practiced it legally in the 1990s" (Martínez Hernández 2010). Subsequent legislation breathed new life into the island's moribund private sector by allowing unprecedented legal space and business opportunity for Cuba's long-suffering micro-entrepreneurs.

Together with a detailed list of economic reform "guidelines" approved at the April 2011 Communist Party Congress, these announcements ushered in a new understanding of Cuban socialism that sought to recalibrate the "social pact" between Cuban workers and the state (Partido Comunista de Cuba 2011). The idea that socialism meant egalitarianism was openly mocked as a grave error leading to economic dysfunction, lack of efficiency, low productivity, and free-riding—something Raúl criticized as "the exploitation of the good workers by the lazy ones" (Castro Ruz 2008). The guidelines made official something Raúl had become fond of repeating since becoming president in 2008: "We must erase forever the notion that Cuba is the only country in the world where you can live without working" (Castro Ruz 2010a).

Cuentapropismo, or "On-Your-Ownism": A Necessary History

The immediate cause of Cubans' characteristic entrepreneurial bent—often proudly, if guiltily, referred to by Cubans themselves as *el invento cubano*—was hinted at by President Obama himself in his December 17 speech with the words: "*No es fácil.*" This standard Cuban expression of mocking exasperation sums up the daily struggle (*la lucha*) to invent (*inventar*) often extra-legal solutions and creatively resolve (*resolver*) all manner of problems—problems produced by a thick web of legal prohibitions, bureaucratic obstacles, ideological suspicion, and material shortages (some caused by the US embargo itself) that have made Cuba's ubiquitous underground economy necessary.

It is often mistakenly assumed that Raúl's 2010 opening created the hundreds of thousands of private microenterprises that exist today. However, for fifty years, government policies suppressed or outlawed private business, forcing it to operate extra-legally. More recent state policies that legalized entrepreneurial activities under the euphemistic term *trabajo por cuenta propia* (self-employment or, more literally, "working on your own account") simply recognized what already existed in the underground economy.

The contested nature of *cuentapropismo* came to the fore in our interviews with Cuban entrepreneurs following the 2010 self-employment reform. For example, when asked if he would now obtain a license and emerge from the underground, Julián, a shoemaker who had lived for decades informally selling shoes he made himself, replied:

> What you need to be a *cuentapropista* in Cuba is a license and "*mucho invento*" [a lot of inventiveness]: the license bureaucratically empowers you, but that is all appearance . . . What matters is the substance of inventiveness, the miracle not of multiplying fish and bread, but of producing them out of thin air, out of NOTHING! Of course for that, the license is useless; you have to "*ir por la izquierda*" [operate on the black market] or you will only multiply the emptiness in your stomach. This is a country where to survive you have to break the law every day. There's no other way (Vignoli, personal communication, April 2012).

Even Cuba's term for its tiny private sector—*cuentapropismo*—literally implies the condition of being "on your own" (*por cuenta propia*). This casts individual agency either as a suspicious threat to state socialism or as a state abandonment of Cuban workers, rather than a necessary and honorable engine of economic development. When the Association for the Study of the Cuban Economy and the Cuba Study Group co-hosted a group of five enterprising Cuban business-women for a panel in summer 2014, they explicitly asked *not* to be introduced or referred to as *cuentapropistas*, but rather as *emprendedo-ras* (entrepreneurs)—a term that emphasizes their ingenuity, resourcefulness, and market savvy.

The Cuban government has embraced *cuentapropismo* historically only during times of economic crisis when it could no longer provide enough jobs, goods, or services. Indeed, this is one of the mantras most commonly repeated in the press when justifying the downsizing of the state sector and the expansion of self-employment: the state must lighten its load so it can focus only on the fundamentals of the economy. Given such a context, Cuban workers can be forgiven for taking Raúl's calls for greater productivity and efficiency and sharp criticisms of Cuba's "inflated state payrolls, bulky social spending, undue gratuities, and excessive subsidies" as a euphemism for the state's progressive dismantling of the historic social contract with Cuban workers under the Revolution.

Entrepreneurship has an elastic history in revolutionary Cuba (Mesa-Lago and Pérez-López 2013). In 1968, the "Revolutionary Offensive" wiped out virtually the entire private sector (then comprising approximately 58,000 small and micro-enterprises). Then, in 1978, the government allowed a very limited experiment in "self-employment," legalizing just 48 quite marginal private occupations. Most of these were eliminated once again during the "Rectification Campaign" that began in 1986. Later, in 1993, as a response to the economic crisis of the "Special Period," the government reinstituted self-employment—as a "necessary evil" in the words of Fidel Castro—legalizing 117 occupations, which grew to 157 by 1997.

By the early 2000s, however, the government had run many of these small enterprises out of business or back underground, and it officially ceased to issue new licenses for 40 of the total 157 legal self-employed occupations. As a result, the total number of licensed *cuentapropistas* decreased from a peak of 209,606 in January 1996 to 149,000 by January 2004, and it remained at that level in the six years before Raúl Castro changed economic policy once again in September 2010 with a new round of legislation that legalized 178 occupations, which eventually grew to 201. By mid 2015, the total number of registered *cuentapropistas* reached a record half-million, 100,000 of which were licensed employees of other private enterprises (most working in the food service sector).

The Promise and Peril of *Cuentapropismo* Today

Raúl's expansion of self-employment since 2010 differs in key respects from his elder brother's grudging experiments with micro-enterprise during the "Special Period." Licenses are more readily and quickly issued and potential entrepreneurs have a wider array of occupations in which to do business. They face a much improved, if still regressive, tax policy that allows them to deduct a greater portion of their business expenses—especially important for high value-added and input-dependent operations like *paladares* (private, family-run restaurants), *casas particulares* (bed and breakfasts), and *boteros* (private cab drivers). Finally, for the first time since 1968's "Revolutionary Offensive," business owners can legally hire and pay private employees.

Still, many onerous and frustrating obstacles remain that severely (and perhaps intentionally) limit *cuentapropista* growth, wealth accumulation, flexibility, access to affordable inputs and potential markets, employment, and productivity. Thus, while Raúl's reforms seem based on a refreshingly clear and transparent economic logic (especially when compared to Fidel's halting measures from the 1990s), his gradualist approach to economic change obeys an undeniable political logic as well.[2] Indeed, Raúl has explicitly described this delicate balance by repeatedly claiming that reforms will continue to move forward "*sin prisa pero sin pausa*" ("without haste but also without pause").

For example, instead of declaring a broad opening for small and medium private enterprise, together with a short list of explicitly prohibited jobs or sectors, the state published a list of just 201 jobs, outlawing all others by default.[3] The vast majority of Cuba's legalized "own-account" occupations are not entrepreneurial or wealth-generating, but strictly low-skilled, survival-oriented, service sector jobs targeted at Cuba's extremely limited and cash-poor local markets. Nearly all professionals are excluded from the self-employment sector, an especially frustrating policy for Cuba's highly educated workforce. Indeed, only 7 percent of Cuba's nearly half-million self-employed are college graduates. As Julia Cooke (2014) succinctly put it in a *New York Times* editorial, "a Cuban can go into business as a party clown but not a lawyer; she can open a bar but not a private clinic." Indeed, some of the more medieval and laughable of these 201 "private" occupations include party clown, water deliverer, knife sharpener, dandy, fortune teller, mule driver, pushcart operator, parking or public bathroom attendant, palm tree trimmer, charcoal maker and seller, button upholsterer, spark plug cleaner and tester, disposable lighter repairer and refiller, and sheep shearer.[4]

On the upside, Raúl's policies have brought much of Cuba's vast informal sector into the light. An estimated 70 percent of Cuba's new *cuentapropistas* were previously "unemployed"—a status we understand to mean working in the same jobs underground. However, to date, the expansion of self-employment has done little to create new, innovative, modern, or high-skilled employment opportunities for the projected 1.8 million state sector workers slated for layoff. Even under Raúl's more pragmatic leadership, Cuba's *papá estado* (father state) continues micromanaging the limited opening to "on-your-ownism" to protect its control of key economic sectors. Such an approach acts as an effective self-imposed, internal embargo on the productive utilization of Cuba's highly skilled labor force.

The Cooperative Alternative

One of the main ideological hurdles *cuentapropismo* still faces is an understanding of private enterprise as an individualistic contradiction within a state socialist system. Perhaps for this reason, the government is now fostering cooperatives, which are seen as more socially responsible and democratic than private enterprise and constitute a more efficient alternative to state enterprise. Thus, starting in late 2012, the government passed legislation that provided legal space for the existence of nonagricultural cooperatives (NACs) for the first time. Since then, these urban co-ops have become increasingly meaningful players in the Cuban economy and hold great potential for future entrepreneurial development.

To be sure, cooperatives are nothing new in revolutionary Cuba. Agricultural cooperatives were first inaugurated just months after the triumph of the Revolution in 1959. However, most were imposed by the state rather than arising as a result of demands from farmers themselves (Piñeiro Harnecker 2014, pp. 63–64; Ritter 2014). All Cuban agricultural cooperatives have suffered from excessive state interventionism and little autonomy, operating more as state-controlled enterprises than as real cooperatives (Ritter 2014). Consequently, the numbers of agricultural cooperatives and their membership have been dwindling since the turn of the century (Piñeiro Harnecker 2014, pp. 66–69), although at the end of 2011 there were still more than 6000 agricultural cooperatives with a total of over half a million members.

It was only in late 2012 that Cuba began to "experiment" with *nonagricultural cooperatives* focused on the production of goods and provision of services in Cuba's urban areas (*Gaceta Oficial de la República de Cuba* 2012). Although this is a living number and thus bound to change, by mid 2015, 498 such NACs had been approved, with 347 in operation and another 205 under study by the government commission in charge of approvals (Dacal Díaz 2015). The first NACs were formerly state-run farmers' markets that were turned over to the farmers themselves (Betancourt 2015). The new legal regime for nonagricultural cooperatives allows the management of the enterprise by its employees, with the worker-managers making all decisions regarding the setting of prices, the purchase of inputs, what to produce, labor relations, and the pay of members (Ritter 2014, p. 38; Ritter and Henken 2015, p. 182)—a veritable novelty in terms of economic organization and governance.

Although Cuba's NACs are still a work in progress, their numbers are growing, especially in the food service sector, because the government has publicly declared its intention to get out of the restaurant and cafeteria business. Most NACs are concentrated in the sectors of commerce, food service, and technical and personal services (59%), construction (19%), and light industry (10%), with a significant presence in transportation as well (Dacal Díaz 2015).

Cuba's NACs offer several advantages with respect to state employment and *cuentapropismo*. Professionals are legally allowed to work in cooperatives, addressing one of the structural flaws of the *cuentapropista* occupational list—namely, the absence of almost any professions. Furthermore, NACs can obtain economies of scale that are unattainable for the majority of *cuentapropistas*. Given their shared system of management and rewards, NACs should also generate a more egalitarian redistribution of income than does the private *cuentapropista* sector.

In comparison to state enterprises, nonagricultural cooperatives pay taxes and social security, and thus contribute to the state budget. Also, because members share the revenue, they should work with more intrinsic drive. Petty theft—which is endemic in state enterprises—should be absent. Given their small scale and decentralized, autonomous management structure, they should also be more flexible than state enterprises in adapting to market demand. They should usher in a more democratic workplace as well, something absent both in state enterprises and *cuentapropismo*—with the result that workers would no longer be "order takers" but "decision makers" (Ritter 2014, pp. 44–45).

Several unanswered questions and potential difficulties threaten the future development of Cuba's NACs. First, the legal framework that undergirds the NAC experiment is not yet fixed (or constitutional) and is thus susceptible to sudden and unforeseeable change. The vetting process for NACs is still too lengthy, cumbersome, and centrally controlled (Betancourt 2015; Fernández-Aballí Altamirano 2015); there is still uncertainty about the actual speed and depth of the implementation of the nonagricultural cooperative law; and neither the bureaucratic apparatus nor the cultural mindset that undergirds work in Cuba are yet cooperative-friendly.

Second, many NACs are not the result of the free association and choice of ordinary citizens. Instead, their creation can be the result of the state's abandonment of burdensome and unproductive enterprises, which are bureaucratically turned into cooperatives from above, not born from ideas incubated from below. In fact, 77 percent of the existing NACs are former state-owned enterprises that have been "cooperativatized" from on high, whereas just 23 percent are "grassroots" co-op startups (Betancourt 2015). When the state decides to close an enterprise, the employees are often given the option to transform it into a cooperative, pay rent to the owner (the state), pay taxes, and procure raw materials and clientele on their own. If they chose not to form a co-op, then the workers are declared *disponible* (available) and laid off. Moreover, autonomous decision-making and freedom from state intervention are part of the 2012 law, but implementation has been slow and erratic (Nieves Cárdenas 2014b). Thus, it is the state that decides what type of business can be turned into a cooperative through licensing and which cannot.[5]

Finally, President Raúl Castro and his chief economic advisor and chairman of the economic policy commission Marino Murillo have recently underlined the go-slow, experimental nature of the NAC roll-out, publicly reminding Cubans that "we will not massify the creation of coops but give priority to consolidating those that already exist and move forward gradually so as not to spread problems that have appeared" (Dacal Díaz 2015; Martínez Hernández 2015).

Overcoming both Embargoes:
Recommendations for Havana and Washington

Overcoming Cuba's "internal embargo" on the optimal development of island entrepreneurship will require Raúl to undertake a second, deeper, and more audacious round of economic reforms that meet halfway both the new Obama "empowerment through engagement" policy and Cuban entrepreneurs themselves. Specifically, he can do this by:

1) implementing affordable wholesale markets for entrepreneurs, among the loudest and most consistent demands of Cuba's new breed of *cuentapropistas*;
2) providing direct access to foreign exchange, investment, credit, and imports and exports—all fiercely guarded state monopolies;
3) opening the professions to private enterprise;
4) relaxing the onerous tax burden on microenterprise, which currently discriminates against domestic ventures in favor of foreign investors; and
5) allowing foreign investors to partner with Cuba's nonstate sector, opening new sources of capital and technology.

Progress in all these areas will be greatly facilitated by a more open relationship between the United States and Cuba. Access to higher levels of remittances, investment, credit, banking services, and markets would give Cuban small businesses desperately needed wholesale inputs and places to sell their products. Indeed, to varying degrees, all of these options became theoretically possible during the first half of 2015, when Obama's historic policy changes were implemented and financial companies like MasterCard and American Express, Internet behemoths like Netflix, Google, and Twitter, and the New Jersey–based telecom IDT all began to actively engage the Cuban government with business proposals.

One particularly innovative strategy of US entrepreneurial engagement has been successfully deployed in Cuba by the San Francisco startup Airbnb. Despite the fact that the US embargo still outlaws American tourist travel to the island, on April 2, 2015, the Internet-based private home reservation and payment service announced that it had begun to legally offer Americans the ability to stay in more than 1000 "real Cuban homes." The number of Cuban *casas particulares* to join Airbnb more than doubled to 2000 by June 2015, making Cuba the company's fastest growing market (Whitefield 2015).

This entrepreneurial coup amounted to a rare all-around "win" as it put hard currency directly into the pockets of Cuban entrepreneurs and gave US travelers access to authentic, affordable housing as an alternative to state-run hotels. In fact, in the three months following the April launch, Airbnb claimed that its Cuban hosts earned an average of $650, with hosts taking in $200 per booking and average room prices in Havana amounting to $41 per night (Whitefield 2015). Airbnb's move also provided the Obama administration with a marquee example of how its new regulations could be used by American companies to engage and empower Cuba's emergent entrepreneurial class while simultaneously providing the Cuban government with excess housing capacity to supplement the island's overburdened hotels at a time of booming foreign arrivals. In fact, as of mid 2015, international arrivals to Cuba were up 15.4 percent compared to the first half of 2014, with arrivals from the United States up a whopping 50.1 percent (Perelló Cabrera 2015a). The emergent bed-and-breakfast sector is well positioned to absorb a significant share of new arrivals given that it currently accounts for 23 percent (18,742) of the total 80,832 available hotel rooms on the island (Perelló Cabrera 2015b).

Airbnb was able to move so quickly by nimbly exploiting both the letter and the spirit of the new regulations that permit Americans to purchase services directly from Cuba's private sector. The company did this by plugging into the country's pre-existing network of *casas particulares* and facilitating connections between homeowners and "hosting partners," third parties with Internet access who manage inquiries and bookings (Whitefield 2015). The company also partnered with Va Cuba, an established money transfer company based in Miami, allowing hosts to quickly receive cash payments (Kessler 2015). Finally, Airbnb also proactively engaged officials in both the US and Cuban governments to obtain legal approval for their innovative project. Indeed, the Cuban Airbnb success story could become a model for other US companies that seek to use creative web strategies to partner with Cuba's emerging nonstate sector.

However, for this still largely symbolic opening to become a real one that impacts the bottom line for the majority of Cuban startups (not just ones who sell lodging services to authorized travelers via the Internet), more needs to happen on the US side. The main challenge in this vein is the still piecemeal reform of overall US policy. The continued existence of the embargo undermines President Obama's efforts to engage Cuba, forcing him to make policy with one hand tied behind his back.

On the bright side, the US list of goods and services eligible for import from Cuba's private and cooperative enterprises, released on February 13, 2015, is purposely a "negative" one. That is, instead of listing what is permitted in exhaustive detail (as the Cuban Government has done with its list of 201 self-employed occupations), the State Department only lists exceptions, allowing Cuban entrepreneurs to use their imaginations, be creative, and think outside the box (in other words, to keep "inventing" and finding solutions where there apparently are none).[6] However, the fact that these provisions apply only to goods and services that originate in Cuba's "private sector" (something for which importers must show documentary proof) could be interpreted by the Cuban government as a "Trojan horse of trade" aimed at undermining the state enterprise sector (and the government monopoly on imports and exports) by empowering *cuentapropistas* to become more independent from the state. So far, even though the State Department has said it would allow Alimport, the Cuban government import-export monopoly, to act as a middleman, there is no evidence that any trade with Cuba's entrepreneurial sector has taken place beyond the "suitcase commerce" that approved travelers may engage in.

Although most of the services on Cuba's self-employment list are decidedly low-skilled and extremely local in their application, others such as telecommunications agent, real estate broker, photographer/videographer, computer programmer, bookkeeper, and document translator are both potentially lucrative and will be increasingly "exportable" abroad as Cuba's Internet penetration and speed increase. Given the strong linguistic, cultural, and familial bonds between Cuba and South Florida, it would be easy to imagine Cuban American businesses in Miami outsourcing certain "back office" computer and technical services to Cubans on the island as a way to simultaneously cut costs and support their compatriots. Under Obama's new regulations, this kind of "offshoring" of services to Cuba is now legal.[7]

The State Department has also clearly stated that the import list is a "living document" that will be expanded over time as it receives feedback from Cuba's private sector and as conditions (and laws) change on the ground in Cuba. As the US list expands, we envisage a series of positive spillover effects within Cuba, incentivizing the concomitant expansion of Cuba's own list of permitted self-employment occupations to include more modern, professional, value-added categories of economic activity. In the short term, this should increase the number of licensed *cuentapropistas* (which has virtually flat-lined since 2012 after phenomenal growth [González-Corzo 2015]). It should also allow them—together with Cuba's new nonagricultural cooperatives—to link with US suppliers and markets. In the medium to long term, US engagement could stimulate the growth of viable and dynamic modes of entrepreneurship (such as food service, hospitality, and transportation).

Strengthening viable entrepreneurship means establishing a new relationship between Cubans and the state, transforming citizens from passive recipients of subsidized goods into active participants in the nation's economy. Raúl has repeatedly reminded Cubans that the days of "undue gratuities and excessive subsidies" are numbered. So should the days of a paternalist state that centralizes and monopolizes all vital economic activities. US engagement with Cuban *cuentapropistas* could help tip the balance in this direction. Increased American involvement with Cuban entrepreneurs could also bring about a transfer of intangible but essential "know-how" in terms of specific technological advancements and products and in terms of the market ethos that is emerging despite an unstable, ad hoc, and not yet fully legitimate and legal environment for private enterprise.

Conclusion: Making the Lives of Ordinary Cubans *"Un Poco Más Fácil"*

It remains to be seen whether Raúl has the political will to intensify the internal reform process. The prohibition of private economic activities in sectors the government prefers to keep under state monopoly allows it to exercise control over Cuban citizens and impose an apparent order over society. However, this comes at the cost of pushing economic activity (along with potential tax revenue) back into the black market, where much of it lurked prior to 2010. However, the acceptance and regulation of the many private activities dreamed-up and market-tested by Cuba's always inventive entrepreneurial sector would create more jobs and better quality and variety of goods and services at lower prices while also increasing tax revenue. However, these benefits come at the political cost of allowing greater citizen autonomy, wealth, and property into private hands and open competition against state monopolies.

The historic change in US-Cuban policy announced on December 17, 2014 will inevitably change the political calculus that underlies the pace and depth of the island's economic reform. As external obstacles to Cuba's economic revitalization are eliminated, the onus for Cuba's chronic economic problems will fall increasingly onto the Cuban government itself, spurring demands for deeper reforms. Fidel Castro's legitimacy and legacy were tied more to political and ideological achievements (like the defense of Cuban sovereignty and provision of universal social services) than they were to economic growth. Raúl, however, knows that his own legitimacy and legacy are riding on the economic achievements he can bequeath to a new generation of Cuban rulers when he leaves office in 2018. This makes the stakes of engagement with the United States very high indeed.

Obama's courageous move to replace a failed past US policy of isolation and impoverishment aimed at regime change with one of empowerment and prosperity aimed at the Cuban people is a necessary step toward "making the lives of ordinary Cubans a little bit easier, more free, more prosperous," as he declared on December 17, 2014. However, this historic change remains insufficient to spark real job creation, wealth formation, economic growth, and sustainable development on the island unless Raúl Castro is equally bold in eliminating the still onerous internal obstacles to a more enterprising Cuba.

Notes

1. For the full video and text of President Obama's speech, see the White House's foreign policy page (https://www.whitehouse.gov/issues/foreign-policy/cuba). For a fact sheet detailing the administration's "new course on Cuba," see https://www.whitehouse.gov/the-press-office/2014/12/17/fact-sheet-charting-new-course-cuba.

2. On Cuba's alternating "pragmatic" cycles of policymaking that obey economic logic versus "idealist" cycles, which follow political logic, see Mesa-Lago and Pérez-López (2013).

3. For analysis by Cuban economists that makes similar criticisms and recommendations, see Pavel Vidal and Omar Everleny Pérez Villanueva (2010).

4. For the full list of Cuba's 201 self-employment occupations, see Feinberg (2013) and Ritter and Henken (2015).

5. For example, in 2014 in Cienfuegos "70 state-owned cafeterias, restaurants and barbershops will be turned into cooperatives, while only five applications for 'cooperatives in construction' have been approved by the territorial government" (Nieves Cárdenas 2014a).

6. The US State Department section 515.582 list of Cuban goods and services eligible for importation is available at http://m.state.gov/md237471.htm, together with a Fact Sheet: http://m.state.gov/md237473.htm.

7. For two excellent articles by *Miami Herald* reporter Mimi Whitefield that try to make sense of this emerging legislation, see "New import rules for Cuba represent historic change," February 13, 2015, and "Cuban entrepreneurs can sell everything from shoes to soap in the United States," February 23, 2015.

References

Betancourt, Rafael. 2015. "Non-Agricultural Cooperatives in Cuba's New Economic Strategy." Panel presentation given at the Brookings Institution Seminar: "Time to Invest in Cuba?", Washington, DC, June 2. https://www.youtube.com/watch?t=11&v=UmMt60iQ5IA.

Castro Ruz, Raúl. 2008. "Discurso pronunciado por el General de Ejército Raúl Castro Ruz, Presidente de los Consejos de Estado y de Ministros, en las conclusiones de la primera sesión ordinaria de la VII Legislatura de la Asamblea Nacional del Poder Popular." Havana, July 11. http://www.cuba.cu/gobierno/rauldiscursos/2008/esp/r110708e.html.

———. 2010a. "Discurso pronunciado por el General de Ejército Raúl Castro Ruz, Presidente de los Consejos de Estado y de Ministros, en el Quinto Período Ordinario de Sesiones de la VII Legislatura de la Asamblea Nacional del Poder Popular." Havana, August 1. http://www.cuba.cu/gobierno/rauldiscursos/2010/esp/r010810e.html.

———. 2010b. "Discurso del General de Ejército Raúl Castro Ruz." *Juventud Rebelde*, December 18. http://www.juventudrebelde.cu/cuba/2010-12-18/discurso-raul-castro-ruz/.

Cooke, Julia. 2014. "In Cuba, Unequal Reform." *New York Times*, April 2. http://www.nytimes.com/2014/04/02/opinion/in-cuba-unequal-reform.html?_r=0.

Dacal Díaz, Ariel. 2015. "Las cooperativas, sí... pero no." *OnCuba*, June 11. http://oncubamagazine.com/sociedad/las-cooperativas-si-pero-no/.

Feinberg, Richard. 2013. "Soft Landing in Cuba: Emerging Entrepreneurs and Middle Classes." Brookings Institution, November. http://www.brookings.edu/~/media/research/files/reports/2013/11/cuba-emerging-entrepreneurs-middle-classes-feinberg/cuba-entrepreneurs-middle-classes-feinberg.pdf.

Fernández-Aballí Altamirano, Carlos. 2015. "New Entrepreneurship in Cuba: CnA Cooperativa Industrias Purita Case Study." Presentation given at the annual meeting for the Association for the Study of the Cuban Economy, Miami, Florida, July 31.

Gaceta Oficial de la República de Cuba. 2012. Number 53, December 16. http://www.cepec.cu/sites/default/files/GO_X_53_2014.pdf.

Goldberg, Jeffrey. 2010. "Fidel: 'Cuban Model Doesn't Even Work for Us Anymore.'" *The Atlantic*, September 8. http://www.theatlantic.com/

international/archive/2010/09/fidel-cuban-model-doesnt-even-work-for-us-anymore/62602/.

González-Corzo, Mario A. 2015. "Recent US-Cuba Policy Changes: Potential Impact on Self-Employment." *Focus on Cuba*, 239. http://ctp. iccas.miami.edu/FOCUS_Web/Issue239.htm.

Kessler, Sarah. 2015. "Airbnb's Secret to Scaling in Cuba." *Fast Company*, July 8. http://www.fastcompany.com/3048272/innovation-agents/airbnbs-secret-to-scaling-in-cuba.

Martínez Hernández, Leticia. 2010. "Trabajo por cuenta propia, Mucho más que una Alternativa." *Granma*, September 24. http://www.cubainformacion.tv/index.php/economia/32027-trabajo-por-cuenta-propia-mucho-mas-que-una-alternativa.

———. 2015. "Raúl: 'Lo que hacemos debe ser sometido constantemente a la crítica constructiva por parte de todos.'" *Granma*, May 31. http://www.granma.cu/cuba/2015-05-31/raul-lo-que-hacemos-debe-ser-sometido-constantemente-a-la-critica-constructiva-por-parte-de-todos.

Mesa-Lago, Carmelo, and Jorge Pérez-López. 2013. *Cuba Under Raúl Castro: Assessing the Reforms*. Boulder: Lynne Rienner.

Nieves Cárdenas, J.J. 2014a. "Reviewing Cuba's 'Experiment' with Non-agricultural Cooperatives." *Havana Times*, May 9. http://www.havanatimes.org/?p=103534.

———. 2014b. "Cuba y cooperativas 'sin papeles.'" *Havana Times*, May 20. http://www.havanatimes.org/sp/?p=96006.

Partido Comunista de Cuba. 2011. "Lineamientos de la política económica y social del partido y la revolución." Adopted during the Sixth Congress of the PCC, April 18.

Perelló Cabrera, José Luis. 2015a. "Actualización del turismo en Cuba." Working paper draft provided by the author, July 4.

———. 2015b. "El sector privado y el turismo en Cuba ante un escenario de relaciones con Estados Unidos." Presentation given at the annual meeting of the Association for the Study of the Cuban Economy, Miami, Florida, July 30.

Piñeiro Harnecker, C. 2014. "Las cooperativas en Cuba." In *Reformando el modelo económico Cubano*, edited by Mauricio Font and Mario González-Corzo, 63–83. New York: Bildner Center for Western Hemisphere Studies, City University.

"Pronunciamiento de la Central de Trabajadores de Cuba: Reducirá Cuba medio millón de plazas en el sector estatal." 2010. *Granma*, September 13. http://www.cubadebate.cu/noticias/2010/09/13/reducira-cuba-medio-millon-de-plazas-en-el-sector-estatal/#.VRZEFCgq83Q.

Ritter, Archibald R.M. 2014. "Potentials and Pitfalls of Cuba's Move toward Non-Agricultural Cooperatives." *Cuba in Transition* 23: 38–49. http://www.ascecuba.org/c/wp-content/uploads/2014/09/v23-ritter.pdf.

Ritter, Archibald R.M., and Ted A. Henken. 2015. *Entrepreneurial Cuba: The Changing Policy Landscape*. Boulder: FirstForum.
Vidal, Pavel, and Omar Everleny Pérez Villanueva. 2010. "Entre el Ajuste Fiscal y los Cambios Estructurales se Extiende el Cuentapropismo en Cuba." *Espacio Laical*, October-December. http://www.espaciolaical.org/contens/esp/sd_112.pdf.
Whitefield, Mimi. 2015. "Airbnb Cracking the Cuban Market." *Miami Herald*, July 5. http://www.miamiherald.com/news/business/biz-monday/article26213032.html.

Chapter 13

Onstage or Backstage? Latin America and US-Cuban Relations

Andrés Serbin

On December 17, 2014, three days after Havana celebrated the tenth anniversary of the official creation of the Bolivarian Alliance for the Americas (or ALBA, its acronym in Spanish), Presidents Barack Obama and Raúl Castro announced that, after more than half a century of hostilities between the United States and Cuba, the countries had begun bilateral talks to reestablish diplomatic relations. The announcement—and the secret talks that led to it—may have come as a surprise for Cuba's closest ally in the region, the Bolivarian government of President Nicolás Maduro in Venezuela, but it was long desired by Latin American and Caribbean governments. Although most of these governments, particularly the more left-leaning ones, continue to denounce the US embargo on Cuba in regional and international forums, expectations had been on the rise since President Obama's attendance at the fifth Summit of the Americas held in Port of Spain in April 2009, where he promised a different, more open approach to US-Latin American relations. Hopes were high that Cuba, the only country in the hemisphere excluded from the Inter-American system, could return to the fold and participate in the Summits of the Americas. This was further evident at the sixth Summit, held in Cartagena de Indias in 2012, where Latin American and Caribbean leaders increased pressure on the United States to include Cuba in any future Summit and the host, Colombian

President Santos, paid a special visit to President Castro in Havana before the gathering. Meanwhile, in June 2009, the thirty-ninth Organization of American States (OAS) General Assembly, held in San Pedro Sula, Honduras, decided unanimously to cancel the 1962 resolution to exclude the Cuban government from the organization, confirming that most Latin American and Caribbean governments—and not just those aligned with ALBA—were committed to Cuba's rapid reincorporation into the hemispheric community. The overturning of Cuba's exclusion from the OAS and the pressure by Latin American and Caribbean countries in preparation of and during the previous Summits were important steps to include Cuba for the first time at the seventh Summit of the Americas held in Panama in April 2015.

Within this context, and after eighteen months of secret interventions by the Vatican and Canada, US-Cuban bilateral talks were officially announced in December 2014. A key pending question is whether Latin American and Caribbean governments contributed in any way to this dialogue, given their increasing autonomy from the United States and the rapidly changing hemispheric relations during the first decade of the twenty-first century. To answer this question, it is important to elaborate on two important factors that played into this process: (1) the changing landscape of regional governance after the end of the Cold War and the events of September 11, leading to the gradual strategic disengagement of the United States from Latin America (as its priorities in the region narrowed to the war on drugs and immigration and focused on its closest neighbors) and (2) the cautious approach taken by some key Latin American and Caribbean countries in influencing the US position toward Cuba. The two factors are intertwined. Latin American new regionalism emerged through the creation of several regional organizations—such as ALBA, the Union of South American States (UNASUR), and the Community of Latin American and Caribbean States (CELAC)—that excluded the United States and Canada. And several Latin American and Caribbean countries—particularly Brazil, Mexico, and Venezuela—played leading roles in this process (Serbin 2009, 2010a).

However, a third factor should not be underestimated. Since the 1970s, when Cuba began to establish closer ties with the Caribbean Community (CARICOM) countries, until the late 1990s, when Cuba was admitted to the Latin American Integration Association (ALADI, for its acronym in Spanish), Havana developed a consistent foreign policy strategy of broadening and deepening its relations with Latin America within its international policy of "concentric circles"

(Serbin 2011, 2013a). This strategy was closely related to the process of economic reforms associated with the "*modelo de actualización económica y social*" (Alzugaray 2014).

Cuban policy toward the region benefitted from the electoral accession to power of like-minded left-wing or populist parties and movements that sympathized with Cuba's revolution within the framework of the so-called pink tide (Cameron and Hershberg 2010; Cannon and Kirby 2012).

Additionally, the strategy of gradual reintegration of Cuba into Latin America and the Caribbean was linked to the country's growing array of political and economic ties with a broad spectrum of emerging powers, particularly from the Global South. Capitalizing on the links forged during its "globalist" strategy from previous years, Cuba first tightened ties with China (which became its second trade partner) and re-established its links with the Russian Federation, which in 2014 forgave 90 percent of Cuba's outstanding debt with that nation (Alzugaray 2014, p. 77; Domínguez 2001; Serbin 2001). Since the early 1990s, the island has successfully used soft power to condemn and restrict US positions within the United Nations and other multilateral forums. This policy was originally designed to safeguard the Cuban political process through diversifying and rebalancing its foreign relations within an emerging multipolar and polycentric international system (Serbin 2011, 2013a). In later years, it also became a fundamental instrument for strengthening the island's economic reform process by diversifying its trade partners and attracting foreign investment (Alzugaray 2014; Serbin 2013a).

Cuba commenced the process of full reincorporation into the Latin American and Caribbean community by participating in the Iberoamerican Summit in Guadalajara in 1991. Subsequently, Fidel Castro attended presidential inaugurations in different Latin American and Caribbean countries before his retirement, and Cuba began to participate officially in regional multilateral summits and meetings, including those of the Association of Caribbean States (which was created in 1994 with Cuba's strong support), Caribbean Community (CARICOM), and the Mercado Común del Sur (Mercosur). Once in office, Raúl Castro followed suit, particularly regarding attendance at regional gatherings, and also through a series of official visits to several Latin American and Caribbean countries (Alzugaray 2014, p. 73).

In Latin America, and particularly South America, the development of a new and distinctive form of regionalism was simultaneously a sounding board and a key factor in paving the way to renewed Cuban presence in the region.

The New Latin American Regionalism and its Impact on Hemispheric Relations

Since the 1950s, Latin American regionalism has evolved in three distinct stages. The first phase took place between the 1960s and 1980s (when US hegemony remained strong) and was built around a desire for greater autonomy through the creation of regional markets and strategies of industrialization and import substitution. A second phase took shape at the end of the 1980s and the beginning of the 1990s. Heavily influenced by the so-called Washington Consensus and the concept of "open regionalism" espoused by the Economic Commission on Latin America (ECLAC), a neoliberal approach was introduced that focused on trade liberalization, economic opening, and the elimination of trade barriers. However, after negotiations concerning the Free Trade Area of the Americas collapsed during 2005, new forms of regional political cooperation, as well as social and economic integration, began to emerge. Dubbed "postliberal" or "posthegemonic,"[1] these new forms of regionalism have centered on creating organizations that prioritize political coordination, intergovernmental arrangements, and a new regional agenda predicated on a stronger role for the State.

During the first decade of this century, the international environment advanced this process through the increasing global demand for commodities, the growing links with China and the Asian-Pacific region, and the sustained economic growth of most regional economies. China became an important trade partner, eventually displacing the European Union in several Latin American and Caribbean countries, and particularly in South America.

This period signaled profound changes in the international system. After the end of the Cold War, and especially after September 11, 2001, the United States reoriented its strategic priorities, giving less attention to Latin America (apart from its closest neighbors Mexico, Central America, and the Caribbean). Such a withdrawal weakened both US-Latin American relations and the Inter-American system in general, the latter of which was strongly criticized, particularly by the ALBA governments. At the same time, the euro crisis precipitated a decline of European presence in the area. Links among Latin American states grew, but not through a single and coherent process of regional integration, which eventually resulted in the "segmented proliferation" of weak and unstable models of region-building (Malamud 2013).

Meanwhile, India, Korea, and particularly China increased their presence in Latin America, as Japan had done earlier, although they initially limited themselves principally to economic ties. Other actors, such as Russia and Iran, also established closer ties with the region. For its part, Latin America was looking for new partners in a world characterized by the "rise of the rest" (Zakaria 2008).

Even though Latin America and the Caribbean in general withstood the effects of the 2008 global financial crisis better than did the developed countries, the "commodities boom" and economic growth in most of these countries were short-lived. Even as the region absorbed China's increasing presence (boosted by more than a decade of sustained economic growth in this country) and links with the Asia-Pacific grew and developed, the international economic environment started to change. Chinese growth decelerated while the US economy showed signs of recovery, and the euro zone—notwithstanding the crisis in Greece—also started to show incipient signs of revitalization. Weaker demand from China's slowing economy produced a downturn in commodity prices.[2] As a result, in the first quarter of 2015, the region's annual growth rate was projected to be significantly lower than the 1.1 percent posted in 2014. Following years of abundant liquidity in international financial markets and access to credit at low interest rates, concerns have arisen once again over the date of a possible increase in the benchmark interest rate by the US Federal Reserve, as well as the timing and size of subsequent increases. It is unclear what impact a hike would have on financial markets, but the combination of these factors has effectively marked the end of a favorable international cycle for the region (ECLAC 2015).

Looking for Increased Autonomy

Nevertheless, during the past two decades, the international system has shown greater signs of multipolarity and polycentrism (Serbin 2010a). Latin American countries, particularly in South America, took advantage of the new international situation to exhibit greater autonomy from the United States (Tickner 2015). In this context, over the past decade, regional organizations with varying political, economic, and ideological approaches were created in Latin America and the Caribbean. In 2004, Cuba and Venezuela formed the Bolivarian Alternative for the Peoples of Our America, later renamed the

Bolivarian Alliance for the Peoples of Our America (ALBA) (Bagley and Defort 2014). The Venezuelan-funded organization promoted South-South cooperation and assistance, all while espousing strident anti-US rhetoric. In May 2008, after a long process led mostly by Brazil, UNASUR was founded in Brasília, bringing together 12 South American states.

In February 2010 in Cancun, all of the Latin American and Caribbean governments collaborated to form CELAC, another inter-American organization that, like ALBA and UNASUR, excluded the United States and Canada. CELAC took over the role of the Rio Group, which had served as a forum for political coordination and consultation since the 1980s. Since its inauguration, and even with an evident lack of an institutionalized structure, CELAC has developed a series of extra-regional dialogue initiatives with actors such as the European Union, China, India, and Russia, a process that in 2015 culminated with a Sino-Latin American Summit in Beijing and an EU-CELAC meeting in Brussels. Finally, the Pacific Alliance—founded in 2012 by Colombia, Chile, Peru, and Mexico—started out fundamentally as a revitalized free trade agreement between these countries, but also as a political counterbalance to the Bolivarian sympathizers on the Atlantic side of the Americas. Several observer states like Panama and Costa Rica are currently in the process of joining the bloc, because Pacific Alliance members stand to gain from the Trans-Pacific Partnership (Serbin 2013b, 2014).

The dominant trends of regional political coordination and increasing autonomy from the United States (whether cautious or stridently radical), with the exception of the Pacific Alliance, have prevailed in Latin America and the Caribbean for the past 15 years, notwithstanding the region's persistent fragmentation and lack of consolidated institutions. Before the most recent changes in the international environment, this situation allowed Latin American and Caribbean countries to implement more proactive and assertive foreign policies vis-á-vis the United States, from open contestation to partial and critical accommodation. The new policies were clearly illustrated by tensions and divergent positions within the OAS, which were usually aimed at contesting US positions.

Within this context of contestation, Cuba (as mentioned) has been consistently invited by Latin American and Caribbean countries to attend regional summits and high-level meetings, and it has become a regular participant at most of the major regional political events, with the exception of OAS meetings. Cuba and different Latin American countries and regional organizations have also signed various treaties and agreements, and Cuba was one of the founders of CELAC. Cuba's process of inclusion within the Latin American and Caribbean community culminated at the third Summit of CELAC, which was held under Cuban pro-tempore presidency in Havana in January 2014. Latin American and Caribbean presidents and heads of states participated, and the Secretary General of the OAS attended. At the event, participants declared their support for the Cuban government and denounced the US embargo on the island. The Summit was not only a show of the region's support for Cuba but also an important signal to the United States that Latin America and the Caribbean were committed to fully reintegrating Cuba into the hemispheric community.

Key Latin American Players

In the crusade for Cuba's inclusion in the Latin American and Caribbean community, Venezuela (and particularly Hugo Chávez's charisma and regional influence) played an important role, especially since the creation of ALBA (Serbin 2010b). But Brazil's subtle and cautious support and leadership, especially that of Lula da Silva, were also key factors in this process, even if the country's stance toward the United States was less openly antagonistic. More cautious still was the Colombian government's position, even after President Santos' re-election in 2014. Although the United States has historically been one of Colombia's allies, Cuba has played a fundamental role in peace negotiations between the Colombian government and the FARC and ELN guerrillas, and has helped significantly to mitigate past tensions between Colombia and Chávez's government. Before the creation of CELAC, Mexico was initially excluded from the process, despite its important historic ties with Cuba, but it finally followed suit in supporting Cuba during the Calderón and Peña Nieto administrations, as did the rest of the South American and Caribbean countries—Bolivarian or not—and some of the Central American nations. The Panamanian government's decision to invite the Cuban government to attend the seventh Summit of the Americas, notwithstanding US reluctance, catalyzed the regional process of support for Cuba's full inclusion into the hemispheric community, although influential media and politicians expressed distrust regarding Cuba's commitment to democracy, its human rights record, and the scope of economic reforms on the island.

However, there is no way of measuring the real influence of individual Latin American and Caribbean governments in the process of re-establishing Cuban-US bilateral relations. What is clear is that most of them supported ending the Cuban government's suspension from the OAS and, through statements and declarations by the newly formed regional organizations, were crucial for creating an environment that pressured the United States to allow Cuba's full reincorporation into the hemispheric community, as illustrated by the seventh Summit of the Americas. In any case, even if the protracted bilateral talks that culminated in the December 2014 announcements were solely the result of sovereign decisions made by both the United States and Cuban administrations without any direct external intervention, pressure, or facilitation by the Latin American and Caribbean governments, the changes in the regional environment since the beginning of the century were propitious for initiating this process and became a key factor in influencing the current US administration (see Hershberg, this volume).

Opening Pandora's Box

The most anticipated moment of the seventh Summit of the Americas was the symbolic handshake between Barack Obama and Raúl Castro, leaders of two countries separated by decades of diplomatic confrontation. However, although Cuba was on the top of the "to-do" list for the United States in Panama, it was actually part of a wider and more ambitious agenda: re-establishing US presence in Latin America and the Caribbean and limiting China's growing regional influence (Serbin and Serbin Pont 2015).

The re-establishment of diplomatic relations between Cuba and the United States following Panama's Summit of the Americas seems promising in terms of the "normalization" of hemispheric relations, a process that has indeed prominently included Latin American and Caribbean countries. Nevertheless, several questions remain unanswered after the December 2014 announcement.

The first one is related to the beginning of a new phase of hemispheric relations, mostly due to a more assertive US presence in the region. Within this framework, Cuba's diversified foreign policy (both regional and global) could be challenged by the rapprochement between Havana and Washington. Traditional relations with partners such as China, Russia, and even the European Union might be readjusted. Likewise, new priorities and adjustments may be made in light of the weakening role of the regional organizations that supported Cuba's stand, the disappearance of Lula's and Chávez's regional leadership, and the domestic political turmoil both in Brazil and in Venezuela, among other relevant Latin American and Caribbean players.

The second unanswered question is in regard to whether Cuba will be able, under the new conditions, to combine the demands of an economic reform process with the continuation of an autonomous, balanced, and diversified foreign policy. Although autonomy was a priority of Cuba's foreign policy for decades—and a symbolic reference for most countries in the region—Cuba's recent internal reforms and foreign policy changes prioritize other objectives to an extent that it is difficult to appraise their effects in the near future.

Finally, since Lula and Chávez left the regional scene, hegemonic competition in the hemisphere has eased considerably. There are no emergent new leaders to drive the new regionalism in Latin America and the Caribbean, mostly because domestic political and economic priorities of the main regional governments are already affecting the performance of regional organizations. ALBA, for example, has suffered from the decrease in international oil prices and subsequent loss of Venezuelan commitments. More recently, UNASUR has not been able to address some of the most urgent regional issues, such as the Venezuelan domestic political crisis and the increasing tension between Venezuela and Colombia after a decision by Maduro to expel Colombian citizens. Colombia's decision to bring the issue before the OAS in August 2015 has failed so far, and the two countries remain at an impasse, with all of the accompanying regional reverberations. Venezuela's government also alienated CARICOM members with Guyana regarding oil exploration. And Mexico is still licking its internal political wounds after the disappearance of 43 students in the town of Iguala and under the impact of the international decrease in oil prices, both of which have seriously weakened Peña Nieto's administration. In sum, the previous decade's wave of a vigorous new regionalism, with all of its imperfections and achievements, seems to be losing momentum now that its main protagonists are focusing on their own domestic issues. The current regional environment begs the question: can Latin American and Caribbean governments sustain the same level of support for Cuba as they have in the recent past?

Looking forward in light of the recent advances in Cuban-US relations and the political success of the seventh Summit of the Americas in Panama, it remains to be seen how future rounds of Cuba-US talks and the "normalization" process will develop and how the current reconfiguration of the regional geopolitical landscape will affect

US-Cuban relations, Cuban foreign policy, and US influence on Latin America and the Caribbean.

Notes

1. On this debate, see the first section of Serbin et al. (2012).
2. Specifically, metal and agricultural product prices began to decrease in the first quarter of 2011 and, although the trend has stabilized, these categories posted losses of 41 percent and 29 percent, respectively, between the first quarter of 2011 and April 2015. After a period of stagnation and gradual decline since 2011, energy prices (comprising crude oil, natural gas, and coal) tumbled 52 percent in the seven months between July 2014 and January 2015. The crude oil price—the largest component in the energy price index—decreased by almost 60 percent during that period. (ECLAC 2015, pp. 15–17).

References

Alzugaray, Carlos. 2014. "La actualización de la política exterior cubana." *Política Exterior* 161 (September–October): 70–82.

Bagley, Bruce, and Magdalena Defort, eds. 2014. *¿La hegemonía norteamericana en declive? El desafío del ALBA y la nueva integración latinoamericana del siglo XXI.* Cali: Universidad ICESI.

Cameron, Maxwell, and Eric Hershberg, eds. 2010. *Latin America's Left Turns. Politics, Policies and Trajectories of Change.* Boulder: Lynne Rienner.

Cannon, Barry, and Peadar Kirby, eds. 2012. *Civil Society and State in Left-Led Latin America: Challenges and Limitations to Democratization.* London: Zed Books.

Domínguez, Jorge. 2001. "Cuban Foreign Policy and the International System." In *Latin America in the New International System*, edited by Joseph Tulchin and Ralph H. Espach, 183–206. Boulder-London: Lynne Rienner.

ECLAC (Economic Commission for Latin America and the Caribbean). 2015. "Economic Survey of Latin America and the Caribbean: Challenges in Boosting the Investment Cycle to Reinvigorate Growth." *ECLAC Briefing Paper*, July.

Malamud, Andrés. 2013. "Overlapping Regionalism, No Integration: Conceptual Issues and the Latin American Experiences." *European University Institute Working Paper RSCAS 2013/20.* http://cadmus.eui.eu/bitstream/handle/1814/26336/RSCAS_2013_20.pdf?sequence=1.

Serbin, Andrés. 2001. "Lejos de Dios y demasiado cerca de … La política exterior de Cuba hacia América Latina y el Caribe." *Foreign Affairs en español* 1.3: 40.

————. 2009. "Tres liderazgos y un vacío: América Latina y la nueva encrucijada regional." In *Escenarios de crisis: fracturas y pugnas en el sistema internacional*. *Anuario 2008–2009*, coordinated by Manuela Mesa, 141–58. Madrid: CEIPAZ-Icaria Editorial.

————. 2010a. "Multipolaridad, liderazgos e instituciones regionales: los desafíos de UNASUR ante la prevención de crisis regionales." In *Crisis y cambio en la sociedad global*. *Anuario 2009–2010*, coordinated by Manuela Mesa, 331–46. Madrid: CEIPAZ – Icaria Editorial.

————. 2010b. *Chávez, Venezuela y la reconfiguración política de América Latina y el Caribe*. Buenos Aires: Editorial Siglo XXI.

————. 2011. "Círculos concéntricos: la política exterior de Cuba en un mundo multipolar y el proceso de 'actualización.'" In *Cuba, Estados Unidos y América Latina frente a los desafíos hemisféricos*, edited by Luis Fernando Ayerbe, 229–68. Buenos Aires: CRIES/Icaria Editorial.

————. 2013a. "Cuba: a atualização do modelo econômico e a politica externa em um mundo multipolar." *Política Externa* 21: 177–208.

————. 2013b. "Los nuevos regionalismos y la CELAC: Los retos pendientes." In *Desafíos estratégicos del regionalismo contemporáneo: CELAC e Iberoamérica*, edited by Adrián Bonilla and Isabel Álvarez Echandi, 47–78. San José: FLACSO.

————. 2014. "¿Atlántico vs. Pacífico?: Mega-acuerdos e implicaciones geo-estratégicas para América Latina y el Caribe." In ¿Atlántico vs. Pacífico?: América Latina y el Caribe, los cambios regionales y los desafíos globales. Anuario de la Integración Regional de América Latina y el Caribe No. 10, coordinated by Andrés Serbin, Laneydi Martínez, and Haroldo Ramanzini Júnior, 15–72. Buenos Aires: CRIES. http://www.cries.org/wp-content/uploads/2014/11/02a-Serbin.pdf.

Serbin, Andrés, Laneydi Martínez, and Haroldo Ramanzini Júnior, coords. 2012. *El regionalismo "post-liberal" en América Latina y el Caribe: Nuevos actores, nuevos temas, nuevos desafíos. Anuario de la Integración Regional de América Latina y el Caribe 2012*. Buenos Aires: CRIES. http://www.ieei-unesp.com.br/portal/wp-content/uploads/2012/10/2012-Anuario-CRIES-1.pdf.

Serbin, Andrés, and Andrei Serbin Pont. 2015. "Obama Is Using Cuba to Counter Russia, Iran, and China's Growing Influence in Latin America." *Forbes*, April 16. http://www.forbes.com/sites/afontevecchia/2015/04/16/obama-is-using-cuba-to-counter-russia-iran-and-chinas-growing-influence-in-latin-america/#a5c2e6445044.

Tickner, Arlene. 2015. "Autonomy in Latin American International Relations Thinking." In *Routledge Handbook of Latin America in the World*, edited by Jorge Domínguez and Ana Covarrubias, 74–84. New York: Routledge.

Zakaria, Fareed. 2008. *The Post-American World*. New York: W.W. Norton.

Chapter 14

Conclusion: Keys to Assessing Progress Toward Establishing Normal Relations between the United States and Cuba

William M. LeoGrande and Eric Hershberg

Events have moved quickly since President Barack Obama and President Raúl Castro announced their agreement to normalize relations last December 17—quickly at least as compared to how little progress was made over the previous fifty-four years. The two presidents have met twice face-to-face for substantive talks—at the Seventh Summit of the Americas in Panama in April 2015 and at the United Nations (UN) General Assembly in September. They have also spoken three times on the telephone—on the day before their historic announcement, before their face-to-face meeting in Panama, and just prior to the Pope's visit to Cuba and the United States in September.

The US Department of State and Cuban Foreign Ministry—both left out of the secret negotiations that led to December 17—have since taken charge of the normalization process. They established a high-level Bilateral Commission scheduled to meet quarterly to take stock of progress and set the agenda for the months ahead. Between commission meetings, working groups of specialists were negotiating their way through the myriad remaining issues between the two countries and trying to unravel what Fidel Castro once called "a tangled ball of yarn" (LeoGrande and Kornbluh 2014, p. 203).

Yet despite what appeared to be a quick start, progress on the diplomatic front proved slower than many people expected. One element of the agreement that emerged from the secret negotiations was that the United States and Cuba would restore diplomatic relations. The two presidents announced that commitment in their simultaneous television broadcasts. Yet it took more than six months to negotiate the details of restoring ties and reopening embassies.

Havana insisted that it should be removed from the Department of State's list of state sponsors of internationalism terrorism, saying it would be hard to imagine normal relations as long as that unjust designation remained. Washington insisted that US diplomats in Havana should have the right to travel freely and meet with people across the island—a freedom that Cuban officials argued had been abused in previous years by US diplomats who provided support to Cuban dissidents.

Eventually, the State Department took Cuba off the terrorism list—an action long overdue based on the facts. The issue of diplomatic travel was resolved by restoring the pre-2003 arrangement (before the George W. Bush administration imposed travel limits on Cuban diplomats in Washington, triggering Cuban retaliation against US diplomats in Havana). Under the new rules, US diplomats could travel freely but most were required to notify the Cuban Foreign Ministry in advance.

Subsequent negotiations in 2015 produced agreements on protection of the marine environment in the Caribbean, restoration of direct mail service, and expansion of civil aviation links.

All the conflictual issues still remaining between the two countries—US economic sanctions first among them—are more complex than simply restoring normal diplomatic relations and will surely take even longer to resolve. At the Panama Summit, just before his private meeting with Obama, Castro expressed his hope for progress in bilateral relations but warned that the road ahead would not be easy. "No one should entertain illusions. It is true that we have many differences," he said. "Our countries have a long and complicated history, but we are willing to make progress . . . We are willing to discuss everything, but we need to be patient—very patient" (Castro Ruz and Obama 2015).

At the ceremony opening, Cuba's embassy in Washington, DC, Foreign Minister Bruno Rodríguez, was equally cautious. "Today, the re-establishment of diplomatic relations and the re-opening of embassies complete the first stage of the bilateral dialogue and pave the way to the complex and certainly long process towards the normalization of bilateral relations," he said. "The challenge is huge because there have never been normal relations between the United States of America and Cuba" (Rodríguez Parrilla 2015).

Speaking to the UN General Assembly in September 2015, Obama touted the opening to Cuba as a triumph of diplomacy over the use of force—a major theme of his address (Obama 2015). Raúl Castro (2015b), by contrast, recited the long list of outstanding issues, noting that relations could never be normal as long as US economic sanctions remained in place and the United States occupied Cuban territory at Guantánamo. He also announced that Cuba would once again offer to the General Assembly its annual resolution calling for an immediate end to the US embargo. The resolution has passed each of the last 24 years, with ever larger margins; in 2015, only the United States and Israel voted no and, for the first time, no one abstained.

Cuban leaders appeared to be approaching the new relationship with the United States in the same way they approached restructuring ("updating") the Cuban economy—slowly and cautiously, testing the political fallout from each step forward. Havana routinely urged Obama to use his executive authority to poke more holes in the embargo, but the Cuban government has been slow to take steps to facilitate the expansion of trade in sectors where Obama has already licensed embargo exceptions. US Commerce Secretary Penny Pritzker used the occasion of an October trade promotion visit to Cuba to urge Cuban officials to adopt measures that would ease the task of conducting business on the island, but her counterparts offered no concrete commitments in response (Hirschfeld Davis 2015).

One reason for the tentativeness on the Cuban side is simple capacity. In 2014, Cuba hosted more than three million foreign visitors and its tourism infrastructure was operating at near capacity. The sudden surge of US visitors after December 17 strained the industry's ability to accommodate them all. With regard to trade, Cuba's import-export agencies attached to the various ministries have thus far only had to deal with the demands of state enterprises. For Cuba's growing private sector to develop robust trade relations with US firms, Cuba's state agencies will have to either scale up dramatically or surrender their monopoly control over foreign trade.

On the political front, Cuban officials remain skeptical of the motives behind US offers to help expand Internet access, recalling, no doubt, that the last two US administrations implemented programs to use digital media to stoke opposition to the Cuban government.

Nor have Cuban officials done anything thus far to enable Cuba's private entrepreneurs to do business with US companies.

The Agenda Going Forward

The Bilateral Commission and working groups have a full agenda of issues to tackle. Foremost among them is the US embargo, which was written into law by the Cuban Liberty and Democratic Solidarity Act of 1996 (also known as Helms-Burton). Obama has called for Congress to repeal it, but with Republicans in control of both houses, and with Republican presidential aspirants blasting Obama for appeasing America's enemies, congressional leaders were unlikely to allow any legislation that made Obama's Cuba policy look like a success. Thus, there was little chance that Congress would lift the embargo or the ban on tourist travel before the 2016 election.

Resolving the claims issue was linked to the embargo since US economic sanctions were originally imposed to punish Cuba for nationalizing US property at the outset of the revolution. A working group on claims was scheduled to review the $8 billion that the United States demands for nationalized property (originally $1.9 billion plus half a century of interest) and Cuba's counterclaims for $117 billion in damage done by the embargo (Foreign Claims Settlement Commission of the United States 2015; Trotta 2015).

A working group on law enforcement cooperation is discussing human smuggling, document fraud, and fugitives. Approximately 70 US fugitives reside in Cuba; most of them are common criminals. However, some—like Black Liberation Army activist Assata Shakur (aka Joanne Chesimard) and Puerto Rican nationalist William Morales—are high-profile expatriates to whom Cuba has granted political asylum. Cuba is not likely to surrender them any more than the United States will surrender Cuban exiles responsible for terrorist attacks inside Cuba.

A working group on human rights has already begun discussing the very different perspectives the two governments have on the balance between social and economic rights and political liberties. As of late 2015, they had not gotten beyond expounding on their disagreement.

Still in place are a number of programs that are vestiges of the old US policy of regime change by economic denial and political subversion: US democracy promotion programs; TV and Radio Martí; and the Cuban Medical Professionals Parole Program. Cuba regards these programs as an affront to its sovereignty and demands their cessation, as Raúl Castro made clear in his September 2015 speech to the UN.

Washington has been unwilling to even discuss these programs. Obama cannot simply halt them because, except for the parole program, they are authorized and funded by Congress. Nevertheless, senior administration officials privately acknowledge that they are incompatible with the new direction of US-Cuban relations.

The 1966 Cuban Adjustment Act allows any Cuban paroled or admitted into the United States, whether they arrived legally or illegally, to become a permanent resident after one year. Cuba has called for its repeal because it creates an incentive for human smuggling. Washington insists it has no intention of changing the law, for fear that any hint of repeal might spark a new migration crisis.

Speaking to a conference of the Community of Latin American and Caribbean States (CELAC) soon after December 17, Raúl Castro (2015a) declared that fully normal relations with the United States would require the return of Guantánamo. The Obama administration, however, insists that Guantánamo "still has operational value" and its return is not open for discussion.

Despite a recalcitrant Congress, Obama still has options to move the normalization process forward during his last months in office. He could exercise his executive authority to promulgate additional regulatory changes, licensing an even wider range of commerce with Cuba. He could restructure US democracy promotion programs to be open and transparent rather than clandestine and covert, facilitating authentic social and cultural linkages rather than funding dissident political activity and trying to foment opposition to the government. He also could relocate TV and Radio Martí from Miami back to Washington, bringing them under the supervision of professional journalists at the Voice of America.

The Road Ahead and Forces Shaping the Future

For both presidents, the normalization of US-Cuban relations is a singular achievement central to their respective legacies. Despite the slow pace of progress, both must feel some urgency to push the process forward, making it hard to reverse. Both, after all, are short-timers. When they met at the UN, Obama had only 15 months remaining in his presidency and Castro was scheduled to step down just 14 months after Obama's departure. The completion of the normalization process—or its breakdown—will be the responsibility of their successors, whose future commitment to it is impossible to predict.

Almost all the leading Republican presidential candidates denounced Obama's opening to Cuba and pledged to roll it back entirely. The diplomatic cost to the United States in Latin America would be enormous if a new president broke relations with Havana but, at the very least, a Republican would likely halt the normalization process in its tracks, leaving relations to languish in a twilight zone between hostility and normality. As noted, even a Democratic president will likely face a Republican House of Representatives and perhaps a Republican Senate as well, making it difficult to end the embargo or legalize tourist travel, both of which require Congressional action.

In Havana, Castro's successor will not command the general's authority and is likely to be much more constrained by bureaucratic and elite politics. Managing the evolving relationship with the United States could become even more politically fraught in an environment where influential leaders see the US policy of engagement as simply the old policy of regime change hiding behind a false facade of friendship. Surely, Fidel Castro is not alone in his skepticism about the empire ever changing its spots.

However, there are deeper forces pressing for change on both sides of the Florida Strait that successor politicians in Washington and Havana cannot ignore. How successful these are in producing an ever deeper degree of rapprochement cannot be predicted in advance, but we can identify likely indicators of progress, some of which are measurable. First, Cuba's successful integration into the global economy will still require an end to the embargo and the expansion of trade and investment from the United States. Cuba's tourist industry will still need access to the US market to fuel its expansion. The ability to trade with the United States is also critical to the island's plans for the modern port of Mariel to become a major logistics hub for large container ships after their transit through the new "Panamax" Panama Canal. US businesses will continue to push for the right to compete in the Cuban market. All of these pressures for advance on the economic front will be facilitated if Cuba manages a smooth transition toward a unified currency, gains access to financial and technical assistance from international financial institutions, and reduces the barriers to foreign direct investment, including by eliminating restrictions on hiring Cuban workers.

Second, Latin American governments will continue to demand that Cuba be fully reintegrated into the hemispheric community. Havana's enhanced participation during the coming years both in the OAS and in less prominent forums for governance that include the United States would signal further progress toward normalization. More immediately, a successful conclusion of peace talks between the Colombian government and the Revolutionary Armed Forces of Colombia (FARC), which have been facilitated by Havana, may add to awareness in Washington of the constructive role that Cuba can play in realizing common objectives. Both governments might find their interests converging on an orderly resolution to Venezuela's political crisis. Cooperation in encouraging their respective allies to seek compromise over conflict would surely add to the incentives for both countries to work collaboratively in the future.

Finally, there is a critical role to be played by civil society. As Cubans and Cuban Americans travel back and forth in increasing numbers, along with other US travelers taking part in people-to-people exchange programs and eventually in conventional tourism, citizens of the two countries will continue to knit back together the social and cultural ties severed after 1959. Polls in Cuba and in the United States show overwhelming support for reconciliation; even a majority of Cuban Americans support Obama's new policy. Ordinary people were ready for reconciliation long before their two governments, and expectations are running high now that the process is underway. That sentiment will become ever more widespread, and politicians will ignore it at their peril. As Secretary of State John Kerry (2015) said at the ceremony raising the American flag to mark the reopening of the US embassy in Havana, "The time is now to reach out to one another, as two peoples who are no longer enemies or rivals, but neighbors—time to unfurl our flags, raise them up, and let the world know that we wish each other well."

References

Castro Ruz, Raúl. 2015a. "President Raúl Castro speaks to Third CELAC Summit in Costa Rica." *Granma International*, January 29. http://en.granma.cu/mundo/2015-10-06/president-raul-castro-speaks-to-third-celac-summit-in-costa-rica.

———. 2015b. "Full text of speech by Raúl Castro Ruz, President of Cuba's Councils of State and Ministers, during 70th Session of the UN General Assembly." *Granma International*, September 28.

Castro Ruz, Raúl, and Barack Obama. 2015. "Remarks by President Obama and President Raúl Castro of Cuba Before Meeting." White House Office of the Press Secretary, April 11.

Foreign Claims Settlement Commission of the United States. 2015. "Completed Programs: Cuba." *The United States Department of Justice.* http://www.justice.gov/fcsc/claims-against-cuba.

Hirschfeld Davis, Julia. 2015. "U.S. Commerce Chief Makes a Pitch in Cuba." *New York Times,* October 6.

Kerry, John. 2015. "Remarks at Flag Raising Ceremony." U.S. Department of State, August 14.

LeoGrande, William M., and Peter Kornbluh. 2014. *Back Channel to Cuba: The Hidden History of Negotiations between Washington and Havana.* Chapel Hill: University of North Carolina.

Obama, Barack. 2015. "Remarks by President Obama to the United Nations General Assembly." White House, Office of the Press Secretary, September 28.

Rodríguez Parrilla, Bruno. 2015. "Statement by Bruno Rodríguez Parrilla, Minister of Foreign Affairs of the Republic of Cuba, at the Ceremony to Re-open the Cuban Embassy in the United States." Ministry of Foreign Affairs, July 20.

Trotta, Daniel. 2014. "Cuba estimates total damage of U.S. embargo at $116.8 billion." *Reuters,* September 9.

Index

CPSIA information can be obtained at www.ICGtesting.com
Printed in the USA
BVOW06s1354260816

460287BV00010B/45/P